A Cambodian Odyssey

A Cambodian Odyssey

and The Deaths of 25 Journalists

Kurt Volkert and T. Jeff Williams

Writer's Showcase

San Jose New York Lincoln Shanghai

A Cambodian Odyssey
and The Deaths of 25 Journalists

Writer's Showcase
an imprint of iUniverse.com, Inc.

For information address:
iUniverse.com, Inc.
5220 S 16th, Ste. 200
Lincoln, NE 68512
www.iuniverse.com

Cover illustration by Kurt Volkert
Cover design by Dina Acreman
Proofreading by Lisa Adlam

ISBN: 0-595-16606-7

Printed in the United States of America

DEDICATION

For Gusta Syvertsen and Gisela, my wife, who were in Phnom Penh
and shared the futile hours of waiting for George
and our other friends who never returned.
—Kurt Volkert

And for all missing journalists.
—T. Jeff Williams

TABLE OF CONTENTS

Part One—T. Jeff Williams

Chapter 1 The Historical Tapestry 3
Chapter 2 Sihanouk's Decline 14
Chapter 3 The Coup 21
Chapter 4 The End of Neutrality 31
Chapter 5 Mercedes Marauders 46
Chapter 6 Weird Things 61
Chapter 7 Dogs of War 78

Part Two—Kurt Volkert

Chapter 1 Death on Highway 3 103
Chapter 2 Return to Cambodia 132
Chapter 3 Cambodia, 22 Years Later 137
Chapter 4 Partial Success 179
Chapter 5 Mrs. Ishii and Sakai's Son 228
Chapter 6 Back to Cambodia 239
Chapter 7 Sakai Goes Home 252

LIST OF ILLUSTRATIONS

Snapshots from Cambodia, 1970 83
Snapshots from the Search Site, 1992 90

APPENDIX

1. List of Foreign Correspondents Killed or Missing in Cambodia, 1970

2. Hand-drawn maps Kurt Volkert made in 1971 to help pinpoint the location of the captured and missing CBS and NBC crews.

3. Transcripts of Interviews:
> Soldier Phun
> The Actor
> Farmer Nin
> Former NBC Driver Chay You Leng
> The (Catholic) Priest
> Soldier Keo Soeung
> A Taxi Driver
> Teacher Sang Soeur

4. Declassified Department of Defense Intelligence Report on 3 Unidentified Missing American Journalists Reportedly Seen in Kampot Province in 1970

FOREWORD

Shrapnel in Our Hearts

By Bernard Kalb

FOR THOSE of a certain age, Viet Nam is a remote date on the calendar; no eyewitnesses could possibly still be around. For others, for those of us who were there during the war, Viet Nam was only yesterday, still vivid, raw.

A certain age, say, 10. "Talk to my daughter," my friend says. "She's in the fifth grade and she has to give a speech about Southeast Asia to her class." Mom leaves me with her daughter, saying she'll be back in a half hour. I begin to share some memories of my decade and a half in Asia, but mostly, inevitably, memories of the war. It is always like that, Viet Nam taking over, memories never exhausted even after all these years. Names and places and images began spilling out about the way it was, about what I had seen close-up. After a while, my friend reappears. "Mom," her daughter erupts, disbelief and astonishment on her face, "he was *alive* during the Viet Nam war."

Alive, yes, but Indo-China will always be shrapnel in our hearts. "A Cambodian Odyssey," defying the quarter of a century since that last U.S. helicopter lifted off from a Saigon rooftop, plunges us deep into the conflict in 1970, with five more years of KIA and MIA still to be achieved. But what we are offered by correspondent Jeff Williams and cameraman Kurt Volkert, both CBS News colleagues of mine during the

Viet Nam days, is not just a shot-list of what it felt like to be out in the "boonies" in this war without a front, the everywhere war; rather, it's a story of how the hell of war tests the correspondents who cover it, forces them to confront the merciless dilemma of deciding just how close to get to the killing, whether getting a minute-fifteen of bang-bang on the evening news is worth risking your life. The merciless, unyielding dilemma—day after day.

Jeff opens with a scene-setter, a political and historical narrative that explains how it happened that war was thrust on a Cambodia desperate to stay out of it, and how Cambodia, just a skip away from the bigger war next door, had reporters crossing the border to cover the expanding conflict. For journalists, Cambodia was even a greater mess than Viet Nam, even more exotically lethal. Viet Nam at least had an organized army, but even more, it had half a million American troops in the country and they still were battling against defeat. By contrast, Cambodia went to war with teenagers in Phnom Penh cheerfully waving wooden rifles, as if they were off to a Sunday picnic, en route to combat in soda-pop trucks.

Then it's Kurt's turn, and his evocative autobiographical account zooms in on a fatal day in May 1970, when all of Cambodia was a no-man's land.

On one level, the story centers on a fundamental conflict over the definition of acceptable danger. "Acceptable?" A million definitions explode in the dictionary of war, and just such an explosion cracks the CBS News crew of Kurt and correspondent George Syvertsen. All of us out there for CBS knew both of them; they were a brave, combat-experienced team. But their disagreement over "acceptable" was not a mere semantic luxury; it could be a matter of life and death. This is a question that still bluntly assaults every reporter and cameraman covering war anywhere in the world. When to stop? Where to stop? Ever to stop? We lived with that challenge all during the war, yet so many of us felt invulnerable—was it innocence, arrogance, the intoxication of war? We were objective reporters, weren't we, not combat soldiers. We gave ourselves exemptions from death. We armored ourselves with naiveté.

"Not me," he remembers Syvertsen saying. "They will never get me."

Only later does Kurt learn that "Syvertsen was under tremendous pressure from the home office in New York to get 'tougher' in his reporting. He was unfairly considered a lightweight and he decided he had to fight for his professional reputation and change the minds of a few New York executives comfortably ensconced in their mahogany foxholes."

There you have it: the different worlds; mahogany versus B-40s. The giant gap between the TV grunts in the field and the button-down brass back home. The pressure to keep turning out stories to beat the competition. The frustrations of the journalists avoiding poisoned punji sticks and their fury at New York's failure to understand what it's really like out in the tall grass, terror all around. Vignette by vignette, what emerges is a first-hand portrait of the culture of TV journalism in a war zone: the obsession with combat footage, reporters dangerously prowling for the big exclusive, coupled with the schizo message from back home; CONGRATULATIONS YOU CLOBBERED THE OPPO-SITION coupled with the predictable bureaucratic self-acquittal clo-sure: BE CAREFUL.

But there's another level to this story, and it is even more psycholog-ically haunting, of Kurt's emotional upheaval to the news the very next day that several CBS staffers have been killed when their jeep, racing through Khmer Rouge territory, is hit by a B-40 rocket grenade. At the wheel: George Syvertsen. Captured and later executed: Tomoharu Ishii, the CBS cameraman from Japan, unhappy about being in Cambodia, but chosen at the last minute to fill in for Volkert.

"Yes, it could have been me," Kurt agonizes. "Or could I have stopped the madness of Syvertsen's expedition that day? Probably not. Nobody wants to be called a coward, but we should remember that cowards often live longer."

Cowardice? Fate? Or the courage to revolt? Whatever demons were driving George died with him; we'll never know whether it was one of those B-40 coincidences or whether he had crossed even his own boundaries of the "acceptable."

But where are the bodies?

Not only of this crew, but of six other TV people racing down that same dangerous highway, one network chasing after another. Some bodies were recovered fairly quickly, but Ishii's and some of the others were not, and this defiant reality would pursue Kurt for more than two decades. What we have here is the diary of his tormented journey from the split-up to the killings, to the search for the bodies—the initial search in 1970 and the return two decades later to look for the bodies still missing.

In all, this book is a tribute to all slain journalists who brought the war to your living room; some caught in a firefight, some shot out of the sky, some who vanished, some executed. Yet even while the shooting was going on, there was a war about the war, about whether the United States had misread history and the dying was all a waste. Those postmortems would all come later, too late to end the killing. But while it was going on in Viet Nam and you were there, the war was surrounding, no escape.

Except when you flew to Cambodia, just an hour away, and you suddenly had the liberating sensation that you were on R&R. There was the illusion then, in the sixties, of a gentle country—but that was before the Khmer Rouge, overnight, bloodied the land; it was as though a giant vacuum had suddenly sucked a whole country into the murderous whirl of war. But earlier, going to Cambodia from Viet Nam, was like swapping worlds.

Phnom Penh was a pleasure, relaxed; the two giant arms of a mammoth clock built into the capital's main sloping lawn welcomed you to Cambodia. The skyline was dotted with fairytale palaces and soaring temples, not with exploding napalm and screaming F-100s. Without feeling guilty, you could talk about the cheese soufflé at Phnom Penh's Hotel le Royal and other specialties the French had left behind, instead of the mimeographed optimism handed out to the press at "the five o'clock follies" in Saigon. If you had an extra day or two, you could fly up to Siem Reap, the stand in awe before the architectural triumph of Angkor Wat.

And Cambodia had something extra; the impresario of the Kingdom, Prince Norodom Sihanouk, the ex-king himself. You could always count on him to give you a story, to mix theatre and strategy in his desperate effort to ward off the conflict threatening to overwhelm his little country. Little? Ah, the Monseigneur, as he liked to be called, would denounce that word and he denounced it with comic fury. "You don't say 'little America,' do you?" he'd lecture visiting Western reporters who would chuckle along with him. "You don't say 'little China,' do you?" And then he'd threaten to put you on his "*liste noir*" and ban you from entering his Kingdom. Or he would hold press conferences and read top-secret cables from abroad to embarrass any of the major powers pressuring "little" Cambodia. Highly unorthodox diplomacy and great showmanship, part of his repertoire in trying to offset his military weakness in playing off the superpowers involved in Indo-China. Going to Cambodia in the late sixties before war splattered over the country was always a kind of surrealistic treat. But then one day the landscape was turned into the killing fields and it all turned deadly serious.

Deadly serious: this book suddenly relocates me from Washington to Phnom Penh, 1970, just after those eight killings and the first of those bodies was recovered. A question, please. Have you ever cremated anyone? But that's phrased—how to put it—much too generously. Try it this way: Have you ever had the assignment of putting a burning match to the remains of two of your colleagues on the cremation grounds in Phnom Penh? Of pouring their ashes into silver urns to be delivered to their grieving families in faraway countries? The pyres burn into the soul. Hour after hour, I watch my friends' flames get smaller and smaller, the smoke thinner and thinner. The sheer duration, the sheer unbearability, suddenly broken when a young Cambodian arrives carrying a small wooden case—the "Johnny Walker" label visible on its side. He pours gasoline on the case. Gently, so gently, he strikes a match. New flames erupt, startle the sky. "*Ma petite fille*." His voice, a whisper.

All unforgettable, and as I write this, tortured memories assaulting, I keep thinking of a certain Secretary of Defense who, much later, decades after the killing stops, finally surrenders: "...we were wrong, terribly wrong." What is his name again?

In this book, Kurt and Jeff bring it all back: the war, the killings, the questions, George, Ishii and all the others.

Bernard Kalb is an internationally recognized journalist, author and lecturer on subjects ranging from the media to United States foreign policy. Mr. Kalb is a former correspondent for CBS News, NBC News and the New York Times. He is co-host of the CNN program, "Reliable Sources," which weekly turns a critical lens on the media. He was a journalist in Asia for 15 years and travels the world moderating Freedom Forum panels focusing on the media under siege. Winner of the Overseas Press Club for a CBS documentary, "Viet Cong," Mr. Kalb is co-author, with his brother, Marvin Kalb, of "Kissinger." He is also a Visiting Professor on Media and Foreign Policy at Hamilton College, NY.

MAPS

Map of Cambodia

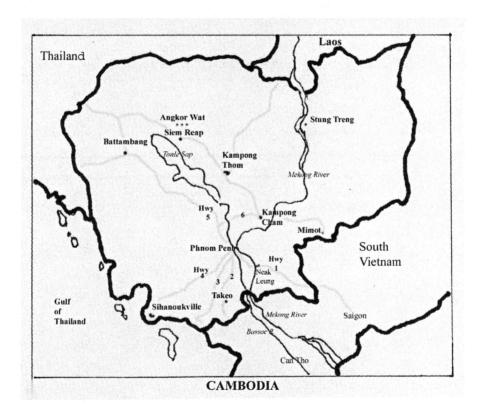

INTRODUCTION

IN THE SPRING of 1970, a coup d'etat in Cambodia, the subsequent U.S.-South Vietnamese invasion and the exponential growth of the Khmer Rouge set in motion a chain of events that culminated in the deaths of between 1 and 2 million Cambodians. In light of that, the deaths of 25 journalists in the first five months of the conflict pales in comparison. But that is what we lived with.

Among those killed were two entire crews with CBS News and NBC News. Those with CBS included George Syvertsen, correspondent; Gerry Miller, producer; Tomoharu Ishii, cameraman; Kojiro Sakai, soundman; and Ramnik Lekhi, a camera stringer from India. Those with NBC were Welles Hangen, correspondent; Roger Colne, a French cameraman; and Yoshihiko Waku, a Japanese soundman.

This book is more than just an account of those dangerous times. It is the personal and often moving record that Kurt Volkert kept during a U.S. Army team's arduous search for the remains of the CBS and NBC News people. Kurt was a CBS News cameraman working with Syvertsen in Cambodia just after the 1970 coup, but he did not accompany him on the fateful day Syvertsen and others were killed. Although some of the bodies could not be recovered at the time because North Vietnamese and Khmer Rouge troops controlled the area, Kurt eventually managed to interview enough people from the area to make a hand drawn map of the killing site. Nearly a quarter century later, his map became crucial to determining where to start the search. In the second half of the book, Kurt recounts the details that led to the deaths of the two news teams, the search for their whereabouts and finally, the recovery effort.

T. Jeff Williams was then an Associated Press correspondent and the only American journalist in Cambodia at the time of the coup. He covered the war there for the following six months and then, after the death of George Syvertsen, became a CBS News correspondent. In the first portion of the book, he recounts Cambodia's centuries of conflict with neighboring Thailand and Vietnam, the events leading up to the overthrow of Prince Norodom Sihanouk and Cambodia's eventual engulfment by the Vietnam War.

Part One

By T. Jeff Williams

CHAPTER 1

The Historical Tapestry

ON MARCH 17, 1970, scores of perspiring American and European tourists trudged through the carved stone labyrinths of Angkor Wat, Cambodia's ancient temple complex. They viewed 12th century friezes depicting past royal struggles for control of the kingdom with admiring murmurs, little aware that another royal power play was at that moment reaching a climax in Phnom Penh, the capital.

On the other side of the world, Prince Norodom Sihanouk, for years plagued by insomnia, spent a restless night in Moscow. He knew, but refused to accept, that a long-developing crisis was reaching a flash point in the country he had ruled since 1941 when the French colonial government placed him, a cherubic youth of 19, on the throne. He was also only too aware that the man guiding the effort to topple him was his royal cousin, Prince Sisowath Sirik Matak, a descendant of the royal Sisowath lineage that the French had passed over in favor of crowning Sihanouk, scion of the Norodom line.

Collaborating with Sirik Matak and playing the front man was Gen. Lon Nol, a deceptively placid looking man who owed his rise to power largely to his long and loyal association with Sihanouk. The two had known each other since July 1953 when Sihanouk, to protest France's refusal to grant Cambodia its independence, had gone into self-

imposed exile into the autonomous military area of Siem Reap. The
province was then commanded by a conservative lieutenant colonel
named Lon Nol. Sihanouk easily charmed Lon Nol into becoming his
ally, and together they plotted the formation of a resistance movement
if France did not agree to independence.

Now, 17 years later, Prime Minister Lon Nol plotted with deputy
Prime Minister Sirik Matak to bring Sihanouk down. Although the
roots of the conflict lay in royal rivalry, there were profound political
differences between the mercurial Sihanouk (the description always
infuriated him) and the right-leaning and conservative Sirik Matak and
Lon Nol. The immediate issue was the large number of North
Vietnamese and Viet Cong forces who used Cambodia as a sanctuary
while attacking U.S. forces in neighboring South Vietnam. Sirik Matak
and Lon Nol wanted the Communists out of the country, by force if
necessary. Sihanouk, always shifting with the political winds, believed
that the North Vietnamese would drive the United States out of
Vietnam as they had France and that he therefore should remain allied
with Hanoi.

Sihanouk, an astute albeit unpredictable politician, had above
everything else consistently attempted to maintain Cambodia's neutrality in the face of Hanoi's emergence as a dominant Southeast Asian
military power. His first concern was to prevent Vietnam or Thailand
from carving off large pieces of Cambodian territory, as they often had
in the past. Sihanouk's efforts to maintain Cambodia's neutrality at any
cost is better understood when seen against the country's larger historical backdrop.

Between Two Enemies

Cambodia lies at the heart of the Indochina peninsula. It also lies
between Vietnam and Thailand, two countries that have repeatedly

trampled Cambodia during their own expansionist periods. Cambodia, however, has also conquered much of Thailand and Vietnam in past centuries and its old enemies haven't forgotten.

Cambodia covers slightly less than 70,000 square miles, approximately the size of Missouri. It is half as big as Germany, but more than four times the size of Switzerland. These comparisons are noted because it invariably angered Prince Sihanouk to have journalists refer to his country as a "tiny" kingdom. More than half of Cambodia is a large fertile basin, the remnant of an ancient seabed that flows from the central part of the country down to the broad Mekong River delta. Steep, jungle-covered hills form Cambodia's northern borders with Laos and Vietnam. To the west, along its border with Thailand, are more plateaus and rugged hills, which have long provided a safe haven for Cambodia's rebel groups. To the south, where Cambodia abuts the Gulf of Thailand, rise the rugged Cardamom Mountains and Elephant Range. To the east, steep, jungle-covered highlands merge with Vietnam's Central Highlands. To the southeast, flat, fertile ground stretches into the Mekong River delta. Later, both American and South Vietnamese military leaders would agree that much of Cambodia was perfect tank country.

The great Mekong River, which rises in the Himalayas far to the north and west, runs through the heart of the country roughly from north to southeast. Where the river sweeps past Phnom Penh it forks off another river called the Bassac. Almost dead center in the country is the remarkable Tonle Sap (Great Lake), which is a reservoir for the Mekong during the monsoon season. During the dry season, the Tonle Sap is drained by a river that flows into the Mekong. When the monsoons arrive, however, the rain-swollen Mekong forces the Tonle Sap River to run backwards and fill the great lake once again. Because of these predictable rains and alluvial plains, Cambodia has long been one of the world's leading rice exporters, often producing two crops a year.

Chinese dynastic records show that Khmer (Cambodian) people had established numerous communities in the region more than a century before the birth of Christ. By the first century A.D., the Khmer people had built a significant city in the Mekong delta area known through Chinese chronicles as Funan. Because it lay on trade routes between India and China, Funan grew and flourished. By the sixth century A.D., however, political strife and internal power struggles led to Funan's collapse. Out of those ruins emerged a new state known as Chenla. It too divided into the Land Chenla to the north and the Water Chenla in the Mekong delta.

For the next three centuries, the Khmers of Chenla continued to expand their kingdom, eventually controlling much of Vietnam, Laos and Thailand. At the dawn of the ninth century, the ruler of a Water Chenla principality defeated an invading force from Sumatra. Riding this military momentum, he quickly exerted his control over all of Chenla and assumed the throne as Jayavarman II in 802. His rule launched the golden age of Kambuja, as the new kingdom was known.

For 400 years, from 802 until the death of Jayavarman VII in 1218, the Khmers established one of the most extraordinary kingdoms in the world. Its power was rooted in Angkor Wat and Angkor Thom, two vast temple cities exquisitely carved from blocks of stone. Strategically located just north of Tonle Sap, which was its breadbasket, even today it evokes a sense of mystery and awe. The roots of silk trees still entwine many of the great stone faces that are turned toward the cardinal compass points, their faint, enigmatic smiles frozen in time. Less visible, but equally remarkable, were the irrigation and transportation canal networks built throughout the region. These engineered waterways allowed the kingdom to expand its agricultural base and support its growing population.

While Jayavarman VII was expending much of Kambuja's human and financial resources on temple construction, however, neighboring Tai tribes were consolidating their own powers. By 1353 the Tais, who had migrated into present day Thailand from southern China, were strong enough to attack and capture Angkor Wat. Although the Khmers recaptured it, the battles seesawed back and forth for 90 years. Meanwhile, more Cambodian territory was lost to a rising kingdom in Laos. Finally, in 1431, the Tais captured and held Angkor Thom. This devastating assault started Kambuja on a decline from which it never fully recovered.

During Cambodia's Dark Ages, the kingdom and its people became vassals of both Thailand and Vietnam. Both powers controlled large sections of the country and often dictated who would sit on Cambodia's throne. Weakened by internal strife, royal intrigue and corruption, Kambuja abandoned the Angkor area and established a new capital called Phnom Penh at the confluence of the Mekong River, the Bassac River and the Tonle Sap River.

For a period under the rule of King Ang Chan (1516-66), Cambodia appeared to be recovering its military strength and pride. King Ang, considered one of the country's great monarchs, moved the capital from Phnom Penh to Lovek, about halfway to the Tonle Sap. The new capital became a fabulously wealthy trading center. Spanish colonialists from the Philippines, Portuguese from Macao, along with Chinese, Arabs, Japanese and Malays crowded the city. Shops were filled with rubies, opals, ivory, lacquer ware, silks, rhinoceros horns and metals. But the wealth attracted those who would take it away, and in 1594 Thailand captured Lovek and placed its own governor in control.

With the fall of Lovek, Cambodia fell under another long spell of Thai and Vietnamese dominance. Vietnam continued to expand its territorial holdings and by the early 1600s had taken control of the Mekong delta, long a Khmer territory. By the late 1700s Thailand placed a puppet king on the Cambodian throne and seized the rice-rich northwest provinces of Siem Reap and Battambang. By the early 1800s, Vietnam fought back against the Thai encroachment and installed its own puppet king on the throne.

Enter France

The battles for suzerainty over Cambodia might have continued for more centuries except for France's intervention. In 1863, France, which earlier had established colonial control over much of Vietnam, made Cambodia a protectorate. The agreement with France was signed by Sihanouk's grandfather, King Norodom, who ruled from 1859 to 1904. When Norodom died in 1904, the French ignored his son as rightful heir and instead placed Norodom's half-brother, Sisowath, on the throne. The French believed Sisowath would be a willing vassal of colonial rule and, indeed, he and his son Monivong, who succeeded him and ruled from 1927 to 1941, caused the French no trouble.

Although the French did little for Cambodian education in general, there was an educated urban elite who learned of such daring concepts as freedom, equality and political independence. During their colonial rule, the French fanned resentment among the people by hiring Vietnamese rather than Cambodians to staff their government bureaucracy. The French also spurred ongoing resentment among the farming class by imposing heavy taxes on them. When France took upon itself the task of restoring the long-lost temples of Angkor Wat and Angkor Thom, it had a completely unforeseen effect: It gave impetus to rebel groups who found a new pride in their history and a belief that the kingdom could be restored to past glories.

But the most significant impact on Cambodia's fledgling independence movement came with World War II and the conquering Japanese army. Indigenous opponents of colonialism from Africa to Southeast Asia were deeply impressed that a small country like Japan could quickly seize so much territory and leave established powers like France, Britain and the United States seemingly helpless to stop it. Following the 1940 establishment of the Vichy government in France, Japan moved into Vietnam and then into Cambodia, where it maintained the Vichy colonial officials in power. Despite its ultimate defeat in 1945,

Japan's military dominance over much of East Asia, starting with China in 1931, set in motion the wheels of revolution around the world.

In April 1941, King Sisowath Monivong died and his son, Prince Sisowath Monireth, expected to ascend to the throne in his place. Instead, the French colonial rulers passed him over and selected Norodom Sihanouk to become king. Again, because of a whimsical decision by the French, the fortunes of Cambodia's two primary royal families shifted from the Sisowaths back to the Norodoms. The irony could not have been lost on young Sihanouk, and certainly not on his cousin Prince Sisowath Sirik Matak, who had expected his royal line to continue in power. But because Prince Sihanouk was just 19 years old and without governing experience, the French considered this great grandson of the first King Norodom to be more malleable. They couldn't have been more wrong.

In early 1945, with defeat facing them, the Japanese dissolved the Vichy French colonial government and urged Cambodia to declare independence. It did so in March, but allied forces, intent on reestablishing French colonial rule, occupied the country in October and put an immediate and rude end to the brief dream. Sihanouk, however, was not easily dissuaded.

In continuing to negotiate for Cambodia's independence, Sihanouk had to balance his dealings with the French against the demands of rebel groups in the countryside that considered him a French puppet. First among the rebel leaders was Son Ngoc Thanh, a shadowy Khmer Krom, or ethnic Cambodian, from Vietnam's Mekong delta. From the time Son Ngoc Thanh founded the kingdom's first Cambodian language newspaper in 1945, he attracted a diverse group of businessmen and student followers united only in their anti-French and anti-colonialist sentiments.

Among those most attracted to revolutionary ideals were several young Cambodians who had gone to Paris to study in the 1950s. One who became most imbued with the persuasive Communist concepts of the time was a youth named Saloth Sar. Later, in the jungles of Cambodia, he changed his name to Pol Pot.

Born in 1928 in Kampong Thom province north of Phnom Penh, Saloth Sar went to Paris in 1949 to study electronics. His attention wandered to other studies until he found his true calling in the practices of Communism and its concepts of revolution. Soviet influence in France then was strong and although Saloth Sar did not obtain a degree, he did obtain a foundation in Marxism. Other Cambodian students there during the same period included Ieng Sary, Khieu Samphan, Hou Yuon, Son Sen and Hun Nim. All took degrees in Paris in such subjects as economics, politics, literature and law. Khieu Samphan and Hou Yuon both earned doctorates. This group, which became the most educated of all Asian Communist leaders, ultimately headed the most bloodthirsty organization in modern Asia, the malevolent Khmer Rouge.

During the brief but heady months of independence in 1945, Sihanouk appointed Son Ngoc Thanh as his foreign minister. But because Son Ngoc Thanh had spent much of the war in Japan, returning allied forces declared him a Japanese collaborator and exiled him to France. When Sihanouk later persuaded the French to let him return, Son Ngoc Thanh almost immediately disappeared into the forests with his Khmer Serai (Free Khmer) followers, which became a persistent but ineffectual anti-monarchist group.

The French colonial government that returned after the war appeared chastened enough to permit the formation of political parties and an elected Consultative Assembly to advise young King Sihanouk. During the tumultuous years between 1946 and 1953, when France finally agreed to Cambodia's independence, Sihanouk proved himself to be a master of playing two sides against each other. He was openly anti-Communist and particularly opposed to Viet Minh troops using Cambodia as a sanctuary in their battles against the French. He requested and received American aid but would not join the American-influenced Southeast Asia Treaty Organization.

By 1953, Sihanouk believed that if full independence were not granted immediately, Cambodia would be caught up in the full-blown war between French and Viet Minh troops in neighboring Vietnam. In March of that year he visited Paris to plead his case but was rebuffed. He then went to the United States, where he was largely ignored. On his return, Sihanouk played a high-risk card and declared he would not return to Phnom Penh until the French relented. The French, who had put him on the throne in the first place, could have removed him, but didn't. Sihanouk moved to the autonomous military region of Siem Reap and took up residence in a villa near Angkor Wat. The military commander of the region was Lt. Col. Lon Nol.

Lon Nol was born in Prey Veng province in 1913 and entered the French colonial service in 1937. He was educated at the elite Lycée Chasseloup Laubat in Saigon, as were both Sihanouk and Sirik Matak. Lon Nol proved adept at dealing with bureaucracy and maintaining contacts. In 1946 he helped Sirik Matak found the Renovation Party, which supported the monarchy. Lon Nol quickly rose through the civil service ranks before joining the army in 1952, where he saw much greater opportunity for advancement and control. He took part in numerous campaigns against Communist Vietnamese forces along the border, which reinforced his long-held resentment toward them. In 1953 he was named commander of the Siem Reap autonomous military region when Sihanouk arrived. Two years later, Sihanouk named him chief of staff of the Cambodian army.

Cambodian Independence

But in 1953, France was increasingly bogged down and financially drained by its war in Vietnam. With Cambodians ready to take up arms against its already beleaguered forces, France recognized that it could not sustain a second rebel front. On November 9, 1953, France bowed to Sihanouk's demands for full independence.

The Cambodian people's elation at their liberation, however, was short-lived. Sihanouk's rule, no longer constrained by French laws, was marked by cronyism, greed and excessive taxation. In a country of less than 7 million then, the social structure consisted of a wealthy elite with close connections to the palace, a small and undeveloped middle class and millions of villagers and peasants. Chinese and Vietnamese controlled most of the country's daily business, including exports and imports.

Reflecting widespread unrest, a large demonstration against government corruption and taxation erupted in the northwest city of Battambang in 1954, less than a year after independence. The uprising was brutally put down by Cambodian troops under direction of Lon Nol.

That same year, the French-Vietnam war ended. Viet Minh units that had been using Cambodia as a sanctuary in the war against the French were ordered out of the country under the Geneva accords. The accords also required that Cambodia, like Vietnam, hold general elections. The astute Sihanouk recognized that under these new rules he would have to both participate in elections and control them, something he could not do as king. He promptly abdicated the throne in favor of his father and assumed the title of *samdech*, or prince.

Declaring that he was Cambodia's future, Sihanouk then formed a political party called the Sangkum Reastr Niyum, which translated as the Popular Socialist Community. The name was at odds with its decidedly right-wing makeup.

Sihanouk had never positioned himself as a god-king, as had his forebears, but instead loved to mingle with the ordinary people. To consolidate his power before the elections, he took his new role as prince and politician to the countryside where the peasants, as they had for centuries, looked to the monarchy for guidance and unity. Smiling and immensely charming, Sihanouk walked through admiring throngs while women draped white frangipani leis around his neck. He told the crowds ribald jokes and hinted strongly at his own sexual prowess while at the same time selling his form of democracy.

Still, Sihanouk left nothing to chance. He established a large secret police force and, to ensure its loyalty, he placed the half-brother of his wife, Monique, in charge. By a combination of popularity, payoffs and police intimidation, Sihanouk's political party, the Sangkum, easily defeated all others in the 1955 elections, including Son Ngoc Thanh's Independence Party. Not partaking in the elections but waiting in the forest were Pol Pot and his small band of fanatical followers.

CHAPTER 2

Sihanouk's Decline

ACUTELY CONSCIOUS of history, Sihanouk's overriding goal at the time was to take whatever steps necessary to keep the kingdom neutral and aloof from surrounding wars. At the 1955 Bandung Conference in Indonesia, Peking and Hanoi assured him that they would respect Cambodia's neutrality. To maintain a balance against his larger Communist neighbors, Sihanouk at the same time agreed to accept U.S. military and foreign aid.

By the early '60s, American foreign aid accounted for 14 percent of Cambodia's national budget and 30 percent of its defense budget. U.S. dollars built the Freedom Highway between the port of Sihanoukville and Phnom Penh. But Sihanouk was increasingly suspicious of the close ties the United States fostered with his military commanders through training and trips abroad. Moreover, he believed that America's expanding support for the Saigon regime and Thailand ultimately represented a threat to Cambodia. South Vietnamese troops had often crossed into Cambodia, killing Cambodian peasants and looting stores while claiming they were just pursuing the Viet Cong.

Late in 1963, two events occurred which further inflamed Sihanouk's distrust of the United States. First was the November assassination of South Vietnam's Ngo Dinh Diem and his brother Nhu following the American-supported coup. Second, two Khmer Serei agents were arrested while traveling secretly to Phnom Penh. The Khmer Serei, organized by Son Ngoc Thanh with CIA backing in South Vietnam, regularly called for the overthrow of Sihanouk. In angry retribution, Sihanouk ordered an end in December to all U.S. military and economic aid. He then used the resulting economic decline as an excuse to nationalize the banks, foreign trade and insurance. To oversee these operations, he formed a state trading company, which in fact allowed him to fill his own coffers even more easily while distributing money and favors to loyal followers. But the accompanying corruption sent Cambodia into an economic tailspin. Foreign investment promptly evaporated, leaving the country even weaker. That all these negative economic indicators could be blamed on Prince Sihanouk was not lost on his cousin, Sisowath Sirik Matak.

Sihanouk's economic restraints resulted in a sharp reduction in business income and foreign military aid. In turn, this resulted in a stronger coalition between Cambodia's conservative businessmen and the pro-American Cambodian military officers. During the National Assembly elections in September 1966, an embattled Sihanouk declared he would not support candidates in his own political group, the Sangkum Party. Capitalizing on this opening, many of the prosperous conservatives bought their way into the National Assembly. A significant number of other candidates were elected to office by campaigning for economic reform, which was an indirect slap at Sihanouk that was supported by urban businessmen. The new and decidedly right-leaning National Assembly named Lon Nol as prime minister and Sisowath Sirik Matak, the avenging royal cousin, the deputy prime minister. Concerned by this conservative upsurge, Sihanouk promptly formed a left-leaning shadow cabinet as a form of self-defense.

By this time, however, Sihanouk's touted neutralist policy was unraveling. After breaking diplomatic ties with the United States in May 1965, he secretly granted Hanoi rights the following year to ship food and military supplies through Sihanoukville to North Vietnamese regulars

inside Cambodia. Not only the North Vietnamese Army (NVA) bene-
fited. Sihanouk put Gen. Lon Nol in charge of overseeing these shipments. It was like putting a wolf in charge of the sheep. Lon Nol
promptly skimmed large amounts of the supplies for himself, which he
resold on the black market. Some of the proceeds certainly went to
Sihanouk, while other amounts were distributed among Lon Nol's military cronies. North Vietnamese Prime Minister Pham Van Dong once
complained directly to Sihanouk that he had forwarded a large amount
of cash to Lon Nol specifically to buy rice for Viet Cong forces in
Cambodia, but the rice had never been sent and the money never
accounted for.

But all was far from peaceful in Cambodia. In 1967, an anti-government riot broke out in the town of Samlaut in the restless province of
Battambang, which lies along the Thai border. The uprising almost certainly helped consolidate the Khmer Rouge among the peasantry. The
northeastern province is a major rice producing area and the disparity
between wealthy absentee landlords and their sharecropper tenants was
pronounced. Economic pressure on the poor village and farming classes
became even more severe in 1966 when Lon Nol ordered that all rice
must be sold to the government at below-market prices. Lon Nol took
this step for two reasons: First, farmers had sold more than half the previous year's crop on the black market to evade heavy government taxes
and most of that rice went to the Vietnamese Communists. Second, Lon
Nol could get the rice cheap and sell it abroad at higher prices, pocket-
ing the difference.

On April 2, 1967, several hundred angry villagers and farmers killed
two army soldiers who were following orders to seize rice crops, then
took their weapons. More villagers joined the protest and other government offices were razed, including a military guard post. As the protests
spread among reports of more weapons being seized, there was fear the
uprising would spread to the province's capital, Battambang City. As he
had done in 1954, Lon Nol immediately ordered troops into the city to

stop the riots and to punish the populace. Thousands of villagers fled into the forest as eight army battalions arrived to crush the uprising. Armed vigilantes were also encouraged to help the army. A few months later, Sihanouk casually mentioned that he had "heard" some 10,000 Cambodian people were killed.

The real significance of the riots, however, was that they did not stop there. Anti-government violence steadily spread to 11 of Cambodia's 18 provinces, undoubtedly inflamed by the small but committed Khmer Communist Party and Pol Pot. Unnerved by the display of opposition to his rule, Sihanouk blamed both the Khmer Rouge, as he called the Khmer Communists, and Hanoi for fomenting the unrest. The demonstration and the resulting attacks on the peasant class played directly into the hands of the Khmer Rouge.

Pressure On Sihanouk

Pressure continued to mount against Sihanouk from all sides. His relations with South Vietnam, Thailand and the United States were steadily eroding. Peking and Hanoi continued to insist on using the port of Sihanoukville to ship unlimited supplies to their forces in Cambodia. Although the United States ceaselessly bombed the Ho Chi Minh trail in the belief that was the primary supply route, documents seized during the 1970 raid on the Viet Cong Embassy in Phnom Penh revealed that 80 percent of the supplies went through Sihanoukville, right under the noses of American intelligence.

Additionally, Hanoi regulars were secretly training the ragtag Khmer Rouge in camps along the Vietnamese borders. Tens of thousands of North Vietnamese and Viet Cong troops took refuge inside Cambodia while striking into South Vietnam. Meanwhile, major U.S. offensives in War Zone C, between Saigon and the Cambodian border, had pushed more NVA regulars back into Cambodia.

Sihanouk had little but his rhetoric and personal wiles to counter the rising threats to Cambodia's stability. His military forces were few in number, poorly trained and badly equipped. Seemingly unable to cope with the rising turmoil, Sihanouk had been increasingly turning away from politics from the late 1960s. He spent hours writing articles for the national magazine he published and wiled away the days by writing and directing long movies starring his Eurasian wife, Monique. More sophisticated students in the cities complained about how boring the films were.

But Sihanouk was not turning away from an easy cash flow. Seeing the economy continue to sink, his advisers recommended major cut-backs in spending, but Sihanouk rejected that idea. Instead, he decided to raise money by opening gambling casinos. Because there was already a vast underground gambling network in Phnom Penh, Sihanouk's logic was simple: Make gambling legal and spread the profits, some for him, some for the state, some for him, some for the police, some for him. Since the gambling was carried out with police protection in exchange for payoffs, and since Sihanouk's brother-in-law, Oum Mannorine, ran the police, the setup was ready-made. Let the gambling godfathers manage the casinos with open police protection.

Huge amounts of money were quickly generated from Cambodians at all levels. Gambling is a national addiction in Cambodia. In the streets and at the Hotel Le Royal I heard shopkeepers and busboys bet on how many times a gecko cry would sound. Once, while I sat with some Cambodian soldiers along a dusty rice field, it began to rain. One of the soldiers quickly traced a large circle in the dirt and then everyone bet how many raindrops would land within the circle in the next 60 seconds. At the Phnom Penh casino, raggedy *cyclo* drivers stood shoulder to shoulder with wealthy businessmen at the gaming tables while they all lost their life's savings. Suicides and anti-Sihanouk bitterness mounted. Historian David P. Chandler said that the Phnom Penh casino alone took in the equivalent of $10 million in 1969, which was 9 percent of the budget revenue that year. When Sihanouk went abroad in January 1970, shortly before the coup, Sirik Matak ordered the casinos closed. After the coup, Sihanouk and Monique were accused of skimming 10 percent off the top of all casino revenues.

Secret Bombing Begins

Although the prince thought himself aloof from politics for the moment, others had Cambodia very much on their minds. On March 18, 1969, exactly one year before the coup d'etat, President Nixon and a select few White House officials, including Henry Kissinger, launched Operation Breakfast. This operation was so secret that neither Congress nor most of the U.S. military command in Vietnam were informed.

The massive bombing program was directed at the alleged Central Office for South Vietnam, known as COSVN. This was supposed to be a vast underground concrete bunker system inside Cambodia that housed the high command for all Communist Vietnamese operations in South Vietnam. Not only was COSVN supposedly bombed, but a vast area inside Cambodia along its southeast border with Vietnam was repeatedly hit with saturation bombing. B-52s flying from Guam, each carrying 30 tons of bombs, rained thousands of 750-pound bombs on the region day and night. The alleged COSVN was never found, much less destroyed, but it provided the White House with an excuse to bomb Cambodia. As the bombing continued, Operation Breakfast was followed by Lunch, then Snack, then Dinner, then Dessert and finally Supper. Collectively called Menu, these operations involved huge bombers making more than 3,600 bombing raids inside Cambodia over 14 months. As time progressed, the bombing struck deeper and deeper in the kingdom. Apart from heavy civilian casualties, Menu's chief result was to drive NVA regulars deeper and deeper into Cambodia.

As the Vietnam War threatened to spill openly across the kingdom, Sihanouk was forced to reconsider his tattered weave of alliances, particularly his close ties with North Vietnam. Despite Hanoi's massive 1968 Tet offensive, South Vietnam had not fallen, and indeed now seemed stronger than ever. Meanwhile, North Vietnamese and Viet Cong troops operated at will in the eastern third of Cambodia, which Sihanouk's puny army was helpless to prevent.

On the political front, Hanoi and Peking also actively supported the Communist Khmer Rouge, which Sihanouk considered a threat to his country's shaky stability. Further aggravating the uneasy political situation was the country's depressed nationalized economy, which saw foreign reserves slide from $100 million in 1966 to $74 million in 1969.

Meanwhile, Prime Minister and Defense Minister Gen. Lon Nol remained openly opposed to Sihanouk's steady shift to the left to appease Hanoi. Lon Nol regularly denounced North Vietnam's blatant use of Cambodia to move troops and store supplies, even though he and fellow officers profited highly from the shipments. He spoke openly and critically against Hanoi, claiming it had 40,000 troops positioned in the kingdom.

Faced with these dilemmas, Sihanouk relented to pressure from the right and reestablished full diplomatic relations with the United States in June 1969. Two months earlier, President Nixon had held open the door for renewed relations by telling Sihanouk that the United States respected the "sovereignty, neutrality and territorial integrity" of Cambodia. Although both were well aware of it, neither head of state thought it necessary to mention the secret and ongoing B-52 bombing of Cambodian territory.

CHAPTER 3

The Coup

IN THE FALL OF 1969, the National Assembly increasingly insisted that Sihanouk order Hanoi to remove its troops from Cambodian soil. Supporting this rightist pressure were Sirik Matak and Lon Nol. Students and intellectuals growing more restive under Sihanouk's repressive political control added to the sense of rising instability.

Faced with these mounting attacks on his authority, Sihanouk and his wife, Monique, left Phnom Penh in the first week of January 1970 for another "rest cure" in France. The prince departed believing that without his presence, disorder between left and right in Phnom Penh would become so intense that he would be asked to return as a peacemaker. But this time, it wouldn't happen. Deputy Prime Minister Sisowath Sirik Matak, Sihanouk's royal cousin, was determined to force him out of power and tilt Cambodia back to the right. Sirik Matak knew it would best be done when Sihanouk was out of the country and unable to physically rally the populace to his side.

Sirik Matak was the complete opposite of Sihanouk. Elegantly slim, impeccably dressed, calm and composed, Sirik Matak was a leader in the business community. His opposition to Sihanouk's economic centralization had rallied many of the business leaders to his side. A soft-spoken man, he was more comfortable as a puppet master pulling political strings from behind the stage than he was standing in the spotlight. He had Lon Nol for the visible role. Politically to the right, Sirik Matak supported the United States' efforts to defeat the Communist Vietnamese presence in the region. However, Sirik Matak was also very much a realist: He knew he could not pull off a coup d'e-tat without unequivocal backing from the army, and that required Lon Nol's commitment to his cause. Although Lon Nol owed his rapid rise through the ranks to Sihanouk, he deeply resented the prince's close ties with Hanoi and his secret support of the Communist Vietnamese inside Cambodia. Bland, predictable and filled with dreams of restoring Cambodia's lost grandeur, Lon Nol was a ready-made ally for the quick-witted Sirik Matak.

Some years earlier, Lon Nol had suffered serious injuries when a Jeep he was riding in overturned. Now, by coincidence or design, he had gone to Neuilly-sur-Seine in France for medical treatment in December 1969, just a few weeks prior to Sihanouk's departure. While in France, he met with Sihanouk, which sparked reports that the two had collaborated on a scheme to force Communist Vietnamese troops out of Cambodia. The speculation was that on his return to Cambodia, Lon Nol would stir up anti-Vietnamese riots to reflect the country's deep resentment against Hanoi's abuse of Cambodian territory. For his part, so the story went, Sihanouk would then fly to Moscow and Peking to plead that they pressure Hanoi into removing its troops from Cambodia. Those events, in fact, did play out. But if that plot did occur between the two, as some intelligence officers insist did happen, then Sirik Matak saw it as an opening to direct the riots not only against Cambodian Vietnamese, but also against the embassies of Hanoi and the People's Revolutionary Government of Vietnam, or Viet Cong.

For all his prominence after the coup, it is clear now that Lon Nol neither originated nor developed the plan to overthrow Prince Sihanouk. He not only owed much to his royal mentor, he also was too cautious and too slow to make such a decision. Sirik Matak, on the other hand, was used to quick business decisions and had every reason to get rid of his cousin.

Economic Policies Reversed

With Sirik Matak laying out the plan, the two began their cautious campaign against Sihanouk. One of the first moves, indicative of Sirik Matak's guiding hand, was to reverse several of Sihanouk's economic policies. They first devalued the riel, which virtually eliminated the currency black market. They then ordered government tax collections funneled directly to the treasury, which kept the money out of Sihanouk's hands. Gambling casinos were closed, which shut off another financial pipeline to Sihanouk and his wife, Monique. Finally, Cambodian ambassadors were ordered to report directly to the foreign ministry, not to Sihanouk, which deprived him of valuable intelligence information.

In France, the prince flew into a rage when his chain-smoking cousin, nine years older and unawed, further undercut his authority by bringing Cambodia back into the International Monetary Fund, which Sihanouk had quit in a previous fit of anger.

In February 1970, the National Assembly pushed through a liberal bank law aimed at attracting foreign banks and investment. Sirik Matak followed that by directing that all 500 riel notes (then worth US$9) be recalled. This scheme struck a direct blow at the North Vietnamese and Viet Cong embassies, which had been hoarding the money and bringing in counterfeit bills to finance their operations in Cambodia. This was one of the first practical moves made to restrict Communist Vietnamese influence, moves that Sihanouk never made despite his recent denunciations of Hanoi's military presence.

In mid-February, Prime Minister Lon Nol called all provincial governors to Phnom Penh ostensibly to discuss the military situation in the countryside. The real reason, however, was to assess their attitudes toward Sihanouk. As unpopular as the prince might be with students and businessmen, he was still revered by millions of villagers and farmers. The governors themselves, however, showed no great attachments to Sihanouk, which Lon Nol found encouraging.

Lon Nol, increasingly confident because his open criticisms of Hanoi had triggered no reprisals, then closed Sihanoukville to ships carrying supplies for North Vietnamese troops in Cambodia. Sihanouk had done the same thing a year earlier but did not enforce it.

Continuing to build his case against Sihanouk's policies, but not against the prince personally, Lon Nol announced to the National Assembly in late February that 60,000 North Vietnamese army regulars were operating in Cambodia. His figure was 20,000 higher than he had declared six months earlier. The American Embassy had, just two months earlier, estimated that fully 20 percent of the currency circulating in Cambodia was in the hands of the Vietnamese Communists.

As March opened, Sihanouk felt the political squeeze against him even in far away France. The Cambodian right, deftly guided by Sirik Matak, continued to press Sihanouk to permit rapid liberalization of the economy. On March 2, the emboldened National Assembly voted to bar Sihanouk's return to the country unless he met its demands.

At Lon Nol's urging, the Assembly also insisted that Sihanouk deal decisively with the Communist Vietnamese who had entrenched themselves much deeper inside Cambodia as B-52 bombs hammered them. Intelligence reports at the time showed North Vietnamese forces were operating their own rice farms while sending medical teams throughout the countryside to build popular support.

In response to this rising turmoil, Sihanouk left his retreat and flew to Paris, where he announced he would visit Moscow and Peking to seek their support in forcing Vietnamese troops out of his country. But his last-minute efforts were too little and too late.

In Phnom Penh, Sirik Matak and Lon Nol had already initiated ambitious plans to simultaneously force the Vietnamese out and to topple

Sihanouk. Government agents fanned out through the countryside to stir anti-Vietnamese sentiment among the people. This tactic was aimed at focusing attention on the Vietnamese problem and away from the pending coup against Sihanouk. Sirik Matak and Lon Nol were well aware of the prince's revered status among the farmers and villagers and wanted to head off any demonstrations supporting him by creating the anti-Vietnamese diversions.

On March 8, 1970, the wheels of the actual coup d'etat began to turn. On that day in the sun-baked paddies of Svay Rieng province, in the region known as the Parrot's Beak, Cambodian soldiers disarmed several uncomprehending Viet Cong troops and bravely ordered them to leave the country. Small as the incident seemed, it marked a direct confrontation between Cambodia and Hanoi. This was a decision by Sirik Matak and Lon Nol, and not Sihanouk.

Anti-Sihanouk Demonstrations

Three days later, on March 11, Sirik Matak and Lon Nol ordered thousands of students to march against the Viet Cong and North Vietnamese embassies in Phnom Penh. Mingling among the students were dozens of Cambodian soldiers in civilian clothes who smashed down the embassy door and raced to the second floor to seize papers before they could be incinerated. The terrified Vietnamese employees took refuge in the Polish and Bulgarian embassies.

Still in France but now disdaining to speak with his usurpers, Sihanouk instead cabled his mother, Queen Kossomak: "Personalities … have profited from my absence to realize their designs. I therefore am going to return to the country to speak to the nation and the army, and ask them to make a choice." He added in typically dramatic fashion that he would resign if the people and the army did not support him.

Had Sihanouk in fact returned, it could have been a turning point in Cambodia's history. His popularity in most of the rural areas was immense. Had he immediately rallied the peasants, the army and the National Assembly may well have backed down. To carry this scenario further, there would have been no coup, no North Vietnamese army chopping off provinces in Cambodia, no Khmer Rouge takeover and no holocaust. But Sihanouk did not return.

On March 13, the Lon Nol cabinet cabled Sihanouk to formally inform him of the latest developments. The note was a virtual ultimatum for him to step down. At the same time, Lon Nol imperiously ordered the North Vietnamese and Viet Cong representatives in Phnom Penh to remove all their troops from Cambodia in 24 hours. It was bold talk for a general with a weak and untested army. Hanoi's generals must have laughed.

Some observers later speculated that Lon Nol's surprise order against the Vietnamese indicated that the United States was already behind him and was supporting the planned coup. No evidence to this effect has ever surfaced. Moreover, Lon Nol's subsequent bungling of his country's war effort against the Vietnamese and his penchant for calling field officers to tell them how to run battles he knew nothing about reflected his own ineptness, not U.S. involvement. Lon Nol, always imbued with a deep mixture of Buddhism and folk beliefs, believed that sheer faith could rid the country of the Vietnamese. A popular poster at the time showed Vietnamese wearing conical hats with a red star riding tanks but cowering before a glowing Buddha.

At this point, Queen Kossomak intervened at her son's request and asked Lon Nol to halt the anti-Vietnamese demonstrations. It had long been obvious to Sihanouk that however tenuous his neutralist policy might have been, it was suicide to give the powerful North Vietnamese army any reason to enter combat against Cambodia. Sirik Matak and Lon Nol did not accept such a view, but counted on American military backing to bail them out. They ignored the queen's request.

That same day, Prince Sihanouk enplaned for Moscow, declaring, "I am planning to ask the Russian and Chinese leaders to urge the Viet Cong to leave us alone." He added, somewhat plaintively, "The rightists do not need to stage a coup d'etat against me. I am not really attached to power."

On the morning of March 14, Lon Nol cabled Sihanouk that he was sending two envoys to meet with him. They were to tell Sihanouk that he could now return, but with reduced powers. The prince coldly replied that he would not meet with them. It was another small but vital break in the links between Sihanouk and the emerging powers in Phnom Penh. Lon Nol's cable, however, was one of several small indicators that he wanted Sihanouk to remain on the throne, but without real power. Lon Nol had no desire to destroy his long-time mentor, but now he was torn between two loyalties, Sihanouk and Sirik Matak.

The crisis worsened the following day, a Sunday, when North Vietnamese and Viet Cong efforts to negotiate Lon Nol's ultimatum that they leave the country broke down. The Vietnamese said it was impossible for them to depart, particularly on short notice, and they would have to discuss it with Hanoi. Lon Nol's negotiators coldly replied that they had already requested that South Vietnamese artillery units begin firing on Communist Vietnamese forces inside Cambodia. The talks abruptly ended.

That same day, to the astonishment of port authorities in Sihanoukville, an American merchant marine ship loaded with bombs and napalm suddenly steamed into the harbor. Bound for Thailand, the Columbia Eagle had been hijacked the day before by two young American crewmembers who proclaimed they were Marxist-Leninist revolutionaries. Port authorities placed the ship under armed guard while the preoccupied military command tried to sort out what was going on.

On Monday, March 16, events continued to accelerate. At Sirik Matak's order, the National Assembly convened to question Gen. Oum

Mannorine, head of the national security police and half-brother to Sihanouk's wife Monique. That anyone would dare to question one with such obvious palace connections was another clear signal that the momentum to greatly restrict Sihanouk's power was perhaps beyond stopping. Feeling humiliated by having to submit to such questioning, Mannorine returned to his office and ordered all national security troops throughout the country to proceed immediately to Phnom Penh. Recognizing his call as a counter-coup attempt, army authorities promptly seized him and countermanded the order. Sirik Matak then assumed command of the much-feared security police, ending the last possibility of organized armed support for Sihanouk.

On March 17, two cabinet ministers loyal to Sihanouk called for Lon Nol's arrest but were quickly carted away by police. To guard against any popular uprising in support of Sihanouk, the army took up positions around key installations such as the Post, Telephone and Telegraph (PTT) center, the government radio station and several ministries. Crude sandbag bunkers sprouted overnight on the corners of major intersections. Pochentong Airport was ordered closed.

The same day, an angry Sihanouk cabled from Moscow, again to his mother only, to state that "extreme rightists were attempting to inflate the Vietnamese affairs in order to change the politics of Cambodia." Sihanouk's cable offered no suggestion of conciliation.

At the time, there was speculation in Phnom Penh that Lon Nol interpreted the prince's criticism of the anti-Vietnamese demonstrations as a sign that he had not been able to secure Moscow's support in expelling the Viet Cong. Had Sihanouk been successful, Lon Nol's reasoning ran, he would not have denounced the anti-Vietnamese outbursts. And if the prince could not win Moscow's support for removing the Communist Vietnamese from Cambodia, then Sihanouk had outlived his usefulness. As Sirik Matak had long argued, there was thus no longer any reason to allow him to remain in office.

No Turning Back

But what was Lon Nol, the stolid, long-time ally of Sihanouk, really thinking? Years later, Australian historian David P. Chandler, a noted authority on Cambodia, interviewed Po Chhon, who was a military aide to Sirik Matak in 1970. In the pre-dawn hours of March 18, Po Chhon said, Sirik Matak and several other aides drove to Lon Nol's house where they roused him from his bed. Sirik Matak then demanded that Lon Nol sign a document calling for Sihanouk's removal from office. Sirik Matak thrust the paper at the astounded prime minister. When Lon Nol hesitated, Sirik Matak took a hard stance. As Chhon described it to Chandler, Sirik Matak again waved the document in front of Lon Nol and declared, "Nol, my friend, if you don't sign this paper, we'll shoot you!" Lon Nol, who by many accounts was prone to weeping, burst into tears and signed. There was now no turning back for either of them.

That morning the National Congress again convened at Sirik Matak's orders and at 11 a.m. took up "the case of Norodom Sihanouk." After two hours of denouncing the prince, his wife, his relatives and his policies, the Assembly delegates at 1 p.m. voted overwhelmingly in favor of withdrawing all confidence in the man who for 29 years had personified Cambodia.

The bloodless coup was so swift that even the large French Embassy staff and its 100-plus military advisers were caught unaware. They, like the rest of country, heard of the stunning decision from a government radio announcement. Phnom Penh remained calm, some factions likely uncertain whether to believe this report and others hoping it was true. The large number of armed soldiers patrolling the streets undoubtedly also had something to do with the passive response.

Halfway around the world in Moscow, Premier Alexei Kosygin broke the news of the coup to Prince Sihanouk as the two rode together to Sheremetovo Airport. One can imagine a certain smug satisfaction on

Kosygin's part in delivering such monumentally bad news. The Soviets, like the Americans, had long ago tired of trying to accommodate Sihanouk's erratic ways. While remaining polite, the Kremlin was unsympathetic to Sihanouk's plight and had every intention of continuing to support the NVA troops inside Cambodia.

On his arrival in Peking, Sihanouk was warmly greeted by Premier Chou En-lai and whisked to a guesthouse. There, Sihanouk slipped into his usual contradictory roles as he attempted to unravel the chain of events. First, he announced: "I have absolutely no intention of seeking to resume power." Later he promised to "participate in the sacred struggle our people will wage from inside and outside the country to obliterate this coup d'etat."

Sihanouk quickly called for the formation of a liberation army named the National United Front of Kampuchea (FUNK). He followed this by organizing a royal government in exile, which went by the unfortunate acronym of GRUNK. Cambodia's defense ministry countered by changing the name of the Royal Khmer Armed Forces (FARK) to Khmer National Armed Forces (FANK). At the risk of making it all sound like a Gilbert and Sullivan opera, the new lineup was FUNK and GRUNK against FANK and FARK.

Meanwhile in Phnom Penh, the Chinese Embassy quietly made an offer to Lon Nol: Permit Hanoi to continue using the Cambodian sanctuaries and Peking would not support Sihanouk. Lon Nol rejected the offer. Peking promptly recognized Sihanouk's government in exile, as did Hanoi and North Korea. The small kingdom, which had long escaped the full fury of the conflicts in Vietnam, now plunged toward war.

CHAPTER 4

The End of Neutrality

AS AN ASSOCIATED PRESS correspondent based in Hong Kong during this time, reports of Lon Nol's ultimatum to Communist Vietnamese troops in the kingdom made me wonder: Was Cambodia turning away from its leftist neutralism? If so, why? Getting into Cambodia was difficult because Sihanouk, in one of his anti-American snits, had banned all American journalists. But there were always alternatives. Posing as a tourist, I slipped into Cambodia on March 15 for a closer look at what was going on. At Pochentong Airport, a rotund airport security official who resembled comedian Buddy Hackett squinted long and hard at my Olivetti typewriter and camera. Both were dead giveaways for a journalist. Although seemingly aware of my deception, he allowed me to pass after extensively grilling me about what I was really doing here.

From the cramped backseat of my taxi, I found Phnom Penh's wide, uncrowded boulevards to be a welcome relief from the congestion in every other Asian capital. Here there were more bicyclists and *cyclo pousées*, three-wheeled pedicabs, than cars. The scent of jasmine drifted on humid river breezes and bright orange flowers spilled from the flame-of-the-forest trees along the streets. Two-story villas painted in pastel colors and sprinkled with wrought iron balconies reflected the 90 years of French colonial dominance.

The only hints of unease were sandbagged bunkers along the major thoroughfares. Even so, the soldiers in and around the bunkers showed no evidence of concern. Some smoked and laughed while they played cards; others reclined on the sandbags for an afternoon siesta in the oppressive heat. The more enterprising soldiers had gathered bamboo poles and palm leaves to erect crooked shade roofs over their bunkers. One of the soldiers, spotting me in the little Citroen taxi, quickly brought his AK-47 up as I passed to practice sighting. But he grinned as he did so.

I checked in at Hotel Le Royal, a grand, five-storied building with gables, terraced balconies and gardens that covered a full block. I took a bungalow in the back beside a frangipani tree hung with white blossoms. In the center of the garden was a swimming pool where Air France stewardesses in bikinis languidly spread sun lotion on themselves. The tile-roofed bungalow was spacious, with high ceilings and an overhead fan to stir the humid air. A white mosquito net suspended from the ceiling draped over the bed and the tile floors were cool beneath my bare feet.

AP did not have a stringer in the country and I could not interview government officials without the risk of being identified as an American journalist and expelled. I did have a contact at the U.S. Embassy, however. Bob Blackburn was a veteran political officer whom I had known since we were both in Jakarta during the overthrow of President Sukarno.

That evening over gin and tonics in the Royal's garden, we couldn't help quoting Yogi Berra's line that it seemed like déjà vu all over again. Another country, another autocrat on the way out. In recounting the fast-moving developments of the past two weeks, Blackburn said he had followed the crowd on March 11 that had sacked the Viet Cong and North Vietnamese embassies. Although his dark red hair, pale skin and black-rimmed glasses made him conspicuous among Cambodians, no one had discouraged Blackburn from observing.

Following the crowd as it marched from the Independence Monument down Norodom Boulevard, he watched as army troops in civilian clothes led the break-in and then threw thousands of documents from the second story windows.

The following morning, March 16, I took a *cyclo pousée* to the British Embassy. Rolling quietly on rubber tires, it was a pleasant way to travel and afforded me time to observe the city and the people. The tree-shaded streets and tiled sidewalks were clean and uncrowded. Women, graceful in their bright sarongs, smiled and called to friends as they made their way to the central market. Shopkeepers smiled and gave me a cordial wave as I passed. In some parts of Asia, a blond Westerner was still enough of a curiosity to invite stares and laughter. Here, the people were simply friendly.

Halfway to the embassy, I came upon a crowd of men in dusty work clothes and sandals marching down Norodom Boulevard, the same route Blackburn had followed a few days earlier. They carried banners written in Cambodian script that I could not read, but the hand-drawn placards they waved left little to the imagination: The crude drawings showed Cambodians in peasant garb wielding long knives against Vietnamese, identified by the typical Vietnamese conical hat. This seemed worth checking out.

I handed the *cyclo* driver a few riels and hurried to catch up with the marchers. As I walked along with them, trying to determine what was developing, a scuffle suddenly broke out in the middle of the crowd. People milled back and forth around the fight, making it difficult to see what was happening, but I caught glimpses of two men being savaged with short wooden staffs. The struggle was quick, violent and almost noiseless. The marchers flowed around the beaten men without even breaking stride. When the crowd had passed, two lifeless bodies lay on the hot concrete street. Blood pooled around their heads.

Catching up to the crowd again, I asked one of the men in my bad French what had happened. He replied with a shrug that the two victims had shouted for the overthrow of Prince Norodom Sihanouk.

This was bewildering. Was Sihanouk in or out? It took me awhile to grasp the paradox that this man presented. While much of the country's urban population resented Sihanouk's authoritarian rule and economic corruption, millions of peasants still revered him. This crowd, which had been bussed in from the countryside, was strongly pro-Sihanouk, something apparently overlooked by the Lon Nol supporters who had brought them here. In Asia, nothing is as it seems.

The crowd, with no further thought to the bludgeoning, soon arrived at a two-story residence that was the embassy of the Provisional Revolutionary Government of Vietnam, or Viet Cong. The tree-shaded building was deserted, but hundreds of pieces of paper from the previous assault still littered the front yard. The crowd milled about, disappointed at having nothing left to trash.

Later in the day, I stopped at the American Embassy, an aging white residence surrounded by wide lawns beside the Bassac River. There were two houses on the grounds. The larger was the ambassador's residence and the smaller one behind, with narrow hallways and small rooms, served as the embassy. Although diplomatic relations had resumed between Cambodia and the United States, Washington had not considered the country worthy enough to be assigned an ambassador. Diplomatic relations were handled by Mike Rives, the chargé d'affaires. An unpretentious man, Rives was a career foreign service officer who spoke French fluently and had established good connections with the Cambodian government and the military.

After a briefing from Rives, I sent several cables to the AP bureau in Saigon, attempting to describe what was happening in the city without it sounding like a news story. I couldn't refer to tanks parked around the city, so I called them "George Patton vehicles." Between that and other convoluted paraphrases, I doubt that the reports made much sense.

Signal to Washington

On the morning of March 18, Mike Rives was summoned to the Ministry of Defense. There, as I learned later, several of Lon Nol's senior aides assured him repeatedly that Cambodia would remain a close friend of the United States. Rives, an astute analyst, rightly concluded from this odd behavior that a significant political move could well be under way, possibly a coup. After learning that, I headed toward the French Embassy but was given little more than coffee and a perfunctory greeting. But even the French, with more than 100 military advisers working with the Cambodian army, were not tipped in advance of the impending coup. That embassy, along with all others, heard about the change in power the same way everyone else did: from the government radio announcement. The fact that the French were given no advance notice while the Americans were given a significant hint indicated that the new government wanted to align itself with the United States, not its old colonial ruler.

Phnom Penh took the National Assembly's vote of no confidence in Prince Sihanouk calmly. The large number of armed soldiers positioned throughout the city may have had much to do with that.

I wondered at the time how Sihanouk must have reacted to the news in private, after Kosygin had informed him of the coup. It should not have been that big of a surprise, considering the number of informants he had embedded in all levels of the government. Still, he must have been at once shaken, furious and plotting his return to power.

I first met the prince in 1964, about a year before he severed diplomatic relations with Washington. The occasion was the visit of China's Foreign Minister Chen Yi. I was then the AP correspondent in Bangkok and flew to Phnom Penh to cover the visit. At the time, Sihanouk seemed to be everywhere, meeting the Long March veteran at the airport, escorting him about the city in an American convertible and hosting him that evening at a state dinner.

After Chen Yi retired to his guesthouse, Sihanouk came outside in the warm night air to talk informally with a group of reporters and guests. Wearing a white evening jacket and easily shifting between French and English, he was immediately on stage. Sihanouk never seemed to have calm, collected conversations. As he spoke, his eyes opened wide, as if daring anyone to disbelieve him. He denounced the American military presence in Vietnam and Thailand. He also warned several times that the United States should not regard Cambodia as a mere pawn for its regional objectives. Warming to his topic, his high-pitched voice rose and fell excitedly as he delivered his punch lines. He shouted that France had been driven out of Indochina and the United States would soon follow. His eyebrows shot up and down for emphasis and perspiration beaded his brow.

Incongruously, an American with an accordion draped around his neck suddenly appeared and Sihanouk, his attention diverted, dropped his harangue. The American had arrived on a State Department tour and Sihanouk, an accomplished musician, kept him around. Now, at the prince's command, the American began playing. Inevitably there was "Lady of Spain," followed by some Cambodian folk songs, which made Sihanouk ecstatic. The prince then took the accordion himself and played several numbers, beaming and nodding at us like the veteran performer he was. But that was years ago and now Sihanouk had lost his stage.

On March 18, after learning of the coup, I went directly to the Post, Telephone and Telegraph, or PTT, to file the story. The fortress-like two-story concrete building was darker than usual because it was closed. No telephone, no telegraph, no way to send the coup story. It was a journalist's nightmare: big story, no competition, but no way to get it out. I took a taxi to Pochentong Airport hoping to find someone to hand-carry my stories to Bangkok or Saigon, but the airport was closed.

The following day, cable connections were restored, but not the telephone. I took my reports to the cable office where I was directed to a small room. There, a newly appointed censor went through each story with painstaking slowness, penciling out any references to a military presence in the city or mention of a coup d'etat. The National Assembly, he lectured, had only voted no confidence in the prince.

To send the complete story and photos without censorship, I cabled the Saigon AP bureau and arranged for one of their drivers to meet me at the Vietnam-Cambodia border. After a four-hour trip in a hired car that took me across the Mekong on a creaky old ferry and past miles of dry paddy fields, I handed over the packet to the Saigon driver with no problems from the border guards.

But right at the border, just inside Cambodia, was another story: a large flea market displaying scores of automatic weapons, including Chinese- and Russian-made AK-47s, American M-16s and wooden crates of ammunition. Smiling salesmen held up deadly B-40 rocket launchers, a favorite VC weapon. Others offered me Light Anti-Tank Weapon rocket launchers. These handheld launchers, being American made, were naturally disposable. Rickety wooden tables were covered with flak vests, uniforms, boots, medical bags, C-rations and ponchos. Vietnamese merchants stood beside their wares, nodding and smiling as they urged me to buy. The new Cambodian regime didn't have to ask Washington for military supplies; it could just send a truck convoy to the border. For the right price, anything was available.

Journalists Begin Arriving

Within a few days, the new government opened the airport and all communications. Dozens of journalists, cameramen and television crews dragging cameras, lights, recorders and cables flooded into Phnom Penh. Most of them established headquarters at the Hotel Royal or the nearby Hotel Monorom. The Air France stewardesses and the French businessmen who lolled about the pool at the Royal with their Cambodian mistresses were openly contemptuous toward the brash Americans. La Cyrene, the excellent French restaurant beside the hotel pool, was now crowded with free-spending journalists.

In an attempt to exert some measure of control over the journalists, the Ministry of Information declared that everyone must obtain press credentials. It also established a daily military briefing session in a stuffy little room upstairs in an empty government-owned building. The briefings were conducted by a Cambodian army major with a particularly unfortunate name for a military spokesman: Am Rong. Moreover, Maj. Rong was a gentle soul who had studied film production in Paris and was not cut out for the give and take of press conferences with skeptical international journalists. Because Am Rong's English was marginal, a Cambodian enlisted man who had studied in the United States assisted him. Rong never seemed right as he bravely announced Cambodian military successes to a disbelieving and occasionally abusive press corps.

Although Sihanouk's overthrow provoked no visible opposition in Phnom Penh, the coup was violently opposed in other cities. Two busloads of peasants coming to Phnom Penh to support Sihanouk were fired on by army units and more than 100 were killed. In Kompong Cham, mobs rampaged on March 26 and 27, killing two National Assemblymen. Police fired on the rioters, killing several dozen, but then fled as the crowd swelled to thousands. The protesters were whipped to a frenzy in part out of genuine emotion at the thought of their beloved Sihanouk being unceremoniously deposed, but also in part by Communist agitators. The maddened crowd eventually caught Gen. Lon Nol's youngest brother, Lon Nil. Because he owned a rubber plantation there, he had apparently been sent by the general to report on the growing unrest. After beating him to death with clubs, the mob reportedly cut out his liver and offered pieces of it to willing takers to show their contempt for the new government. More riots were reported in other cities.

As Sirik Matak had feared, the rural populace was rising in support of Sihanouk, who was directing radio broadcasts into the rural areas calling for them to rise up against Lon Nol. In a misguided effort to divert attention away from Sihanouk, the government redoubled its efforts to stir resentment against the Vietnamese. Posters showing Vietnamese in conical hats being bayoneted or knifed by Cambodian villagers were plastered on buildings and trees all over the country.

Once, returning to the hotel after a late dinner on the floating Mekong Restaurant, I decided a poster would be a good souvenir. I had no sooner pulled one off a tree than half a dozen plainclothes policemen who had been hiding in shadowy doorways suddenly surrounded me. A car arrived in minutes and I was bundled off to a police station where the watch officer questioned me in Cambodian. When I said I didn't understand, he shifted to French. When I had trouble following all his rapid questions, he shifted to excellent English. After an hour of explaining that I was not a saboteur, he released me. He also let me keep the poster.

Lon Nol considered the anti-Vietnamese campaign an excellent way to keep the people's minds off of Sihanouk. He coupled it with newspaper and magazine articles warning how treacherous the Vietnamese could be. Anti-Vietnamese posters and leaflets were air-dropped over the countryside. The campaign worked well. Too well.

Mekong Massacre

I saw the first grisly evidence of this pogrom in April while crossing the Mekong River at Neak Leung, about an hour's drive below Phnom Penh. Standing on the vibrating steel deck of the old French car ferry, I noticed other passengers pointing upstream. What at first I thought were logs were actually bodies of men, hundreds of them, twisting and turning on the current and bumping against the ferry. Women put handkerchiefs to their mouths and turned away. All the bodies were bloated, indicating several days in the turbid water. Some floated individually, others in rafts of 10 or more tied together. Most had their hands bound behind their back. Gaping wounds could be seen on some. A few of the victims were women but the others overwhelmingly were men. Where bodies became caught in weeds along the riverbanks, villagers gingerly pushed them back into the current with long bamboo poles.

By the time I left to break the story, I had counted more than 300 bodies and still more were coming.

In the following days, another AP reporter who had arrived from Saigon for a short stay, John Vinocour, and I pieced together reports from military and diplomatic sources that showed how Cambodian troops had rounded up an estimated 800 Vietnamese men from villages surrounding Phnom Penh. All were herded aboard navy landing crafts moored on the Mekong. After their hands were bound behind their backs and groups of 10 or more were tied together, they were forced at bayonet point to jump from the landing crafts into the river. Once in the water, soldiers opened fire on them with automatic weapons, killing many outright and wounding hundreds of others. Tied together as they were, all soon drowned. It was an ugly foretaste of the murderous mindset that eventually swept the entire country.

While this anti-Vietnamese campaign briefly diverted attention from Sihanouk, it did nothing to stop North Vietnam's rapid troop deployment deeper and deeper into Cambodia. Pouring south along the Ho Chi Minh trail complex from Laos and into northeast Cambodia, NVA forces quickly secured the northern Mekong River cities of Stung Treng and Kratie, then moved into the upland rubber plantations.

By May, North Vietnamese forces controlled most of the northern and northeastern quarters of Cambodia and were pushing steadily closer to Phnom Penh. American electronic intelligence gathering planes monitoring Communist ground troops in Cambodia recorded a sharp increase in activities. Part of this was the NVA providing more arms and training to the Khmer Rouge, which until this time had consisted of fewer than 4,000 men and women hiding in the forests. The Khmer Rouge were further aided by Prince Sihanouk who, from his new base in Peking, called for a popular uprising against the Lon Nol/Sirik Matak government. Thousands of poor farmers and villagers who had been bombed by American and Vietnamese planes left their land to join the Khmer Rouge, believing they were fighting for Sihanouk.

For its part, the Lon Nol government controlled several key cities in the southern half of the country and made half-hearted attempts to protect the long and vulnerable highways connecting the cities. But with poorly trained Cambodian troops stretched thin over the long distances, any highway traveler was subject to an ambush. It was something that journalists covering the expanding war were to learn only too well.

In order to expand its small armed forces, the government responded to the NVA attacks by mobilizing all men 18 years and older. Many older civil service men were also mobilized. In poignant contrast to the anti-war rallies and draft dodging in the United States, thousands of Cambodian high school and university students went cheerfully off for military training. Students and bureaucrats marched about parks and school grounds with smiles on their faces, blissfully unaware of what faced them. They were issued olive drab uniforms but little else in the way of equipment. They trained with wooden sticks instead of rifles and most wore rubber shower sandals or thin-soled street shoes instead of boots. After two weeks of inept training, they were issued a hodgepodge of Soviet, East German, Czech and Chinese weapons, most of which required different size ammunition, and shipped off to the battle lines.

The woefully unprepared new troops rode off to war in the backs of confiscated Coca-Cola delivery trucks, laughing and singing as if headed to a grand picnic. Several young men, eyes bright with anticipation of adventure, assured me that they would be back in a couple weeks after having driven the cowardly Vietnamese from their country. Many held up Buddhist amulets they wore around their neck that had been specially blessed. "If I put this in my mouth during battle, I will be invincible," one fresh-faced boy assured me.

It was pitiful to see them depart so full of confidence and so ignorant of what lay ahead of them. As brave as they were, the battle-hardened North Vietnamese would simply shred them.

The Invasion

The intense and secret 1969 bombings inside Cambodia, known by the code name Menu, had forced the Communist forces back from the South Vietnam border. The April 29 invasion by U.S. and South Vietnamese forces drove them even deeper into Cambodia. The bombing and invasion took some pressure off U.S. troops in South Vietnam, but these initiatives spelled disaster for Cambodia.

President Richard Nixon, National Security Assistant Henry Kissinger and a select few military commanders had decided that Vietnamese Communist troops would no longer be permitted to use Cambodia as a sanctuary. Otherwise, the argument ran, the planned withdrawal of American soldiers, part of "Vietnamization," would be threatened. In a nationwide television address on April 20, Nixon declared that peace was in sight and the U.S. troop withdrawal would continue. After noting that the enemy continued to escalate its activities in Laos and Cambodia, he prophetically warned, "I shall not hesitate to take strong and effective measures" against them.

Ten days later, which was April 29 in Cambodia, Nixon told a stunned American television audience that American and South Vietnamese forces had crossed into Cambodia "to attack the headquarters for the entire Communist military operation in South Vietnam." Although few American or Vietnamese military leaders really believed such a headquarters existed, it was a convenient ploy for Nixon. He also declared that the move was "not for the purpose of expanding the war into Cambodia, but for the purpose of ending the war in Vietnam." Visibly perspiring, the president went on to declare that the United States must not act "like a pitiful, helpless giant."

American and South Vietnamese infantry units first rolled across the border near the Fish Hook. The flat land consisted largely of dry rice fields, which field officers considered lovely tank country. The armored columns rolled through small villages with generally light opposition. In the United States, however, opposition to Nixon's decision grew swiftly and finally culminated in the deaths of four Kent State students after National Guard troops fired on them during a campus demonstration.

Unable to find the mythical Central Office for South Vietnam (COSVN), the invasion force continued to advance deeper into Cambodia. Several arms and supply caches were discovered and destroyed, but the Military Advisory Command, Vietnam (MACV) later acknowledged there was ample evidence that the North Vietnamese, informed ahead of time, had already transferred most of their supplies to safe locations.

As U.S. and South Vietnamese armored units pushed into the rubber plantation towns of Snoul and Mimot, both near the border, they received light to moderate enemy fire. Norman Lloyd, a CBS cameraman who had just arrived in Vietnam from his native Australia, was with a group of journalists accompanying the American tanks near Snoul. After an initial contact with the enemy, the tanks stopped short of the town and set up a night defensive perimeter. Shortly before dark, a Chinook helicopter arrived and an Army officer urged the journalists and television crews to load up and return to the base camp to file their stories. Norman, however, mingled among the troops and remained behind.

Minutes after the journalists departed, a flight of F-4 Phantoms streaked low overhead to bomb and napalm Snoul. During the night, flames from the burning town were clearly visible. In the morning, the armored units moved into the town with no opposition. The only sign of people, Norman said, were the bodies of one man and three children that the enemy had piled in the middle of the road into Snoul.

In retrospect, it's easy to fault U.S. officers using such firepower on a seemingly defenseless area. But with the war clearly winding down in 1970, who wanted to risk being killed while fighting in Cambodia, clearly a questionable extension to an already divisive war.

Meanwhile, South Vietnamese troops were intent on settling some old scores with Cambodians. South Vietnamese armored personnel carriers returning home were often stacked high with stolen motorcycles, televisions and anything else that could be sold. The Saigon troops took particular delight in destroying everything Cambodian, including firing on fleeing refugees in retaliation for the Cambodian slaughter of Vietnamese residents.

Following the invasion, the United States abruptly decided Cambodia was now a valuable ally and markedly increased military assistance to the Lon Nol government. Washington had initially provided $9 million in military aid and quickly followed that with $40 million more. In one secret deal, the United States reequipped the entire Indonesian army with M-16s in exchange for all its Soviet- and Chinese-made AK-47 rifles, which were then shipped to Cambodia.

Before the coup, Cambodia's budget for 1970 was then the equivalent of $170 million, with the military taking one-third of that. When the military gobbled down its budget in the first three months after the coup, the entire budget was revised upward to nearly $400 million. At the same time, government revenues from taxes, custom duties and tourist dollars fell by half. Rice and rubber production, which normally brought in 70 percent of export earnings, were at a near halt. Invading U.S. and South Vietnamese forces mauled most of the country's five major rubber plantations, but when they eventually left, the North Vietnamese resumed control of the plantations.

As the North Vietnamese regulars consolidated their hold on the northern half of the kingdom, Lon Nol's inexperienced and poorly equipped troops quickly learned they were no match for the advancing NVA.

The war was coming to Phnom Penh. The good news was that driving to the combat areas took less time; the bad news was that you might not make it back.

CHAPTER 5

Mercedes Marauders

AS THE WAR swiftly expanded, journalists and television crews arrived in larger numbers. Some were new to Asia and others had considerable experience in Vietnam. Many thought it would be an easy war to report. But covering the war in Cambodia was distinctly different from doing so in Vietnam, and many journalists never learned this. In Vietnam, journalists traveled on U.S. or Vietnamese military transport, including cargo planes, helicopters and armored personnel carriers. You were always surrounded by well-armed troops with lots of support, including artillery, helicopter gunships and fast-movers like F-4 Phantoms loaded with 250-pound bombs and napalm canisters. In Vietnam, you might be surrounded by the NVA too, but you were among superbly trained and disciplined American soldiers. Finally, if the situation turned desperate, U.S. Army helicopter pilots would fly through unbelievable amounts of enemy fire to get everybody out.

In Cambodia, on the other hand, our transportation was a rented four-door Mercedes diesel sedan. That was it. There was no backup. If the Mercedes stalled on an empty road, you were stuck. No one was coming to pick you up. The primary goal in covering Cambodia was to travel to the combat areas and back without being shot or captured. To do that, you had to drive from Phnom Penh down long, empty highways with no security to wherever you believed a battle was going on. You didn't know what you would find when you got there, if you got there.

Enroute, you first went through some slipshod army checkpoints, which were usually just some empty 55-gallon oil drums in the middle of the road with a bamboo pole across them. The checkpoints were manned by two or three soldiers lolling in the sandbagged bunker shaded against the fierce sun by a piece of scrounged tin. Sometimes the soldiers would check press credentials for lack of anything better to do, and other times they would languidly wave you through. Few soldiers spoke French, so trying to determine whether enemy troops were nearby was usually a game of charades. If the soldiers smiled and waved you through, that could mean a) it was calm out there, b) they didn't know what was out there, or c) they wanted you to check it out for them. But if they made shooting sounds and drew their fingers across their throats, it might be time to reconsider your travel plans.

Still, you couldn't accept government claims of victory; you had to check it out yourself. So you drove mile after mile past dreary rice fields and through small villages that clung to each side of the road. To survive, you had to learn to read the landscape: were people working in the fields or were they empty? Why had the oncoming traffic, sparse at it was, suddenly stopped? Did the people in the village you drove through appear relaxed or afraid? You also drove at high speed, particularly if the tropical darkness seemed about to overtake you. Never wanting to be caught in the countryside at night, you raced through empty towns, swerving or stopping for nothing short of a human or a barricade. Chickens and little swaybacked pigs scurried across the road in front of you at their peril.

The Executions Begin

Early April was a particularly bad time for newsmen. On April 5, French photographer Gilles Caron with Agence Gamma became the first reporter captured and killed in Cambodia. Caron, who had gained prominence after his coverage of the 1968 Paris riots, was seized while crossing the Parrot's Beak, a section of the Cambodian border that points right at Saigon. Ten more newsmen would be captured in the next two weeks. A lucky few were held for just an hour or two and then released.

With a few exceptions, the journalists who died in Cambodia were not killed in the line of fire, a risk understood and accepted by most correspondents. Instead they were captured and brutally executed. From the few remains found and from interviews with Cambodians at the time, the newsmen were normally killed by being clubbed to death. None was held as a prisoner of war and later released or exchanged. Each was simply murdered.

In the summer of 1970, 25 journalists were captured and ultimately killed. Of this number, 20 died in April and May. They included men from the United States, France, Germany, Japan, Switzerland, Austria, the Netherlands and India. To keep track of the missing and to register new arrivals, several journalists formed a Committee for the Safety of Foreign Correspondents in Cambodia. Art Dommen, Los Angeles Times, Dick Hunt, NBC, and Steve Bell, ABC, were among the organizers. The committee also prepared some precautionary guidelines for journalists to follow in the event they were captured. Many of the cautions were just a matter of common sense, which some newsmen displayed a profound lack of in their actions. One such advisory included a lengthy suggestion to speak politely to anyone who stopped your car at gunpoint. Personally, I was invariably polite to anyone who pointed an automatic weapon at me.

On April 6, the day after Caron was captured, Americans Sean Flynn and Dana Stone also disappeared in the same area. Flynn was tall and rakishly handsome like his matinee idol father, Errol Flynn. Sean and I had gone sailing together several times off China Beach in South Vietnam but had never worked together. He talked sometimes about sailing his father's all-black 60-foot sloop in the Mediterranean, which was a far cry from the little 14-foot rental boat we had. Still, to liven things up, Sean would lay the sailboat over in the choppy sea until water flowed over the gunwales. A freelance photographer from a wealthy family, he didn't need the money. He was in Cambodia, as he had been in Vietnam, just to test himself against dangerous odds.

Tim Page, a veteran photographer and close friend of Flynn, once recounted in an interview with David Gergen how Flynn had accompanied a group of Special Forces and Hmong mercenaries in an attack to take back a South Vietnamese outpost that had been overrun by the North Vietnamese. "As they rolled up the hill to retake the outpost, they came under very intense fire, and all around there, all the Western officers were taken out, at which point Sean picked up the charge, Arrowflex in one hand, an M-16 in the other and won the attack over the top of the hill." That is someone pushing his luck.

Captured with Flynn was Dana Stone, a flint-hard New Englander who had seen a great deal of combat in Vietnam as a still photographer. In Cambodia, he had begun shooting as a freelance cameraman for CBS. Stone and Flynn were close friends and often worked together despite being such a study in contrasts. Stone was the exact opposite of Flynn. Neither well traveled nor sophisticated, he was short, wore thick glasses and spoke with a pronounced New England twang. But he was tenacious, a fine photographer and known for his endurance under any conditions. Marines called him the "mini-grunt." I knew Stone from Vietnam, where we had often crossed paths. When I heard he had been captured, I felt dismayed. I believed him to be too experienced to let himself be caught. If it could happen to

Stone, it could happen to anyone. In the end, Stone had stuck with his daredevil buddy. To their deaths.

Riding their rented Honda motorcycles, the two had accompanied a government-sponsored tour to Svay Rieng province on April 6. The outing, which included a large army escort in ancient pre-World War II armored cars, was organized to show foreign newsmen that Cambodian soldiers were securing the countryside. But security in Cambodia was always relative. Just past the town of Chi Phou, a roadblock was seen in the distance. It appeared to be a car parked sideways on the highway. Everyone got off the bus to decide what was next. Sean and Dana, impatient with the delay, drove their bikes down the road to scout it out. They stopped short of the car and then returned to report that they had seen no sign of bad guys. But roadblocks were a bad sign, so the press tour continued to sit on the road.

Sean and Dana, however, said they would have another look. To get photos of enemy troops inside Cambodia would be a real coup. Both were wearing army boonie hats and a mixture of U.S. military garb and civilian clothes. No one remembers exactly what they wore that day, but Flynn commonly wore tiger-stripe army pants favored by Green Berets in Vietnam. With cameras over their shoulders, the two gunned their bikes down the road, slowed to go around the car and were never seen again.

Henry Kamm, a New York Times correspondent who previously spent many years covering Europe, knew the East German reporter in the press tour. Kamm asked the German and two Soviet journalists to accompany him to the roadblock, where they would plead for the release of the others. Kamm's reasoning was that perhaps the Vietnamese and Cambodian communists up the road would listen to their Marxist allies. The German and the two Soviets begged off. So, incidentally, did the Cambodian army unit accompanying the press tour. Despite protests, they turned around and headed back to Phnom Penh, abandoning the journalists.

Two Japanese journalists, perhaps not understanding the severity of the situation because of their poor command of English or perhaps thinking they would be accepted as neutrals, drove their car slowly down to the roadblock and then around it. Akira Kusaka and Yujiro Takagi, both with Fuji TV, were never seen again and, like most of the others, were assumed to have been executed.

That same day, in a different part of the same Svay Rieng region, French photographer Claude Arpin, a former French paratrooper who was stringing for Newsweek, and Guy Hannoteaux, a veteran correspondent with L'Express, drove out from Phnom Penh in search of Caron. Both were captured and killed.

The Svay Rieng area around Chi Phou was clearly dangerous and there were no battles to cover there, which meant there was no urgent need to go there. Still, the unwary or foolhardy drove into the area, a long and lonely distance from Phnom Penh. On April 8, just days after seven journalists disappeared there, two more disappeared and were believed killed. These were Dieter Bellendorf, a camera stringer for NBC, and Georg Gensluckner, an Austrian freelance cameraman.

A Lucky Few

A few weeks after Flynn and Stone disappeared, a CBS crew drove to the area in hopes of a story. Since everything seemed quiet, they stopped by a rice mill to see if they could do a little story on it, something to justify their time in the field. Correspondent Bert Quint recalled later that as they started walking over to the rice mill, several men carrying AK-47s suddenly stepped from the nearby tree line. On hearing Bert's exclamation, cameraman Carl Sorensen spun toward them. The enemy troops, apparently thinking the camera and long lens on Sorensen's shoulder was a weapon, fell to the ground. That act gave the CBS crew just the few seconds they needed. With Flynn and Stone on their minds, they decided not to be captured and raced for the car. As they piled in, the soldiers opened fire. "It was lucky they were on full automatic, which was not as accurate," Quint said. As it was, one bullet shattered the rear window, literally parted Quint's hair and then went through the arm of French soundman Patrick Forrester.

Three others with good fortune were Richard Dudman of the St. Louis Post Dispatch, Elizabeth Pond, Washington Post, and Michael Morrow with Dispatch News Service. All three were captured May 7 while driving into Cambodia from Vietnam as they attempted to follow the invading U.S. and South Vietnamese forces. The three were released June 15 and Dudman later reported that all times they were in the hands of North Vietnamese. Their cause was perhaps also aided because all three were known critics of the American military role in Vietnam and because Morrow spoke Vietnamese fluently.

In May, CBS's Kurt Hoefle, Don Webster and Skip Brown were pulled over at gunpoint by the Khmer Rouge. Kurt Hoefle, a German citizen, coolly convinced the Khmer Rouge that all in the car were Germans and they were allowed to go. In many cases where journalists were stopped and then released, North Vietnamese officers were present and sometimes, but not always, overruled the more bloodthirsty Khmer Communists who considered the journalists to be imperialist spies. Newsmen who were captured and not released were generally held only for a few days at most before the Khmer Rouge executed them. There were unconfirmed reports of some journalists being held prisoner for two or more years, but if so, none returned alive.

For a long while, most of us thought that Sean and Dana were probably alive. I expected them to come blasting into the hotel driveway any day now to tell us about their ultimate scoop: traveling with the enemy. But as days and weeks passed, we knew it wasn't likely. The one person who never gave up hope, however, was Dana's wife, Louise. For six months she remained in Cambodia to doggedly gather every scrap of information she could about their fate. She regularly arranged for flyers to be distributed throughout the area where they were captured, offering a reward for information on the two. Later, when she moved back to Saigon, she kept up the search, sending out leaflets and asking anyone who went into the Svay Rieng area to seek information about the missing pair. We admired her unflagging determination and hoped that if we disappeared, someone would do as much for us.

Help or Hindrance?

Many of us wondered whether some of the captured journalists were secretly kept alive for months, if not years. An equally nagging question was what the U.S. government did, or did not do, to seek their return. In 1973, three years after most of the journalists disappeared, a group of journalists headed by CBS's Walter Cronkite met with Henry Kissinger to seek his assistance in getting the journalists freed. Others who attended the meeting with Kissinger were Peter Arnett of the Associated Press, Richard Dudman of the St. Louis Post-Dispatch and Zalin Grant, a freelance writer and former U.S. Army intelligence officer in Vietnam. Grant, who spoke fluent Vietnamese, had been engaged by the Committee to Protect Journalists in Cambodia to gather what information he could on missing newsmen. He wrote an account of the meeting with Kissinger:

"The weight of our evidence, which was fragmentary and carefully stated, indicated that some of the newsmen were still alive three years after their capture and that Hanoi clearly had knowledge of their fate. We were at the White House to turn over the information to Henry Kissinger and to ask him to intercede with North Vietnam.

"Henry Kissinger appeared persuaded by our evidence and the likelihood that some of the newsmen were still in Communist hands. He promised us he would make representations to Hanoi in the strongest way. Thus, the four of us battle-grizzled reporters were as shocked as the youngest and most naïve POW wife when we got a look at the letter Kissinger sent the North Vietnamese. It read:

> 'A group of American journalists, representing many members of their profession from all political persuasions, have come to me to inquire if anything further could be done to determine the fate of some of their colleagues who have been missing in Cambodia. Investigations and searches that they have conducted independently have led them to believe that their colleagues might be alive. They asked me whether the DRV [North Vietnam] was in a position to assist in this matter. I told them that we had no basis for believing these American journalists were alive or that the DRV was in a position to assist. Nevertheless, I told them I would make one further inquiry.'

"No basis for believing the Americans were alive? That was certainly not what he told us. Kissinger's letter was a clear invitation to the North Vietnamese to deny, as they did, that they knew anything about the newsmen. The normally unflappable Cronkite was outraged. So were the rest of us. Cronkite tried, without success, to get an explanation out of Kissinger for what we felt was a double cross.

"Footnote: Fifteen years later, on April 20, 1988, Colonel Joseph Schlatter, head of DIA's POW/MIA office, testified before Congress that a number of the post-1975 'unresolved' first-hand sighting reports of Caucasians still being held in Indochina pertained to journalists captured in Cambodia. The classification 'unresolved' was as close as DIA came to conceding that an intelligence report about unaccounted-for MIAs could be true."

C'est La Guerre

As the Cambodian conflict spread, the Lon Nol government quietly abandoned any plans it had to retake the northern and eastern portions of the country. It had all it could do to maintain connections to Battambang in the northwest and the port of Sihanoukville to the south. It managed to hang on to provincial capitals like Svay Rieng, Kompong Thom, Kompong Cham, Kampot and Takeo. But the highways were long, and defending them was difficult.

In early May the North Vietnamese demonstrated their power to strike anywhere they pleased by capturing Neak Leung. This was a large town alongside the Mekong River about 60 miles southeast of Phnom Penh. It was also a vital ferry crossing for Highway 1, which ran from Phnom Penh through the Parrot's Beak to Saigon. The sleepy river town was always a favorite stopover of mine. While waiting for the ferry to make its way slowly across water, now brown with the arrival of the monsoon season, I would sit at a some rickety tables in a noodle stall and watch the cheerful and handsome Cambodian people. War or not, they had to eat and the market was always filled with beautifully stacked piles of vegetables. Women squatted in front of their wares and warded off flies with palm leaf fans.

While I ate a bowl of spicy soup, smooth-skinned children would stand next to me and smile as they petted the blond hair on my arms. The great Mekong, brown and swollen with the arrival of the monsoon season, swept silently past just a few meters away. The busy market town was a small oasis from the war. Then one day, it all changed. North Vietnamese forces struck the town one evening just to show they could. The Cambodian defenders around Neak Leung were ill prepared for any assault and were overrun in a single night.

Neak Leung's fall severed the supply flow to Cambodian troops beyond the Mekong and the government geared up to take it back. The North Vietnamese had no intention of making a stand there; they just wanted to make a statement. The river town was recaptured a few days later, but only after Cambodian and South Vietnamese planes turned the few concrete buildings into bombed-out shells. Later, a South Vietnamese riverine force moved in and made it their operations base. Well-armed and well-equipped, the South Vietnamese troops swaggered about town buying what they wanted from peddlers while Cambodian soldiers in rubber sandals watched with a mixture of envy and bitterness.

The battle for Neak Leung along the Mekong River made good television film. At one point I was near the front with a British television team. The correspondent was, as he confided to me, brand new in country and brand new to television. I don't remember his name but I'll call him Brian Jones. He was trying to do an on-camera close and the nearby rattle of friendly machine gun fire made it sound attractively dangerous.

Taking the microphone from the soundman, Jones crouched against a dirt embankment and on cue from the cameraman said, "This battle for the river city has raged all day, but Cambodian troops remain pinned down by the intensive enemy fire you can hear around me. This is Brian Jones in Nok Long." The Cambodian rifle fire had continued throughout his close and he looked pleased.

The cameraman said, "It's not Nok Long, it's Neak Leung. Do it again."

Brian Jones took the microphone again, brushed his lank blond hair back and repeated his close, ending with, "This is Brian Jones in Nook Loong." The cameraman, a paragon of patience, said, "It's Neak Leung, not Nook Loong. Give it another go."

A little flustered now, Jones repeated to himself, "Nick Long, Nick Long."

"No, it's Neak Leung. Two syllables in each word."

"Nee-ak Lee-ung."

The cameraman pointed his finger at Jones again to indicate he was rolling film. As the Brit once more began his on-camera close, the firing around us came to an abrupt halt. It was absolutely still. Brian finished up and managed to say at the end, "Nee-ak Lee-ung." He looked pleased until the cameraman said, "The shooting stopped. We are not under 'intensive enemy fire.'"

"Bloody hell!"

We sat there for a while and when the firing picked up again Jones repeated his routine, but ended up saying, "This is Brian Jones in Nick Nong." He threw down his microphone and the soundman buried his head to smother a laugh. I left as Brian began again, saying, "Take 8."

Takeo and Col. Blood

Vietnamese in Cambodia, regardless of how many generations they had been there, were now the scapegoat for everything that was wrong in the kingdom. An ethnic Vietnamese family's worst nightmare too often arrived in the form of Cambodian soldiers. Takeo was a horrific example.

Takeo was a pleasant little city halfway between Phnom Penh and the Gulf of Thailand. Its tree-shaded streets were usually busy with small trucks and motorcycles going about daily business. I was returning from Sihanoukville, where I had gone to see the hijacked American munitions ship, the Columbia Eagle. As I drove through Takeo, it seemed strangely quiet. Few people were on the streets and most shops were shuttered. I drove cautiously about, wondering if North Vietnamese troops or Khmer Rouge had seized the area. At an intersection I saw Don Kirk, with the Washington Star. He was a good newsman, although sometimes lacking in social graces, as we all were in that high-pressured environment. I had known him in Jakarta, where he was once unceremoniously evicted from the palace after casually scooping up a piece of cake that had just been set down in front of then-President Sukarno. I flagged him down.

"What's going on?" I asked.

"Nothing," he replied. He seemed evasive.

"The town's too quiet."

"Yeah, well, I'm headed back to Phnom Penh," he said. "You should go back too." With that, he drove off. It's not unusual for newsmen to avoid tipping off the competition, but Kirk's behavior at the time seemed odd.

Certain that something was up, I drove around the quiet city until I came to a long, one-story school building with a number of Cambodian soldiers milling about the grounds. Adjoining the school was a small hospital. Several orderlies or doctors in white coats lounged against the low brick wall that separated the hospital from the school. I asked one what was happening and he replied in French that there were some wounded people in the building. He gave no further explanation.

I walked into the school. Wooden shutters had been pulled tight over the windows and the tile corridor was gloomy. As I walked along, I looked in several empty rooms but found nothing. I kept walking, growing increasingly uneasy. I don't remember which I heard first, the buzzing flies or the moaning. Near the end of the corridor in a barren assembly room were about 30 Vietnamese men, women and children. Almost all had been shot and horribly wounded. They had no food, no water. None had been given any medical treatment. They had been left to die.

Three young boys, perhaps 6 to 12 years old, lay curled in the fetal position on the blood-caked floor, breathing shallowly, eyes unfocused. Parts of their arms and legs were blown away. A woman with her lower jaw missing held her hands over her eyes, keening as she rocked back and forth. Blood, black and stiff, caked their bodies. Flies swarmed over them. Along the pockmarked walls were more bodies, obviously dead.

A thin, elderly Vietnamese man with a gray goatee raised his one good arm as I approached. The bullet-shattered bones of his left shoulder were exposed. He whispered to me in French that the Cambodian soldiers had herded them into the room the previous night and then opened fire on them at pointblank range. "Why did they do this? Why did they do this?" he kept repeating. He said many more had been killed and already taken away.

I ran down the empty hallway to the medical technicians lounging outside and asked them to treat the wounded. They smiled nervously and shook their heads. When I insisted, they nodded toward some Cambodian troops sitting under a shade tree at the front entrance. I hurried over to ask where the commanding officer was, but then easily spotted him. Lounged in a canvas camp chair and smoking a Salem cigarette was a lean officer, around 40 years old, with a pocked face. His eyes were bloodshot and he seemed exhausted.

I asked him what had happened, why so many were killed and wounded. He listened without looking at me. After a long pull on his cigarette, he replied that the Viet Cong had attacked the night before and these people were caught in the crossfire.

"*C'est la guerre,*" he added.

"There are many wounded in there," I said, "including children. Why won't you treat them?"

"We have no medical supplies to spare," he replied, dismissing the subject. I persevered but my words no longer registered on him. He seemed drugged. I had the distinct impression that his exhaustion came from a night of murdering trapped Vietnamese. Several other officers standing nearby looked at the ground, embarrassed. We later named this officer Col. Blood.

After returning to Phnom Penh and filing the story, I told several other journalists at the Royal about the shooting, then went back with them for more details. The government at first said attacking Viet Cong had shot the Vietnamese. The spokesman, Maj. Am Rong, took fearful verbal abuse from the press over this stand. Later, he said the matter was being further investigated.

News stories about the massacre sparked outrage in Saigon, particularly among South Vietnam air force pilots. These pilots, who had regularly attacked North Vietnamese positions inside Cambodia, now took special delight in strafing and bombing Cambodian villages in retaliation. As international opinion swelled against the Lon Nol government, it declared that 450,000 Vietnamese residents in Cambodia represented a subversive risk. More than 200,000 Vietnamese were eventually rounded up and shipped to South Vietnam while thousands more were held in detention camps.

A few weeks later I was with Cambodian troops trying to dislodge a large Khmer Rouge and North Vietnamese unit from the Elephant Mountains between Phnom Penh and the Gulf of Thailand. The battalion commander implored me to have the U.S. send American pilots to support them, not South Vietnamese. "The South Vietnamese pilots are not as accurate, not as careful as the Americans," he said. What he was really saying was that the Saigon pilots didn't give a rat's ass who they bombed, Cambodians or North Vietnamese. As far as they were concerned, both were enemies.

All this weighed on my mind when enemy fire and mortars soon pinned us down and the commander called for air support. The planes that eventually arrived were South Vietnamese T-28 propeller-driven planes laden with bombs. The planes began diving toward the entrenched enemy but their bombs were well wide of the mark, which was about 50 meters directly ahead of us. Then one plane rolled over high in the sky above and into a dive directly above me. As he powered toward earth I could see the windshield glinting in the sunlight and the bombs mounted underneath the wings. After he released the bombs and pulled up, the bombs seemed to keep coming straight at us. Specifically at me. I thought, "This does not look good," but the bombs hit the enemy just ahead of us. The pilot was dead on target, unless he was really aiming at us and missed.

CHAPTER 6

Weird Things

THE CAMBODIAN army was not only poorly trained but also consisted of many "ghost" units. Many military commanders, masters at skimming profits for themselves, had readily seen that with so much American aid pouring in they could inflate their personnel numbers by 50 percent or even 100 percent and receive wages to pay their nonexistent troops. The cash went directly into their pockets. Extra weapons and ammunition that also arrived could be sold on the black market. Lon Nol never attempted to stop the practice; it was how he built and maintained loyalty among his subordinates.

The ineptness of the Cambodian army commanders and their poorly trained soldiers was made particularly evident at Saang, an unhurried town along the Bassac River just a half-hour's drive south of Phnom Penh. In mid-April, NVA soldiers and a few of the growing numbers of Khmer Rouge occupied the town. When a Cambodian counterattack finally got under way, a few shots from enemy forces in the town immediately brought the three Cambodian battalions to a halt.

After several days of desultory exchanges and no advances, a new commander arrived to take charge. He was Col. Sosthene Fernandez, a short, rotund officer with a beaming smile and a Filipino father. Spreading his maps on a camp table in his tent, he explained to us in excellent English how he would use psychological warfare to capture the city. "You will see tomorrow," he promised.

The next morning as some journalists gathered near Sosthene's tent, there was no military action evident. There was also no breeze off the Bassac River, which promised another day of intense and humid heat. Finally, in the late morning, two stakebed trucks arrived from Phnom Penh carrying 60 or 70 Vietnamese men and women. They ranged in age from teenagers to middle-aged. Many of the women wore black pants and a white shirt, their standard working clothes. All stood on the blacktopped road, nervously watching the Cambodian soldiers watching them.

The Vietnamese were handed leaflets while Sosthene explained to us what was about to happen. These people, he declared, would march down the road into Saang and tell the Communist Vietnamese they must leave immediately. "They both speak Vietnamese so they will understand," he said, beaming. It was his newly invented psy-war tactic. The fearful Vietnamese seemed stoically resigned to their fate. With Cambodian weapons at their backs, the group shuffled down the empty road. Many of us were certain we would witness a massacre. One who didn't think so was Dennis Cameron, a beanpole of a freelance cameraman who decided to walk with them near the front. Cameramen, both still and television, often walk point on some operations. Anything for action photos, until you get a little older and wiser. And around here, if you don't get wiser, you don't get older. Dennis towered over the group. An easy target, I thought.

About 100 meters down the road, just as they were going around a bend in the road before Saang, several shots rang out from inside the town. Cambodian soldiers around us immediately opened up, even though they could see nothing but trees. The Vietnamese had flung themselves down on the road. After just a few minutes the firing stopped. One after another the Vietnamese got slowly to their feet and ran back to us. Many were now barefoot, their sandals littering the road.

Amazingly, only a few were wounded and none critically. Even Dennis had escaped unscathed, with close-up pictures.

In the following days, Sosthene decided to drive the enemy out of Saang by demolishing the town with Cambodian air support, which consisted of some old Soviet MiG fighters and American T-28s. To better see what was going on, I accompanied a platoon that had been ordered to advance on the town from the Bassac River. As we left the cover of banana trees, the NVA saw us and directed more fire our way. As bullets snapped overhead, I found myself lying behind a paddy dike next to a 22-year-old army private hugging his AK-47. He had been a university student until a month earlier and spoke English. His name was Kong Deth and his only wish at the moment was that he would stay alive and return to see his mother and father again.

We lay in the dirt, sweating, for about 30 minutes until a sergeant shouted something at us. I assumed he wanted the squad to move forward, which was easy for him to say from his protected spot. Kong Deth pulled out the Buddhist amulet he wore around his neck and put it in his mouth. He did not seem entirely confident that it would make him bulletproof. As more orders were yelled our way, he and the others raised themselves slightly behind the dike and opened fire. Kong Deth emptied his entire clip before pressing himself down again. There was no response from those inside Saang. Meanwhile, along the riverbank behind us, other members of his platoon might as well have been on a training run. Several had their shirts off and were unconcernedly filling plastic canteens with the murky Bassac River water and pouring it over their heads.

With that action bogged down, I made my way back to the main road, where an old armored car was being readied for action. Two photographers, Larry Burroughs of Life magazine and Kent Potter of UPI, were standing nearby watching. Less than a year later they and two other photographers would be killed when the helicopter they were riding in was shot down inside Laos. Larry, slim, bespectacled and exceptionally perceptive, always managed to find both the humor and pathos in a situation, traits that made him one of the world's greatest photographers. I first met him in 1965 in Malaysia where, tired after following a political demonstration for hours, he suddenly appeared, bounding past me. "Stay at the front," he said cheerily, "You'll never see anything back here!" I took his advice to heart.

About six months later, just before Larry was killed, he arrived in a Jeep near the Laotian border where I was accompanying South Vietnamese troops about to invade Laos during Lam Son 719. He miraculously produced and handed me a cold beer before driving on. CBS cameraman Norman Lloyd and I walked away from the South Vietnamese tank unit and sat down in a dry creek bed to share the beer. I had just opened it when a cluster bomb, dropped by an American jet pilot who thought we were the enemy, hit the South Vietnamese unit dead center. Dozens were killed and wounded, but a friendly beer from Larry may have saved us from serious injury or death. Two days later Larry was shot down and killed, along with photographers Kent Potter of UPI and Henri Huet of AP.

But there, just outside Saang, we watched as the driver closed the armored car hatches and drove forward less than 20 meters before stopping. From inside came loud, metallic noises as the gunner loaded a round. The little cannon belched and somewhere in or beyond Saang there was an explosion. In reply, a few shots came our way. One round hit the armored car with a loud clang. The driver put the vehicle in reverse and began backing up. That was not what one Cambodian officer had in mind. He walked along beside it, yelling for it to stop. The driver, locked inside, either could not or would not hear him. In frustration, the officer snatched large rocks from beside the road and bounced them off the armored car. The driver paid not the slightest attention as he continued backing down the road until out of range of both rocks and bullets.

On my way back to Phnom Penh, I stopped to watch a little riverboat with a one-lung engine pull up to the bank. Four dead Cambodian soldiers were put on it. The people loading the bodies were local Vietnamese.

Phnom Penh Transformed

Lon Nol's government badly needed a clear victory to boost morale. It was something they had not achieved in six weeks of fighting. The military hoped that Saang, the largest set-piece battle of the war and close to the capital, would be a turning point, but it was not to be. Although Lon Nol's troops took over the destroyed town two days later, the North Vietnamese had long since withdrawn, their point made.

As always, the widening war most heavily impacted the civilians who were caught between combatants. Tens of thousands of refugees poured into Phnom Penh. The city, which had been peacefully remote only two months ago, now seemed bursting at its seams. Thousands camped along the Bassac and Mekong River banks. The monsoon rains had begun and the capital's parks were filled with thousands more trying to survive under pieces of plastic. Exhausted women with small children lying beside them on woven mats fanned smoky fires to boil a handful of rice and vegetables, or just leaves. The men, confused and lost, squatted in small groups smoking and talking. Army trucks bullied their way through the city, forcing *cyclo* drivers and cars out of their way. My favorite restaurant, La Taverne, in the little square facing the PTT, was now ringed with barbed wire. American and European hucksters, trying to sell the government everything from helicopters to toothpaste, took over the tables and sped about in big Mercedes cars. As did we journalists.

Driving to and from the war continued to be hazardous to health. One morning I ran into Jon Swain and thought he looked particularly ragged. A British subject, Jon was bilingual in French and arrived in

April as the Agence France Presse correspondent in Cambodia. This particular morning, he was sore all over. He said he had been late returning to Phnom Penh from down south and found himself about to be caught by the quickly falling tropical night. No one wanted to be out after dark, especially alone. Hoping not to be spotted by Khmer Rouge, he turned off the car's lights and drove like a maniac through the gloom. Speeding in this manner, he hit an unseen ditch or bomb crater in the middle of the road, which nearly removed both axles and sent the car spinning on it's side. After climbing out of the wreckage, he staggered away and lay all night in a nearby rice paddy, listening to soldiers passing in the dark. In the morning, when the enemy troops disappeared, he flagged down a passing Cambodian patrol and made his way home. Years later, Jon caught the last flight from Bangkok into besieged Phnom Penh the night before it fell and wrote of the terrible days that followed before he and others were expelled.

Journalists took refuge from the pressures in various ways, from booze to marijuana to something even more exotic: opium. The opium dens that had permeated China had disappeared with the communist takeover but here in the warm back streets of Phnom Penh, pipe dreams were still available. Madame Chum ran the city's best know *fumerie* from her pleasant, two-story villa. Upstairs, visitors were guided across a room lit only by a few kerosene lamps to a woven mats on the floor. Several women in sarongs moved silently about the room attending to the clients.

I lay down on the mat and rested my head on a wooden box that served as a pillow. One of the women, very thin, knelt beside me to prepare my pipe. She rolled a brown ball of opium the size of a large marble between her fingers and then stuck it on the end of a steel needle. She held the opium over a lamp flame until it glistened and began to melt, then deftly put it in the end of a long-stemmed opium pipe and handed it to me. I took a long draught and looked around the room. The pipe promptly went out. The woman lighted it again with no display of impatience at my novice approach. But she instructed me with sign language to keep puffing on it.

I would smoke four or five pipes in an evening, which was nothing compared to the 20 or more pipes that an addict would have. Afterwards, I lay back on the mat in the smoky room to watch shadows dance on the walls and listen to the quiet murmur of others. People lay only a few feet apart, each living their own dream. Madame Chum's clientele included members of the diplomatic corps, journalists and businessmen, both Europeans and Cambodians. Opium was a light escape, but I found it was not for me. It didn't relax me. Instead, my mind whirled with the disasters that I saw overtaking Cambodia and its wonderful people. I finally stopped going after Kevin Buckley, the Newsweek correspondent lying a few mats away, asked me to stop talking. I hadn't realized I was.

Amidst this chaos, it was a delight to stumble on something out of the kingdom's royal past. One Sunday morning while walking beside the open and unguarded palace grounds near the Bassac River, I heard a percussion orchestra playing traditional Cambodian music. I followed the sound across a grassy field to an open-sided pavilion with spires and small bells on the orange tiled roof. Inside, about 50 young women in gold brocade sarongs and multitiered headdresses swayed in unison with the music. With each step of their bare feet on the marble tiles, their heads and arms turned in elaborately stylized dance movements. Their palms faced out and their wrists and fingers bent backward in stylized elegance. It was a performance steeped in history and tradition, much like the dances that have been performed before Cambodian royalty since the earliest kingdoms. This time, however, there was neither king nor audience. The performers were eerily alone on an empty palace stage.

White House Interest

The White House suddenly took more interest in Cambodia than it ever had before. Gen. Alexander Haig, Kissinger's deputy, flew into Pochentong Airport in May for talks with Lon Nol. Haig, wearing military fatigues and spit-shined boots, was met at the airport by the American chargé d'affaires, Mike Rives. Haig loved to project a high profile, I'm-in-charge image and clearly had no time for Rives, a low profile career diplomat. Although Rives had an excellent understanding of where events were leading Cambodia, Haig snubbed him and spent his short visit assuring Lon Nol of Washington's support.

Lon Nol, however, appeared to have difficulties grasping reality. A senior CIA friend told me that Lon Nol's house had been bugged shortly after the coup and that listeners heard him cry himself to sleep virtually every night, often calling out for his late wife. Additionally, Lon Nol was quickly shown to be out of his depth as a military leader. As the war expanded, he felt it necessary to demonstrate his ability to lead by involving himself with all sorts of minutiae. Field commanders confirmed that it was not unusual for them to receive a call directly from Lon Nol at any time of day or night. The prime minister would then proceed to tell them in detail how to run the battle even though he had no idea of what was actually happening there. Lon Nol also progressively withdrew into mysticism and astrology, which in his mind were well entwined with Buddhism. Buddhists were invincible, he believed, and thus Cambodia would certainly crush the Vietnamese, northerners, southerners or indigenous to Cambodia, it didn't matter. All Vietnamese were enemies of Cambodia.

How little Lon Nol actually knew about the war in his country was revealed a few days after the U.S. and South Vietnamese invasion on April 29. At a press conference inside his residence, Lon Nol slumped on a couch in the sunken living room and described to us at length Cambodia's new close friendship with South Vietnam. Gloria Emerson, a lanky and persevering New York Times correspondent, grilled him in French that grated the ear but got the questions across. The most startling piece of information that emerged was that no one had given Lon Nol advance notice of the planned invasion, or incursion, as Nixon's spin-doctors insisted it be called. Neither the White House nor President Thieu apparently thought he could be trusted with such information. The Cambodian prime minister heard about it first from news reports.

As part of Washington's belated interest in Cambodia, a Senate investigation team arrived in Phnom Penh to learn everything about the country in 48 hours. The first evening of their visit they asked several journalists to join them for dinner. The journalists suggested a popular Corsican restaurant that specialized in couscous. What they didn't mention was that the specialty couscous was cooked with marijuana seeds. The evening proceeded with progressively high hilarity as the visitors from Washington praised the couscous and helped themselves to more. Neither the journalists nor the Senate investigators gleaned the slightest bit of useful information during the evening, at least nothing that anyone could remember.

Even Vice President Spiro Agnew arrived for a visit. His Secret Service guards, apparently expecting the city to be overrun at any moment, stepped off the plane with Uzi submachine guns conspicuously at the ready. Ignoring the Cambodian welcoming committee, they hustled Agnew onto a Huey helicopter that had been specially brought in from Saigon just to transport him the five miles to the palace guesthouse. Wherever Agnew went during his two-day visit, Secret Service agents made a show of displaying their Uzis.

During Agnew's official call on newly appointed acting President Cheng Heng, one Secret Service agent, either out of boredom or suppressed desire, repeatedly aimed his weapon at Cheng Heng's back. Rives, more protocol conscious than any of Agnew's party, was aghast and quietly rebuked the agent. The agent complained to Agnew, who complained to Nixon, who complained to the State Department. That isolated episode of bureaucratic backstabbing ended the career of Mike Rives in Phnom Penh. A few months later, Ambassador Emory Swank replaced Rives.

But ambassadors were of relatively little value to the Nixon White House. The president, with Kissinger loyally following along, appeared intent on making his own policy regarding Cambodia, including secretly bombing it, invading it, flooding it with military support and then finally abandoning it. The net effect of the Lon Nol/Sirik Matak coup and the U.S.-South Vietnamese invasion was to shatter Cambodia's tenuous neutrality. One person who dared to stand up to this secret and unethical diplomacy was Marshall Green, then Assistant Secretary of State of East Asian and Pacific Affairs. Green, whom I had known well when he was ambassador to Indonesia, was an exceptionally astute analyst of political developments in Asia. He was also too much of a professional to make his views an open issue. But in his State Department capacity he warned the White House that widening the war into Cambodia would prove ruinous in the long run. Nixon and Kissinger were incensed that anyone would challenge their policy. To show who was boss, Kissinger put a black mark against Green's name, which ensured that he would not be named ambassador to Japan, an appointment Green had anticipated and deserved.

Columbia Eagle Hijacked

Apart from the overall tragedy that Cambodia endured, strange things were always happening. Graham Greene would never have invented them for his novels on Southeast Asia. As an example, four days before the March 18 coup, an American merchant marine ship, the Columbia Eagle, was steaming past Cambodia in the Gulf of Thailand with a load of napalm and bombs for U.S. forces in Thailand. Two young American crewmen on board, in a fit of misguided devotion to the anti-war movement and a juvenile belief in Marxist-Leninism, decided to hijack the ship. Brandishing pistols, they seized control at 1:15 p.m. on March 14 and blew the "Abandon Ship" signal. Of the 39 crewmen on the freighter, 24 immediately went over the side in lifeboats and were soon picked up by passing ships. Meanwhile, the two hijackers then ordered the Columbia Eagle into the small and bleak port of Sihanoukville on March 15. Standing at the ship's bridge as port authorities cautiously came aboard, the two happily prepared themselves for a grand welcome from Sihanouk's anti-American government. Their timing couldn't have been worse.

Lon Nol and Sirik Matak, already absorbed in planning their coup, had no time or inclination to deal with this Twilight Zone incident. The Cambodian port authorities, not having the faintest idea what to do with these people, locked the American captain and his crew in one part of the ship and the hijackers in another. A few weeks after the coup, Capt. Donald O. Swan and his crew were sent home. The hijackers, however, were moved to a heat-drenched prison ship on the Mekong River near Phnom Penh, where I went to visit them.

The floating prison was a rusting landing ship tank anchored, or perhaps sunk, beside the riverbank. Some corrugated tin panels were stuck haphazardly around the superstructure in a futile effort to ward off the relentless tropical sun. Inside, the steel ship was a veritable oven. Locked away near the hijackers in an equally cheerless steel-walled room was Gen. Oum Mannorine, former national police commander and the half-brother of Sihanouk's wife, Monique. This is where Sirik Matak sent Mannorine after his abortive counter-coup effort.

The two hijackers were wary, but anxious to talk to anyone other than their guards. In the weeks they had been there, they had seen a U.S. Embassy representative only for a few minutes. The two sat on plastic chairs, each wearing just a pair of dirty shorts. The air was thick. Clyde McKay, 26, of Escondido, California, and Alvin Glatowski, 20, of Long

Beach, California, both appeared unrepentant despite their rather desperate situation. Still, life could have been worse. They had used some of the money that their captors had allowed them to keep to buy a small television set. With it, and joined by the guards, they could watch Armed Forces Television Vietnam programs beamed into Cambodia. The two said they did not know each other before shipping out, but soon found they shared similar revolutionary views. Importantly, McKay had smuggled two pistols aboard ship.

McKay, the bigger and more outspoken of the two, told me, "The seizure of the Columbia Eagle is part of the prelude to an American revolution. A revolution must take place if Nixon and his henchmen are to be stopped from unwittingly escalating their war against socialism to a nuclear holocaust." His words sounded practiced.

Glatowski, thin, pale and unshaven, mostly wondered if he would ever see his wife again or the baby that was born after he sailed.

Before the Khmer Rouge finally overran Phnom Penh in 1975, McKay escaped and was not heard of again. Glatowski was returned to the United States and jailed for mutiny and hijacking.

A Touch of Rabies

Lots of weird things happened for no reason. Going into my bungalow at the Royal one evening just after sunset, I heard a cat meowing near my feet. I reached down in the darkness and the cat immediately sank its teeth into the base of my thumb. Although the puncture wounds didn't bleed much, I needed to know that the cat was not rabid. With the help of half a dozen waiters and room attendants, we finally captured the ungrateful beast and delivered it to a veterinarian for testing. The results were positive: The cat had rabies, I had rabies.

Standard rabies treatment then was a series of 14 shots placed in the abdomen with a long needle. A *very* long needle, friends assured me.

One shot every day for two weeks. The hotel gave me the name of a doctor and I went to see him. His office was on the ground floor rear of an old two-story villa with bougainvillea climbing the faded yellow walls. The empty waiting room consisted of four wooden chairs against one wall. The doctor, a thin French-Vietnamese man with graying hair, eventually appeared and asked me to step into his office. With the window shutters closed against the afternoon heat, the light was dim.

Sitting across from him at his wooden desk, I explained why I was there and produced the veterinarian laboratory findings. The doctor studied the form. He had a long, sad face that did not inspire confidence. "Rabies," he murmured.

"Will I need the whole series of inoculations?"

"*Oui, certainement.*" He pulled open several desk drawers and rummaged through each with a silent intensity. At the same time, he seemed rather pleased. "It is not too often I see rabies. Ahh, here it is." He held up a brass syringe large enough to dose a bull. The needle alone looked to be more than 6 inches long. Maybe 2 feet. The thought of coming to this dark office for 14 days to have Doctor Death plunge an antique brass needle into my gut was not appealing. And what was he going to clean it with, Brasso?

I excused myself and caught a flight to Hong Kong the next day. There, a British doctor asked his colleague to hurry into the examination room so they could both delight in hearing me describe the proposed rabies treatment. The doctors then handed me a small syringe and showed me how to give myself subcutaneous abdominal injections. The next day, I returned to Phnom Penh and gave myself daily shots for the following two weeks. Modern medicine was good.

Angkor Wat Unvisited

With the arrival of the war, Cambodia's tourism revenues plummeted to nothing. Even before the war, the tourism business had been marginal because of the country's uncertain politics. The chief draw, as always, was the famed Angkor Wat ruins. I hadn't seen them myself and now it seemed too late. Reports from the area said North Vietnamese troops had occupied the great temple complex. To see what the current status was and in hopes of getting a close look, AP photographer Max Nash and I caught a rice transport flight to the provincial capital of Siem Reap, located close to the ruins. Commercial flights had stopped. Horst Faas, AP photo chief in Saigon and a renowned collector of antiquities, sent me a cable just before I left: "Advise soonest if Angkor Wat accessible; will send large truck." He was only half-kidding.

We had no trouble finding a hotel room in the small and nearly deserted city. After a dinner of tough chicken and rice, I went for a stroll in the cooler night air. The long street in front of the hotel was empty at 8 p.m. except for some men sitting in the shadows, smoking and talking among themselves.

Across the road, streetlights cast deep shadows through trees in a spacious park and a chorus of frog bellows rose from a nearby pond. As I walked along the edge of the park, I began to discern mounds of fresh red earth in the shadows. Thinking that the army must be digging fortifications, I took a closer look. They were graves, dozens of them. In the faint light I could see small markers at the head of each grave. They were military grave markers. The war was closer to Siem Reap than many realized.

In the morning Max and I met with the area military commander for a briefing. An army major, he was unusually frank about the country's precarious position. The reason so few people were around Siem Reap, he said, was because they were taking refuge inside Angkor Wat.

"The people go into the temples because they are afraid of our artillery fire," he said. "We fire anywhere the North Vietnamese soldiers are, even if they are in our villages. The North Vietnamese are free to move about the countryside, but we are tied up in this town. We can't move without getting into trouble."

I asked if the villagers and farmers in the area were cooperating with the Cambodian army. "No, the people do not support the army. We do not have enough guns to provide them security. We need more guns."

"Why don't you try to build popular support among the people, perhaps by not shelling them indiscriminately?" I asked.

"You don't win wars with people, you win with guns," he said with some frustration. It was an unwitting reversal of one of the basic rules of guerrilla warfare as laid out by Mao Tse-tung.

I explained to the major that we wanted to see Angkor Wat. After some consideration he replied that he had a reconnaissance patrol leaving in an hour and we could accompany them.

In the interval we took a *cyclo* to a nearby compound where French archaeologists were restoring pieces of stone sculpture brought from Angkor Wat. Parts of carved stone statues lay in profusion around the open courtyard, some without heads, others missing arms, hands or legs. It looked depressingly like the aftermath of battle. An unsmiling Frenchman gave us a perfunctory tour of the work site. I asked if he were still able to go into the great temple complex now that the North Vietnamese occupied it. He shrugged off the question and instead lectured us about the American folly of fighting in Vietnam.

I told him that I had never been to Angkor Wat but hoped to see something of it when we joined a Cambodian patrol shortly. He turned away with a derisive laugh and said something over his shoulder. I didn't catch it. Max, who had grown up on the streets of Paris, translated. "He hopes we like dog meat." What the Frenchman meant was that the Vietnamese, who relish dog meat, would likely capture us.

The recon patrol consisted of a dozen men, with one radiotelephone operator. It was nearly noon before we began walking. The sun was fierce. The great ruins were only about seven miles north of us.

The narrow road to Angkor was raised above the surrounding rice fields, which were entirely empty. The fact that the Cambodian army regularly shelled its own people probably had something to do with that. The soldiers strolled on both sides of the road, seemingly unconcerned about the lack of farmers in the fields. I walked between the two files, but stayed away from the radio operator. He was always the first target.

As we rounded a bend in the road, the carved stone towers of Angkor Wat rose ahead of us above some palm trees. I began to feel we would get lucky and walk right inside. Far ahead of us appeared two Cambodian monks walking toward us in their saffron robes. Heat shimmering on the pavement made it appear that they were walking on water. As we drew abreast of each other, the soldiers placed their hands in front of their faces and bowed. The monks did the same in return. The patrol leader, a sergeant, questioned the monks at length and finally, irritated, sent them on their way with a wave of his weapon. He had asked about the number of Vietnamese or Khmer Rouge troops inside and the types of weapons, but the monks said they didn't know.

"It's always the same," the sergeant said. "They tell us nothing."

Still, we continued down the road, completely exposed. The red stone temples, seat of so many ancient Khmer empires, grew closer. I was hot and sweaty and thirsty and nothing was happening. Were we actually going to make it to the temples? We stopped again, still in the middle of the road, while the patrol leader radioed in his situation. I didn't like to think about the possibility of a sniper sitting up there drawing a bead on me. We were about to continue on when an explosion in the field beyond the road sent up a geyser of red earth. A mortar round.

The patrol came to a stop. I always hated getting mortared. It seemed so random. Either you got it or you didn't. Another round hit on the other side of the road, still some distance from us. The mortar team did not appear to be too accurate or we were just beyond range. Either way, it was time to move. They could get lucky.

We turned around and walked back down the hot, empty road. I never did get to see Angkor Wat.

CHAPTER 7

Dogs of War

EVEN AS JOURNALISTS disappeared, were killed, or just had enough and left, more arrived to take their places. AP rotated several people in to cover the story, including John Wheeler, Lewis Simons and photographers Ghislan Bellorget and Max Nash. One constant among the change, however, was a puppy that became a mascot for the journalists at the Royal. He was just a shorthaired black and white mongrel with one lop ear and a permanent grin on his face. Each evening when we gathered for drinks, he made his way around to check on who was there. As a result of hip dysplasia he didn't walk or run normally, but hopped instead. Pushing off unsteadily on his back legs, he started in one direction. When his front legs engaged, he swerved back in another direction. Another push from the back legs sent him veering sharply off course only to be righted again. We liked him because he walked the same way many of us did after a late night of drinking.

I found the pup in a farming community populated by Cambodian-Vietnamese who had disappeared. When I arrived, some Cambodian soldiers were loading two recently shot pigs into the back of a truck. An officer stood in the dirt path between the rows of empty thatch huts. He had a bullwhip and was practicing his aim by snapping at flies that settled on the dusty ground in front of him.

Asked where the villagers were, he said they had all been shipped to a relocation camp. "Many VC here," he said in English. "We help them. Send them to camp."

In looking through the desperately poor houses with just dirt floors and a bench or two, I saw cooking utensils, rolled bedding and clothes in some of them. Maybe the Vietnamese had been relocated, maybe not.

At this point, a little puppy hopped around the corner of a hut and stood looking at me, swaying from side to side on his fragile hind legs. He seemed to be laughing. On impulse, I picked him up and put him in my jacket pocket as I left. Back in Phnom Penh, I took him to a vet for some shots. They wanted to know his name and I said, "Hopalong Cassidy." They thought he must be a fine dog to have such a long name.

It seemed stupid to give a dog scraps when so many people were hungry, but we did. After a few months, Hopalong disappeared. I was sure he hadn't run off but had been stolen. Maybe he had become attractively fat. Several days later, he reappeared, dragging a rope around his neck that had been chewed in half. The journalists gave him extra scraps as he made the rounds with that goofy grin of his. A few days before I eventually left Cambodia, he disappeared again. I like to think that a boy who really wanted a crippled dog took him.

Syvertsen Crew Arrives

In the middle of May, another CBS News team rotated in, this one from Tokyo. The correspondent was George Syvertsen, along with cameraman Kurt Volkert and soundman Thanong Hiransi, a Thai. All were experienced in combat conditions, having done tours in Vietnam. Two Japanese crewmembers, cameraman Tomoharu Ishii and soundman Kojiro Sakai, had arrived a day earlier. Ramnik Lekhi, a camera stringer from India, was already there. Shortly after the Tokyo crew arrived, producer Gerry Miller arrived from Rome. Rounding out the large CBS crew were two more cameraman, Skip Brown and Kurt Hoefle, plus correspondent Don Webster. Bernie Kalb, a veteran correspondent based in Hong Kong with long experience in Asia, was also often there. CBS didn't do things halfway in those days.

Both Miller and Syvertsen were former AP correspondents who had shifted to CBS News. With our common background, we spent several evenings talking about different countries and stories we had covered. Both of them had spent their time in Europe while I had always been in Asia. They often said I should switch to television news and talked about how different it was from the wire service, which required filing stories at any time of day or night to meet a deadline somewhere in the world. Gerry had just joined CBS and was especially enthusiastic. With CBS, he said, you just had to make one show, "The CBS Evening News with Walter Cronkite." None of us had an inkling that in two weeks they would be dead and that as a result, I would be asked to join CBS.

Gerry was a particularly affable fellow with a great bushy mustache and dancing eyes behind round spectacles. It was his first time in Asia and his first time in a bang-bang situation. "Is this really a war zone? Am I really in a war?" he used to ask, excited at the prospect. Syvertsen was his counterpoint, quiet and intense. George quickly sized up the competition and mentioned to me once that his biggest concern was Welles Hangen, the NBC correspondent. I didn't disagree. Welles and I had been on several stories in different parts of Asia at the same time and I knew him to be a thorough and scholarly journalist. He also looked the part, rather like a tall professor, with horn-rimmed glasses and a soft-spoken demeanor.

Syvertsen quickly made it a point to cover the heaviest fighting, as if trying to catch up with others who had been there longer. Some CBS people who had worked with George felt that he was putting undue pressure on himself. He was not only competing against the other networks, he was competing against those in CBS, too. Some thought he was too intent on proving himself, but that was a journalistic sin common to all of us at one time or another. Still, he pushed the limits, which led to a falling out between George and Kurt Volkert.

During the brief two weeks that the CBS crew was in Cambodia, Kurt had increasingly felt that Syvertsen was putting people's lives unnecessarily at risk in his zeal to get some combat footage. Kurt was clear in his own mind that no story was worth getting killed over. War was nothing new to him. Born in Germany, Kurt had lived through World War II as a child, had come to the United States as a young man, joined the army to speed up naturalization and was promptly sent to Vietnam. After his discharge, he returned to combat in Vietnam again as a CBS cameraman. As he once told me, "The only way I haven't seen war is from a submarine periscope."

Shortly after Syvertsen and the seven others were killed, CBS hired me and I relocated to the Saigon bureau. Saigon bureau chief Dave Miller promptly sent Kurt, Thanong and me back to Phnom Penh for ongoing war coverage. I was still new to CBS and the three of us were just then getting to know each other. Immediately on arrival, Kurt let it be known that he was not going to spend any time shooting film. Instead, he was going to pursue his search for Ishii and Sakai, along with Welles Hangen and his crew. I felt some resentment and confusion. We were here to do stories, but our cameraman was essentially abandoning us while he drove up and down highways trying to collect information on his former colleagues.

What I didn't fully understand at the time was Kurt's deep-seated feelings of determination, remorse and even guilt because Syvertsen had angrily taken another camera crew that murderous day instead of Kurt and Thanong. Should Kurt have stopped Syvertsen? Could he have stopped him? No, but it didn't ease matters in his mind.

Determined to proceed with or without Volkert, Syvertsen set out on the last Sunday in May in his rented Jeep. He drove and Gerry Miller, hoping tensions would ease soon, sat beside him. Following behind in the CBS Mercedes driven by Cambodian Sam Leng were Ishii and Sakai and camera stringer Lekhi. Seeing them leave the hotel and afraid of being scooped, NBC's Welles Hangen hastily rounded up his crew and followed. With Welles were Roger Colne, a French cameraman, and Yoshihiko Waku, a Japanese soundman. They all drove south, toward Takeo. It was their last trip in Cambodia.

Because the communist Vietnamese and Khmer Rouge largely controlled the area surrounding the blown bridge where some were killed and others captured, no one could immediately enter the area to recover bodies or look for the missing. CBS immediately rushed several people to Cambodia, including Vice President Gordon Manning from New York and Saigon bureau chief Dave Miller. Manning, long used to CBS's clout in America, expected Cambodian officials to turn cartwheels to meet his demands. But Cambodian officials had never heard of CBS and were not impressed. Wheels turned slowly. The bodies of George Syvertsen, Gerry Miller and Ramnik Lekhi were recovered in a few days, but Welles Hangen and his crew, along with CBS's Ishii and Sakai, were still missing.

Several months after these killings when Kurt, Thanong and I returned to Cambodia, Thanong did the camerawork in Kurt's absence and I did the sound as we continued to gather stories. Meanwhile, it was Kurt's dogged persistence in following up leads that finally allowed him to learn exactly where the captured newsmen had been killed. By searching day after day, he located villagers who had seen the captured men being led away at gunpoint, who knew the house in which they were imprisoned near a Buddhist temple and could tell him about the bamboo grove in which they were all clubbed to death.

With this information, Kurt was then able to draw a detailed map of the killing area. A quarter of a century later, that hand-drawn map was to prove invaluable in finally locating the remains. All but one.

PHOTOGRAPHS

Snapshots from Cambodia, 1970

South Vietnamese troops took over the vital ferry-crossing town of Neak Leung in the summer of 1970. Several Vietnamese officers conduct business over lunch behind author T. Jeff Williams.

Cambodian troops positioned this World War I French tank in a futile effort to defend the outskirts of Phnom Penh. Newsmen, l-r, are unknown, Eddie Chan, ABC, Ghislan Bellorget, AP, Jeff Williams, AP, and Kent Potter, UPI.

Kevin Buckley
Newsweek

Bob Blackburn
U.S. Embassy

Henry Kamm
New York Times

Dick Hunt
NBC News

Jon Swain
Agence France-Presse

Maj. Am Rong, the unfortunately named government spokesman, stands in front of a map while his assistant translates.

Photographer Kent Potter, at left, later killed in Laos when the helicopter he was in was shot down, takes a break with Williams and Bellorget.

Elaborate Buddhist temples such as this one dot the Cambodian countryside.

Waiting in the noonday sun on the road to Neak Leung are, l-r, Jeff Williams, AP photographer Max Nash and CBS cameraman Ramnik Lekhi, who was killed a few days later.

This poster, part of a Lon Nol government campaign against Vietnamese, shows a Cambodian about to plunge his long knife into a Vietnamese.

Snapshots from the Search Site, 1992

Peter Chuun stands near the point where George Syvertsen and his colleagues drove across the stream into an ambush. The bridge has been reconstructed since 1970.

The idyllic beauty of this temple at Wat Po belies the horror of what happened near this holy shrine.

Villagers wheel their bicycles across the same makeshift footbridge near Wat Po that the captured newsmen were marched over.

The river as it appeared before it was drained to begin the search for remains. The river bend near the center is the burial site.

Members of the U.S. Army recovery team begin building a diversion dam prior to draining the river.

With the dam completed, the pump on the far bank continues to drain the river. The field headquarters is near the lone palm tree.

Anthropologist Madeleine Hinkes, surrounded by Cambodian helpers, works in one of the gravesites. Ropes mark out the search pattern grid.

Peter Chuun, Kurt Volkert and Madeleine Hinkes in brimmed hat listen to Capt. John, with shovel, as searchers take a break.

Author Kurt Volkert, standing in a gravesite, takes a short break before heaving up another bucket of mud to be screened for small bones, teeth or anything to help locate remains.

Capt. Hudson, in white T-shirt, considers the team's next move as Sgt. Williams, back to camera, helps Kurt raise another bucket.

This overview of the drained riverbed, the graves, the grid and some of the diggers helps show the immensity of the project.

Anthropologist Madeleine Hinkes holds the skull of one of the missing newsmen.

The bucket brigade hoists load after load of mud to be screened for any traces of the missing newsmen.

Peter Chuun, an NBC editor originally from Cambodia, played an invaluable role in helping during the long process through his knowledge of the people and the country.

Cambodian workers stand near the mud screening area while an armed guard looks on as the last remains are recovered..

At Pochentong Airport in Phnom Penh, a U.S. military honor guard carries a coffin containing the remains of one of the newsmen is carried to a waiting Air Force plane. The remains were flown to Hawaii for identification.

At the conclusion of the search, Kurt Volkert departs the recovery site after leaving a farewell bouquet of tropical flowers.

Part Two

By Kurt Volkert

CHAPTER 1

Death on Highway 3

On a hot spring day 22 years ago, nine men, doing what was just another job, were gathering news for NBC and CBS. They went down [this] road in the Cambodian countryside and disappeared.

Those of us who covered Cambodia never imagined it would turn out to be just a footnote to that Vietnam War people want to forget. It was a particularly dangerous assignment – a lot of newsmen went missing – but we thought, as journalists, it was worthwhile being there.

On that day in May 1970, the network men, three Americans, a Frenchman, an Indian, a Cambodian and three Japanese, were out looking for a story in an area without battle lines. Four [CBS] men were ambushed in their Jeep and killed by the Viet Cong and Khmer Rouge. Their bodies were recovered within a few days. The five who had followed the Jeep were taken prisoner. There were reports they had been killed, but in all these years, their bodies were never found.

Bert Quint, CBS News
May 1992

My Notes:
June 1972
OUR GROUP ARRIVED in Cambodia in the middle of May 1970: George Syvertsen, CBS's Tokyo correspondent; Thanong Hiransi, my Thai soundman; and myself, a Tokyo-based cameraman.

We went to Cambodia full of expectations. We had covered the American incursion from the Vietnamese border and were now eager to report on the war being waged inside the country itself.

We knew that many of the roads leading from the capital of Phnom Penh into the brush were safe one day, unsafe the next. The situation could change even from hour to hour.

But, being old Southeast Asia hands, we looked forward to roaming the countryside without the restrictions that U.S. officials imposed on us in Vietnam. In Cambodia, the war had not engulfed the whole country. Clashes occurred not far from Phnom Penh, so we didn't need choppers or planes to get around. We only had to rent a car and drive to the war.

The contrast with Saigon was already apparent at Phnom Penh's Pochentong Airport. The Cambodian customs officials hardly paid any attention to our bulky equipment. They even seemed glad to see us.

Maybe they viewed our arrival as the U.S. government's promise to help in their fight against the Communists. Their war wasn't going so well, and misery loves company.

We marveled at how times had changed. Only a few weeks ago, with Prince Sihanouk still in power, these same airport officials would have arrested us on the spot. The prince never cared for the foreign press.

Now, after his ouster and the installation of a pro-American military government, we were more than welcome to lend moral support, or so it was hoped, to Cambodia's uncertain struggle against the Viet Cong and its own Communist Khmer Rouge.

At the airport, we were joined by Kurt Hoefle, a CBS soundman from Rome who could also operate a camera. He had flown first class on our plane from Bangkok and looked somewhat disdainfully at our motley crew emerging from coach.

George Syvertsen had his wife, Gusta, with him. The atmosphere was peaceful as our taxis rode through wide, tree-lined avenues toward our hotel, the famous Hotel Le Royal, a relic from the days of the French.

Buses drove past filled with very young government troops, waving and laughing, heading for a war they hadn't yet seen. The waving and laughing would go on for some weeks until the real battling began.

Halfway to the hotel, George's taxi had an accident and couldn't go on. Well, I thought, this isn't the best way to start off in a new country. It looked like a bad omen.

The Hotel Le Royal lay in colonial splendor in a lush, beautiful park, its swimming pool lined with tropical trees and flowers. French planters and their European bikini-clad companions, escaping the scorching heat, sipped drinks under huge tamarind trees, eyeing the sudden intrusion of loud, unkempt foreign newsmen with undisguised distaste.

The management of the Royal barely managed to be polite. Unlike the Cambodian military, they didn't view us as potential allies or even as well-paying customers, but as a possible embarrassment should Sihanouk return to power and ask some tough questions.

Eventually we got settled, and I prepared my camera equipment for the big job.

Gerry Miller, a CBS producer from Rome along with my Tokyo-based colleagues, cameraman Tomoharu Ishii and soundman Kojiro Sakai, had arrived a few days earlier. Ramnik Lekhi, our stringer cameraman from India, was also here.

The same day we arrived, these three had gone to cover the government troops' advance on Kampong Cham, a provincial capital about 120 kilometers north of Phnom Penh.

Journalists from other news organizations who had also covered the advance were back that day by mid-afternoon, but our people were nowhere to be seen. By late afternoon we started to get concerned, especially when other newsmen told us Kampong Cham was held by Viet Cong troops.

George and I knew that Miller and the Japanese crew were new to this war. Ishii and Sakai were both in their 50s. Ishii was a bit frail and had a stomach problem. Both spoke little English, which made it hard for them to communicate with their producer and correspondent. I wondered why they were here in the first place.

Dusk came, but no Miller and crew. We had just agreed to wait for first light and then go look for them when they finally appeared, haggard and dusty. They were a little shaky but unhurt.

In their inexperience, Miller and the crew had separated from the rest of the newsmen to do more filming. First mistake. In the meantime, the road to Phnom Penh was reported to have been cut by the Viet Cong. Hearing that, they decided to stay with friendly forces till the "all clear" was given.

Then they traveled at night. Second mistake, some veteran newsmen said. Slowly it dawned on them how lucky they'd been. Ishii whispered to me just outside the hotel, "Very dangerous. A trap. Road cut."

There were many experienced war veterans among the press in Phnom Penh. Too often, news organizations sent greenhorns to Southeast Asia without giving them a chance to get acquainted with the dangers of covering a guerrilla war.

Quite a few had to find out for themselves what to do when the shooting started—when to duck, when to run, when to call it a day.

Some of our colleagues played soldier, becoming part of the action instead of staying apart and observing it. One good bit of advice I got was: "Don't be on the first tank during an attack. Be on the fifth one and film the first one being hit."

For a newsman to sport camouflaged uniforms, guns and knives, even in situations when a warlike appearance would have been appropriate, was to lose one of his most important credentials: to look and act like a civilian as much as possible. I am certain that some of my colleagues disagree with me.

Most newcomers, however, came to the war, looked and listened. They learned quickly as the war went on. Fear taught them judgment. They learned to take calculated risks but kept in mind that in the end, no story was worth a life.

Working for TV news was very different from reporting for a paper or magazine. If, as a print reporter, you got stuck in a battalion command post during a firefight, you could still get a meaningful story together by listening to incoming radio calls from the companies engaged in the battle somewhere out there in the jungle. This would give you the big picture even if you were many miles from the action.

Information like this, updated every so often, enabled the reporter to describe the drama he could not see.

But TV reporting needed pictures and sound. We had to find a little corner on the battlefield to film our story, often limited to a very narrow angle of vision dictated by the need to survive and get the story back.

For a TV cameraman, to be stuck at a battalion command post meant defeat. You have to get to the forward company, and better yet to that company's forward platoon, and even better, to that platoon's forward squad. A TV newsman's camera and amplifier were his pencil and paper. Only they're heavier.

And so it happened that many a newsman, young to middle-aged, would get off a jet in Saigon or Phnom Penh, half-dazed from the good living on board and jetlagged by a trip halfway around the world, report to his bureau chief, and then suddenly find himself, still half-dazed, on an operation somewhere in the jungle, trying to report on a war he'd only read about or seen on television halfway around the world.

But most of us were full of ambition and curiosity, and we learned fast. Most would become pretty useful newsmen after a short period of time.

After a few days, the CBS task force took shape. Don Webster, the network's Hong Kong correspondent, and Skip Brown, a cameraman from Saigon, rounded out our presence.

I don't know what we would have done without our Cambodian drivers, Joe Puy and Sam Leng, or Sophan, our Cambodian soundman and escort. All three would eventually pay a terrible price for their loyalty when Khmer Rouge troops murdered them after the fall of Phnom Penh.

One day toward the end of May, we got another strong warning that this war on the Cambodian side was more unpredictable than anything we'd experienced in Vietnam.

I was one of the swimming pool warriors that day, anxiously waiting with the other newsmen for our friends and colleagues to return, when Joe Puy, Don Webster, Skip Brown and Kurt Hoefle pulled their black Mercedes into the Royal parking lot.

I looked to see if they were all right. If their clothes were dirty, it meant action, possibly a good story.

They looked clean. Then everyone except Joe disappeared into the little CBS office in one of the hotel's bungalows near the pool. Nothing unusual, it seemed, but something wasn't right.

Joe was talking excitedly and waving his arms to some of his Cambodian driver friends. I picked up the words "Viet Cong." When Kurt Hoefle came out of the office, he looked beat. I led him to my room and gave him a shot of whiskey while he told me his story.

After they had driven past the last government checkpoint on Highway 3, he noticed some armed men who didn't appear to be Cambodian soldiers. Kurt didn't feel good about it, but being new to Southeast Asia he didn't want to be the first one to sound the alarm. After all, Webster and Brown, two experienced Vietnam hands, should know what they're doing.

Still, an inner voice kept telling him to turn around. Then, without warning, a group of black-clad men armed with Kalashnikovs stopped their car. Webster shouted to make a run for it, but Skip, keeping his presence of mind, ordered Joe to stop the car, probably saving their lives. They'd never have escaped the fusillade that any attempt to flee would certainly have provoked.

The Viet Cong were a tough-looking bunch, holding their rifle muzzles to the newsmen's heads through the windows of the air-conditioned car. Kurt thought, this can't be happening. It's only a few miles to the swimming pool back at the hotel. A few days ago, I was in Rome, on the Via Veneto, and now this. It looked like sudden death, or at the very least, captivity. The VC behaved like men more inclined to shoot them than to let them go.

But then Kurt's sense of survival took over. First, he told his U.S. teammates to keep their mouths shut. A German citizen, he took out his passport, shook it in the VCs' faces, shouting that they were all Germans and should be released immediately. After about 20 tense minutes and a heated discussion among the Viet Cong, they were free to drive away.

Joe put the car into gear and slowly but steadily accelerated, driving past other armed men, smiling and waving.

Kurt had been extremely lucky. When he showed his passport to the Viet Cong, he realized too late that it contained some photographs of him posing with Cambodian government soldiers. But, with all the excitement, the Viet Cong didn't notice.

He had saved himself and the others. The lesson of the story was that even old hands could get careless when they were carried away with an assignment. Webster and Brown said that Kurt, despite his inexperience, had kept his cool and done the right thing.

The contrast couldn't have been sharper. One moment, our people were in grave danger and now, half an hour later, they were at the hotel, with French girls crowding around the pool and no sign of the war just 40 kilometers down the road. We partied hard that night!

When Syvertsen heard about this incident, I heard him mutter, "Not me. They will never get me."

May 1970

The road lay before us in the midday heat. The line of Cambodian infantry, spread across the rice paddies on either side of Highway 3, crept slowly forward, ever wary of a sudden ambush.

We had left the comfort of the Hotel Le Royal and joined the rest of the press corps on a Cambodian army sweep of Highway 3 in the direction of Angtassom. The army brigade, directed by a young flag carrier who walked near the commanding officer, was supported by a column of three old U.S.-made tanks. The tanks followed the troops, who had already covered several kilometers without a sign of the enemy.

The sweep by an army brigade must have been a strange and amusing sight to the enemy. In the lead was the commanding officer, accompanied by a soldier carrying a huge Cambodian flag on a long pole. Forty or more journalists from television and the other press crowded around them. Cambodian troops spread across the rice fields on each side of us. Behind the troops lumbered three World War II American tanks, in a column. Following them were a civilian ambulance, a bulldozer and a weird assortment of trucks and buses that served as troop carriers. In the rear were air-conditioned press cars carrying cold drinks and towels.

This ungainly but colorful worm represented one of the best task forces of the Cambodian army. It was not reassuring. I was with four others from CBS: my friend George Syvertsen, who was the team chief of our little group, producer Gerry Miller, soundman Thanong Hiransi, and Ramnik Lekhi, our camera stringer from India.

In the beginning, this new war in Cambodia was a war for control of the highways. There were no fronts and we had to probe the roads cautiously, not knowing what would be around the next bend. The Cambodian army tried to establish, through forays into the countryside, the extent of the penetration by the North Vietnamese-backed Khmer Rouge, a task that demanded more enthusiasm than competence.

The Cambodian troops we accompanied had no radios. Many of the soldiers had no boots or shoes, only rubber sandals, and all wore a variety of helmets and weapons. I had the feeling that the presence of a press corps that had worked with the well-equipped U.S. Army in Vietnam boosted their morale considerably.

These boys playing at war did very little for our confidence, however. I reassured myself that our air-conditioned Mercedes, at the rear of the column, was our ticket out in case of real trouble. That thought occurred to me more frequently as the countryside grew increasingly still and empty.

Oncoming traffic, people working in the fields and curious children, all signs of relative security, had vanished some time ago, along with the easy banter among us. The air danced on the asphalt road as the sun beat down on us. Rice paddies stretched away from us to the horizon.

Only palm trees and quiet Cambodian houses, rising on stilts from the tropical green, broke the monotony of the landscape. To the south-west, in the direction of Angtassom, rose a range of mountains, blue, distant and forbidding.

Suddenly, about 500 meters ahead, four armed figures darted across the road. Probably Viet Cong. Shouts went up. Soldiers started to set up mortars in the rice fields. The tanks, rather than taking the lead, began to drop behind. The Cambodians didn't want to risk losing them.

We stayed with the commander and his earnest young flag carrier, who now waved the flag to get both wings of infantry straddling the highway on line. There was no doubt that the VC were waiting for us in a little cluster of houses hugging the road just ahead of us. The ragged Cambodian troops in their shower shoes and tattered uniforms pushed ahead, almost eagerly. Certainly more eagerly than the press.

The mortars started to fire into the village. Other shots were heard up ahead. As we moved closer to the houses, silence fell again on the parched countryside. We knew that trouble had to come. It was just a matter of getting into the VCs' range. The tanks were now 100 meters behind us. Our CBS group and the rest of the press moved off the road and into a ditch running parallel to the rice paddies.

Then it started. The staccato bursts of automatic weapons wiped out the stillness of the afternoon. Bullets whipped overhead. The

Cambodians shouted and started firing. We hit the dirt of the rice paddy and I tried to get my camera working.

Mud and water were all over our equipment and us. The press corps looked like a colorful carpet spread over the rice paddy. We got ourselves organized and I started filming. It was impossible to see what was happening on the road. The firing didn't stop and the bullets came in low.

George got on his feet. Ignoring the heavy fire, he grabbed the mike to do an on-camera opening to catch the sound of combat.

We risked a look at the road. A green and red bundle was sprawled in the sunlight just behind one of the tanks that had come forward. It was our flag carrier. The first salvo had smashed his head. Other Cambodians were wounded. Their comrades dragged them to safety. The tank rounds had set the flimsy houses afire and the little village was burning.

Then bursts of automatic fire whipped across the hardtop highway. We plunged into the safety of the rice paddy with the rest of the press and stayed there, half-submerged, for almost two hours. There it was easier to stay lower than the grazing fire that seemed to continue forever.

Gerry Miller had never seen a war before. His moustache twitched: "Listen, fellers, is this a real battle?"

"Yes, Gerry, it's a real battle."

"It's really a real battle?" He sounded excited and anxious but unafraid.

"Yes, Gerry, it is a real battle, it's the real thing."

"Listen, fellers," he added, almost embarrassed, "could you say that we are pinned down?"

"Yes, Gerry, you could really say that we are pinned down, so just stay there and don't move. You are really pinned down and this is a real battle. Congratulations."

Syvertsen spoke up. "Let's go forward, up to that crossroad ahead."

I looked and saw a wounded Cambodian being dragged back by one of his buddies. "I wouldn't. What are we going to do if they counterattack? We'll be the only ones there."

George said, "That's a good point."

Tired of the mud and the sun and the stiffness in our limbs, we finally rushed up on the road and hid behind one of the tanks to get a closer shot of the flag bearer lying in the hot sun. ABC, not wanting to miss a good shot either, followed us.

Now there were too many of us behind the tank. Common sense is not one of our strengths when it comes to keeping up with the competition. We ran back to the paddy and waited. Slowly the Cambodian troops made headway. In one brave charge they finally took the village, shooting and shouting.

There were no villagers left. Just dead animals and a few fallen Viet Cong. Smoke and ruins were all around us. Some captured Viet Cong, hands bound behind them, were held at gunpoint in the middle of a nearby stream.

A beautiful sunset illuminated the scene of destruction. With the aftermath of battle in the background, Syvertsen did an on-camera close, saying, "Many brave men will have to die before the road to Takeo is cleared."

Many men did, like our flag carrier. Only George could not know that just a few days later, he and others from CBS would be among the next to meet death on this very highway.

We returned to our car for the drive home to Phnom Penh. Driver Joe Puy waited for us with cold drinks and towels. Then we drove back alone with our thoughts, happy to have gotten out of this one in one piece.

At the Royal, we were greeted by those who hadn't gone out that day. The competition, drinks in hand, listened anxiously to our tale, fearful of repercussions from the home office about the story they'd missed.

I had shot 40 minutes worth of film. A reluctant evening news producer was finally persuaded to use three minutes of it on air, a relatively
short story for that time. He didn't think it was such an important
piece. After all, no Americans had died in the fight. The home front was
fed up with the war, and our reports from the battleground were often
shrugged off as redundant.

This period of time in Cambodia was not a happy one. Quite a few
cameramen and soundmen were concerned about the networks trying
to outdo one another with war stories. We chased after combat every
day, more mindful of what ABC and NBC were doing than of the
importance of what happened in the field. Often the risks taken were
not worth the results.

We drove down those long and lonesome Cambodian highways
where many a newsman had already paid the travel tax with capture
or death. But the lesson wasn't learned, and we continued to go after
combat with a sense of almost missionary zeal that was bound to end
in disaster.

The hotel swimming pool grounds had become the social center of
the press corps almost since our arrival. The well-to-do Frenchmen,
who owned this playground before our rowdy gang crowded them
aside, watched us with both annoyance and amazement.

One of Phnom Penh's best restaurants was beside the pool and, in
spite of dwindling supplies, it became our daily Mecca for food and
drink. This war, conveniently located only a few commuter miles away,
made it easy to shuttle between the equally unreal worlds of hotel luxury and combat in the countryside.

The dangerous atmosphere of competition continued to grow
among the three networks. ABC's Howard Tuckner, a veteran of many
battles in Vietnam, was one of the few TV newsmen who tried to put a
brake on this madness. He suggested that we consult each other, decide
on coverage, go out and get our stories, then return from the field

together. That way we'd avoid the temptation to outstay the other teams and increase the risks.

Although it sounded reasonable enough, no one bothered to listen. The chance to make or save a reputation by more time on air meant more to us than being prudent in a difficult and dangerous situation.

The day before his death, George and I had personal problems for the first time in our two-year friendship. I felt he had shown an increasingly reckless disregard for his own and his team's safety, more than he ever had before.

During the 1968 Tet offensive, in Danang, Hue, Saigon and Cholon, George had displayed great courage as well as sound judgment when we were in the midst of some of the heaviest fighting of the war.

His bravery and concern for his crews were nearly legendary among the cameramen who had worked with him. In Cambodia, however, his behavior changed. He always wanted to be the first, pushing sometimes even ahead of the troops into unknown and treacherous territory.

He was impatient with any delay and obsessed with the desire to seek out the fiercest combat in this war without fronts, U.S. helicopters or air or artillery support. In this struggle, the opposing Communist forces held the upper hand and the Cambodian army we covered was clearly the underdog.

Only much later did I find out that George was under tremendous pressure from the home office in New York to get "tougher" in his reporting. He was unfairly considered a lightweight, and he decided he had to fight for his professional reputation and change the minds of a few New York executives comfortably ensconced in their mahogany foxholes.

George, Thanong Hiransi, Ishii, Sakai and I were nearing the end of our tour and were scheduled to return to Tokyo shortly after spending an eventful month in Vietnam and Cambodia. I urged George to go back, but I also sensed his desire to stick with the story.

George had developed a deep affection for Cambodia and its hard-pressed population. He had served as a correspondent in Poland, and Cambodia's plight reminded him of Poland's in 1939 when that country was hopelessly squeezed between two rapacious powers, the Soviet Union and Nazi Germany. He wanted to do his best to report Cambodia's suffering, but he overestimated America's interest in Cambodia's struggle. As long as American boys were fighting and dying in Vietnam, not many people in the States were particularly interested in dying Cambodian boys.

We disagreed sharply and argued bitterly about covering the battles. In my opinion, the results of our efforts weren't worth putting our lives on the line. Usage logs showed that the film reports from the Phnom Penh side of the war always played second fiddle to pieces about the U.S. side of the incursion into Cambodia.

I felt very frustrated asking George to consider the odds for survival without looking like a coward. I ran up against a brave professional journalist who made up his mind to show the bosses what he was made of, even though he had proved that already many times over.

We argued for long hours, sitting with Gerry Miller in the shade of a huge banyan tree near the swimming pool of the Hotel Le Royal.

It was the most painful conversation I have ever had. I said I was fed up with our unappreciated but highly dangerous assignment in Cambodia and that we should go back to Vietnam and cover the American troops there. It seemed to me a fair alternative. It was part of our job to run risks but to run them for a purpose: to get stories on the air.

George disagreed and strongly implied that he intended to go on following the Cambodian army on a daily basis. He even mentioned that he wanted to persuade our bosses in New York to purchase an amphibious Jeep so that we could just cruise around the countryside, independent of everyone, covering the war wherever we met it.

The craziness of this idea did not fully hit any of us until later, when tragic events confirmed just how unrealistic the atmosphere had become. George then told me bluntly that my reputation would suffer if I "checked out of the Cambodian situation."

He added that he didn't want anyone to slow him down in the field.

We reached an uneasy truce. I agreed to stay on and do whatever I had to do. However, our professional relationship and our friendship were on the rocks. Twenty-four hours later he was dead. Through the following years I often wondered if I could have turned the situation around if I had been more forceful. I still don't know.

After our discussion, Gerry Miller took me aside and asked me if there were any personality problems between George and me. I denied this, recounting my long and genuine friendship with him over the years in Southeast Asia.

Then Gerry asked me if George had always been so obsessive about going after combat. We talked about it for a while and he seemed concerned. I told Gerry it was his job as head of the Phnom Penh operation to put the brakes on George.

Years later I later learned that Gerry had misgivings of his own about Syvertsen. Syvertsen had initially been sent in to replace Saigon correspondent Bert Quint, who had left temporarily to hand-carry a hot combat story back to Saigon. When Quint, who had had some close calls on the disputed roads of Cambodia, was about to resume his post in Phnom Penh, he was stopped literally at the last moment by New York and told that Syvertsen was insisting that he be allowed to continue covering Cambodia.

Miller, upon learning that Quint was not returning to Phnom Penh as scheduled, telexed New York protesting. Quint, he said, should come back to Cambodia because "he is the only one who knows what is safe to do and what isn't."

Cameraman Skip Brown, who also had had several hair-raising experiences with George, noticed his obsession to seek danger as well. We both felt it to be close to a desire for self-inflicted punishment. Day after day we would find ourselves stuck in dangerous situations without reaping any journalistic results worth mentioning.

This bothered Gerry maybe as much as it did me. No one was less willing to take chances than the next guy. We had all covered war for many years and had nothing to prove to anyone. We were grown men in our late 20s to mid-30s who should have known better than to continue this stupid game of chicken. Yet no one wanted to be the first to call it off.

The next morning, May 31, the day of our canceled departure for Tokyo, Thanong and I were ready to accompany Syvertsen wherever he wanted to go. I was waiting for him near the main entrance of the Royal when Gerry Miller came up to me. "Kurt, why don't you go with Don Webster and check out the Vietnamese marines at Neak Leung? Don wants to go on a combat operation with them. You know the ropes, so please go with him. George and I will drive down the road to Takeo with Ishii and Sakai just to have a look."

He said he didn't think Ishii and Sakai should do any more combat, though they hadn't complained. He and George would take Ramnik Lekhi, our Indian stringer cameraman, with them.

As he walked off, Ishii came over and gave me a package of cookies for my 2-year-old daughter, Danika. She and my wife, Gisela, were now in Phnom Penh along with Gusta, George's wife. We had all planned to return to Tokyo together. Ishii looked sad and depressed, probably thinking of his family back in Tokyo.

A few minutes after 8 a.m. George and Gerry, both in khaki shirts, came out of the hotel and got into their rented Jeep. If George saw me he didn't show it. The previous day's conversation still rankled. Maybe it was Gerry's innate sense of tact to keep us apart that day.

Another reason for our regrouping was that Don Webster really did want to go on a combat operation with the Vietnamese troops and since he had a problem communicating with the Japanese crew whose English was weak, he preferred to take Thanong and me.

The Jeep, with George driving and Gerry next to him, left the hotel compound. Sam Leng, our daring and loyal Cambodian driver, followed close behind in the Mercedes with Ishii, Sakai and Lekhi. The small convoy quickly passed from view. I'll never forget the worn look on Ishii's face as he waved his hand and looked out of the window at me.

Kurt Hoefle found me as I was getting my gear ready.

"I wanted to go with Syvertsen, but Lekhi beat me to it. How come you're with Webster today?"

I shrugged off the question.

"I don't really know. Are we ready?"

Don Webster joined us a few minutes later and we drove away. Syvertsen led his group south of Phnom Penh where we had covered our first fight near the village of Tran Khnar and where Don Webster, Skip Brown and Kurt Hoefle were briefly captured and released.

It took almost a year and a half to reconstruct the whole story of George's last trip, though the immediate facts became clear two days later.

What follows is the sequence of events as they emerged from the tales of many witnesses, some of whom spoke directly afterward and some over the years.

It was a Sunday morning and traffic was light as George drove through the nearly empty Phnom Penh streets. The khaki shirts that George and Gerry wore and the grayish color of the Jeep gave the small convoy a fairly military air.

Sam Leng, in his Mercedes, stayed close to George. He had been in many a tight spot since the Cambodian war began and his reputation as a driver was excellent among the press corps. He handled his baby blue Mercedes with consummate skill, driving safely at high speed. Beside him sat Lekhi with a small silent camera.

As Hoefle told me, Lekhi, a freelancer, was not scheduled to go on this trip but decided at the last minute to go anyway to pick up a few extra bucks. He was paid only if he produced film stories. In the backseat sat Sakai and next to the big sound camera, the diminutive frame of Tomoharu Ishii.

Ishii was my colleague on the staff of the Tokyo bureau. He desperately wanted to go home that day. I later read his cable asking New York to let him return to Japan with Sakai. Each passing day showed how unfit they were for the tough, demanding combat conditions in Cambodia. Although they were inexperienced in Indochina, they faced an unpleasant situation without question or complaint. And they trusted their correspondent.

The little caravan passed Pochentong Airport and moved south on Highway 3. Blue mountains and lush countryside concealed the terror ahead. They passed through Tran Khnar, the last populated place under government control.

On the southern edge of the village, a few Cambodian soldiers manning a checkpoint attempted to stop the convoy, but George flashed his press card and drove through without stopping, the Mercedes close behind. It was the 11th checkpoint since leaving Phnom Penh.

Six more kilometers down the narrow highway, the group reached the 13th and final government checkpoint. A small farmhouse surrounded by a garden served as a shelter and communications station. The soldiers had set up a makeshift roadblock, bamboo poles resting across two oil drums. The poles didn't even cross the entire road, leaving enough room for a car to drive around.

As the Jeep and the Mercedes approached, one of the Cambodian guards tried to wave them down. George drove onto the shoulder of the road, nearly scraping the guard. He again flashed his press card and roared on as the Mercedes followed. The soldiers at the roadblock shouted after them but to no avail.

Moving at high speed, George's convoy had now entered no man's land, but he and his doomed companions didn't know it. He and Gerry were apparently confident that the front line was further down the road, where it had been only a few days before.

The soldier at the roadblock had tried to tell them that the Cambodian army had moved back to the little farmhouse and that a strong enemy force was now occupying the flat countryside ahead. For a few kilometers, the road still showed signs of normal activity. Villagers moved about their daily business, washing laundry, cooking and talking. Peasants worked in the fields.

All oncoming traffic, however, had ceased. When the little group rounded a curve about two kilometers south of the 13th outpost, it entered a silent and empty land. The few houses on either side of the road were deserted, their shutters closed. Nobody worked in the little gardens despite the relative cool of the morning.

As the sun rose higher, the humid heat intensified. At about 9:30 a.m., George pulled up to the destroyed bridge at Baing Kasey, near the village of Prey Neak. A marker showed the distance to Phnom Penh to be 54 kilometers. The total silence, the deserted houses, the empty fields and the newly destroyed bridge should have conveyed a clear warning: Turn around, get out and keep going until you are safely back with Cambodian troops at the next checkpoint.

We don't know what went on among them at this point, but George wasn't one to consult others. Besides, the others could not have provided much advice. Maybe they simply voiced their fears.

Gerry, inexperienced but willing, trusted the experience of Syvertsen. Lekhi, new to the country and the war, couldn't have been much help. Ishii and Sakai, probably silent and scared, were prepared to follow their leader stoically, as their authoritarian upbringing had taught them.

Sam Leng, the daredevil driver, the man who'd gotten his passengers out of many a tough spot before, somehow didn't see the danger, either.

Syvertsen decided to get around the wrecked bridge, fording the shallow stream with the Jeep.

He took along Gerry, Sam Leng as interpreter and Lekhi, perhaps to have at least a silent camera on hand should something develop. Ishii and Sakai stayed behind with the Mercedes.

George drove across the stream and then back on to Highway 3 and sped into the silent countryside. Ahead, the houses of Prey Neak village were eerily empty. Not a single soul could be seen.

We can only guess the mood of these last moments in the lives of the men in the Jeep. Ahead of the men stretched Highway 3, straight and deserted. On either side, abandoned wooden houses, their shutters closed. In the distance loomed serenely beautiful blue mountains. It was the end of the dry season and with the first rains, the countryside was lush and green.

Prey Neak appeared like a sleepy and peaceful Cambodian village at midday with everyone indoors to escape the heat. The appearance was misleading. It was only about 10 in the morning, and the entire countryside should have been alive. What were George's thoughts? How did Gerry feel? Ishii and Sakai? Did they recognize the danger all around them? How about Lekhi and Sam Leng? Was George distracted by the adventure of his little expedition? Did he want to tread where no one else would dare? Or was this an urge to push beyond the last outpost and have a look into the unknown—a sensation most newsmen experience at one time or another?

The Jeep raced through the quiet little village. Suddenly, well concealed enemy soldiers opened fire with automatic weapons. George had steered his people right into the middle of an enemy headquarters. A deadly B-40 rocket slammed into the front of the Jeep. By all indications, George apparently flung himself out of the Jeep an instant before the shell's impact.

With the others already dead or wounded, the Jeep careened off the road, crashed into a mango tree and burst into flames. George rolled a few feet across the highway, then managed to get up and stagger toward his killers as if to fight them off. They put him down with a bullet in his back and dumped him into a hole dug beside a rice paddy not far from the road to Takeo.

The enemy, hateful of anything American, let the Jeep burn and then buried Sam and Gerry near a house by the mango tree. Lekhi was left in the Jeep. The burning Jeep could be seen by frightened Cambodian peasants hiding in the fields near the village. The entire incident lasted only minutes.

Earlier that morning, Hangen, an experienced newsman and keen and respected competitor, had heard that CBS was heading south. He collected his driver and crew, French cameraman Roger Colne and Japanese soundman Waku, and set out after the CBS convoy. He didn't see the CBS cars, but knowing the general military situation, he guessed correctly that their destination was Highway 3.

Stopping at the various government checkpoints, he confirmed that CBS was ahead of him. He followed at a brisk pace, unwilling to get beaten on another combat piece. In his eagerness to catch up, he must have ignored the same warning signs the countryside offered: no oncoming traffic, no peasants in the villages or fields, shuttered windows, no children playing. His journey came to an end as his gray Opel pulled up beside the blue Mercedes just short of the blown Slakou River bridge.

Hangen found Ishii and Sakai cowering near their car. Viet Cong and Khmer Rouge forces suddenly appeared and splashed across the stream, firing as they advanced. The terrified newsmen sought cover behind their vehicles.

One round hit a front tire of the Mercedes. Enemy soldiers reached the cars, searched them. They ordered the crews to take their camera equipment and herded them across the small river and up the opposite bank.

The little group was marched southward, around the town where the CBS crew had just been killed, then back onto Highway 3. Villagers later remembered seeing the two tall white men and three smaller Asians, tired and scared, heading on foot for the village of Thnal Bot crossing a rickety foot bridge leading over one of many small creeks in the area. Their guards, the villagers said, looked and acted nervous and hostile.

Three kilometers to the north at the 13th checkpoint, the Cambodian troops listened helplessly to the exploding rocket and automatic weapons fire. Undermanned, they didn't dare send a patrol down the road. With no radios, they could not even report the incident.

Back in Phnom Penh, many newsmen who had decided not to go out that day relaxed around the pool, drinking and watching the Air France stewardesses sunning themselves. It was Sunday, after all, and nothing especially newsworthy appeared to be happening. They were right.

Webster, Kurt Hoefle and I had reached Neak Leung on Highway 1 at about the same time that the lives of our friends came to an end. The South Vietnamese combat operation did not materialize. The ironies of the situation ran deep: George's "nothing day" had turned into a disaster while our exciting prospects for battle had come to naught. Ignorant of the bloody events by the ruined bridge at Baing Kasey and not wanting to waste the day, we decided to do a film report on the many bridges the enemy had destroyed since the Cambodian war began.

Webster had already left for Phnom Penh, where two women, Gusta Syvertsen and my wife, Gisela, waited for their husbands, looking forward to mid-afternoon when the crews usually returned from the field.

Hoefle and I drove down Highway 3 to get our bridge shots. At one checkpoint, Cambodian guards told us that they had seen a Jeep and two passenger cars heading toward Takeo that morning and shortly after heard the sounds of an explosion and gunfire. The cars hadn't yet returned. Villagers also reported hearing light arms fire as the little CBS/NBC convoy disappeared around a bend on the road near Baing Kasey.

Concerned, Hoefle and I drove back to Phnom Penh, intent on proceeding with caution and not jumping to conclusions. Cambodia was full of rumors and we wanted to avoid raising any unnecessary alarms.

Gathering up Don Webster and Thanong Hiransi at the hotel, we retraced the route Syvertsen and his crew had taken after leaving the hotel. We stopped to talk to the Cambodian guards at every checkpoint along the way. As more and more bad news about explosions and gunfire filtered in, we had to admit that the prospects appeared grim.

One fact became clear: Syvertsen had ignored the last checkpoint and driven on, out of sight, beyond kilometer 53 on Highway 3 on this 31st of May. Not only had peasants and soldiers heard an explosion and automatic weapons fire, but other villagers had seen a burning Jeep on the other side of the bridge near Baing Kasey. We hung around the last checkpoint for a while then went beyond it as far as we dared. We met a Cambodian villager who told us he had seen a blue Mercedes near the bridge with a flat tire, but otherwise undamaged.

A Cambodian soldier informed us that they had eventually sent a patrol to investigate the firing and had lost a man near the abandoned Mercedes to enemy fire. He had important documents on him and they wanted to retrieve his body later in the day. Things looked bad.

We again returned to Phnom Penh, where Webster telexed the foreign desk in New York and also informed NBC of all we knew about the incident. I told my wife and Gusta that George and the others were missing. We didn't mention the explosion or the burning Jeep.

The following morning, June 1, Kurt Hoefle and I tried to charter a small plane to fly over the ambush site, but the charter company refused. We would have to fly low and the plane would be exposed to enemy fire. The pilot considered it a bad insurance risk.

On June 2, Hoefle, Sophan, our very reliable Cambodian helper, and I drove down Highway 3 and joined a Cambodian infantry unit that had moved during the night to a position several kilometers beyond the last government checkpoint. They were now in the vicinity of the ruined bridge. Vegetation and a bend in the stream prevented us from seeing the Mercedes.

We again questioned Cambodian officers and troopers, who expressed little hope for the survival of those in the Jeep.

That night, the Cambodian army unit formed a circle near a pagoda just north of the Slakou River. We could feel the tension and fear among the soldiers. The night air was hot and muggy, and sporadic gunfire made everyone jumpy.

At 9 p.m., the company commander, gentle looking in his ragged uniform, established radio contact with a patrol that had left at dusk to scout the area near the bridge. The night patrol reported that Viet Cong and Khmer Rouge soldiers had driven the two passenger cars away but then left the CBS Mercedes, probably because it couldn't ford the rocky river bed with its low ground clearance.

At midnight, the soldiers inside the perimeter became restless and the officers burned joss sticks and chanted prayers. I did not take this as a good sign. My friend Kurt Hoefle didn't look happy either. It would take more than prayers and incense to hold back the Viet Cong should they decide to attack our small force.

For the first time in the war, I accepted an AK-47 and three magazines. This gun wouldn't have helped me very much, since I wasn't at all familiar with it. But it gave me a sense of security—a false one, but a sense of security nonetheless.

About then, 300 Cambodian soldiers emerged from the darkness. The sight of reinforcements made Kurt and me feel more secure. But dawn brought more fear as the entire unit started to move south to recover the fallen trooper and his documents. The battalion advanced in a broad skirmish line toward Highway 3. Hoefle and I joined the command group in between the two lines of infantry marching slowly across the paddy fields.

It didn't take long before we were hit by some of the heaviest mortar fire I'd ever encountered. These were terrifying moments. I just dropped my camera, dove behind a paddy dike and then pulled it toward me by the battery cable, like a poodle on a leash.

Kurt took shelter behind another section of the dike while our faithful helper and soundman Sophan wisely dropped the rucksack with the extra rolls of film, stuck a Buddha amulet between his teeth, and sought cover behind the nearest tree.

A Cambodian infantryman with an AK-47 stood up right next to us and repeatedly hosed down the low underbrush just ahead. Other soldiers cautiously worked their way forward and, during a break in the firing, told Sophan that our Mercedes was only about 40 meters ahead of us. There was no trace of the NBC Opel. A short time later, a Cambodian officer motioned Kurt and me forward and showed us through the undergrowth, tantalizingly nearby, the blue CBS Mercedes. Except for the shot out left front tire it appeared untouched.

Enemy AK-47s opened up again, driving us back. The ambush site remained insecure for the moment. Several wounded and killed on both sides were the result of this foray into hostile territory. The Cambodian troops never did recover their fallen comrade or his documents.

As we retreated to the last outpost in the direction of Phnom Penh, Kurt, Sophan and I talked to frightened villagers who had escaped the shooting. We got always the same answer to our anxious questions. A peasant woman confirmed earlier reports about an explosion and gunfire. She added that after the explosion she saw a column of smoke rising into the air, probably from George's burning Jeep.

As the three of us walked back to our car, I picked up a wounded Cambodian soldier who had been left on the road. He begged for help and I carried him several kilometers until we could deliver him to his comrades.

Back at the hotel, we talked to Syvertsen's wife, who was desperate for news about George and the other missing men. We didn't tell her everything and nothing of our fears. Time for that would come soon enough.

For the moment, we wanted to get her through the day and another night without destroying all of her hopes. At this point we had a lot of circumstantial evidence pointing straight to disaster, but it wasn't enough to draw final conclusions and tell her that George was dead.

Our mood was ghastly. Only Danika, my blonde little daughter, was oblivious to the tragedy just 30 miles or so down the road and to the fear creeping along the corridors of our hotel.

The weather remained serene. The splendor of the tropical flowers refused to reflect the dark cloud we had to live under. Friends from other media knew something had gone terribly wrong down the road, but we kept our own counsel as much as we could.

But the looks on our faces must have told the story. We couldn't avoid giving strong hints to a select few of our buddies in the press corps. After all, we would eventually need their experience, advice and information to piece the story together.

Two pillars of strength were David Miller, the CBS Saigon bureau chief, who had come over at the first sign of trouble, and Skip Brown, cameraman from Saigon, who pursued his own line of investigation. We, the survivors, became a very tight group during these trying days.

On June 3, three days after the attack, David and Skip advanced with Cambodian forces to the Mercedes and the wreck of the Jeep. The Viet Cong and Khmer Rouge, satisfied with the damage they'd done, had withdrawn.

Kurt, Sophan and I joined David and Skip at the ambush site, where a number of other journalists had gathered around the burnt-out Jeep and the Mercedes. Nearby, we found the decomposing body of George Syvertsen. There was no mistake that it was him.

He wore a cargo strap belt, quite unique, given to him by Dana Stone, a gifted still photographer who was another ambush victim on another lonely Cambodian road.

I recognized George's corduroy pants and high-top Hush Puppies, all Syvertsen trademarks. I also noticed George's fingers, very long and distinctive, with index, middle and ring fingers close together, the finger-tips at almost the same level. His fingernails were also peculiar, giving his fingertips the shape of drumsticks. Finally, the size of the body—George stood over 6 feet—left no doubt that this was Syvertsen.

As daylight began to fade, we continued to look for more bodies but found none. The Cambodians looked jittery and wanted to pull back across the river before dusk.

I took off my shirt, tied it to a pole and marked Syvertsen's grave. There was no time to recover the body and prepare it for the trip to Phnom Penh. We got out just before the sun went down.

The ambush site was taken over by Vietnamese and Khmer Rouge forces during the night, but the Cambodian army made it a point of honor to retake it the next day. The cost was 30 dead. The madness of violent death would not stop. George's body was finally brought back to a Phnom Penh morgue.

Skip Brown, David Miller and I went there to identify the body offi-cially. Before entering, we resisted the temptation to take a heavy swig from a bottle of whiskey. George's body rested on a stone slab in a hot, barren room that lacked even the most basic hygienic or medical gadg-ets. The body was covered with a Cambodian flag. Decomposition had set in. The smell was overpowering. Only his pants, belt and shoes were recognizable. We confirmed the identification and fled the room.

That night, to escape Gusta's and Gisela's wailing, Kurt, Skip and I also fled the hotel. There were few tears left in any of us. Instead, we drank ourselves into oblivion.

The next day, we said goodbye to George. South Vietnam's Vice President Nguyen Cao Ky had sent a two-engine propeller plane to return the body to Saigon. The plane was parked in the military section of Pochentong Airport beside obsolete Cambodian MiGs. The Cambodian military authorities permitted our little ceremony only if we promised not to take pictures of their decrepit fighters.

No problem. Except that a feisty little CBS executive from New York insisted we sneak some shots of the planes while we unloaded George's coffin from a truck. There is no piety in our profession. George would have loved it.

We heaved his heavy zinc coffin into the plane and it soon disappeared in the direction of Vietnam, first leg on the long trip home to the States.

I went to the Monorom Hotel, a few blocks from the Royal, where some of our missing and dead had lived. I packed Sakai's suitcases, then Gerry Miller's. His return ticket to Rome was on his bureau. I knew in my heart he wouldn't be using it anymore.

Lekhi, the Indian stringer, was also missing and presumed dead. Looking at his suitcases, I remembered that we had recovered a badly charred set of keys near the Jeep, lying amidst a heap of burned bones. I asked Thanong Hiransi to bring them over. When I inserted them into the locks of the suitcases, they snapped open. Then I knew that Lekhi was also dead.

For David Miller, Ramnik Lekhi was not just another freelance cameraman. Miller met him in New Delhi while he was there on vacation. He visited his home and met his family. He was surprised that one room in Lekhi's modest house was marked "CBS Office." It housed a supply of CBS shipping bags and labels. David was impressed and suggested that Ramnik do a tour in Vietnam. Cameramen in Vietnam considered themselves a select group and the pay was accordingly high. When Ramnik was offered the chance to go to Cambodia, he eagerly grabbed it in the hope of advancing his career.

Ramnik's remains were cremated at a Buddhist shrine in Cambodia. Gordon Manning, in charge of hard news at CBS, hand-carried the ashes to New Delhi.

Ishii lived in the Royal. As I packed his suitcases, I was struck by how neat his room was. Everything was in its place, as if he had to leave for the airport at a moment's notice.

The next day, many of us in our decimated little group left for Tokyo. There was Gusta, poised and quiet, and my wife, Gisela, always a pillar of strength along with our little daughter, Danika. There was also Kurt Hoefle, Skip Brown, Thanong Hiransi and myself.

We must have looked like a beaten little army forced to leave its dead behind. The press corps, which had turned out in force, stood silently as we peered through the windows of the taxiing plane. Lift off. In the distance I saw for a fleeting moment the blue mountains near Takeo. Then they disappeared and with them the immediacy of the drama played out so close to them. As the plane roared upward, the last sight of Cambodia was dry brown earth, palms and the ugly flat expanse south of Phnom Penh.

We were all consumed by a sense of loss, rage and futility. As the plane leveled off, my thoughts turned to our arrival in Tokyo. There I would have to meet face to face with two elderly Japanese ladies and tell them their husbands were missing. At the same time, I would have to tell them there was still hope that Ishii and Sakai may have survived the savagery of the past week. I dreaded the task.

CHAPTER 2

Return to Cambodia

ONE YEAR LATER, in 1971, Correspondent Jeff Williams, Thanong Hiransi and I returned to Cambodia in search of answers. While Jeff and Thanong covered stories on their own to justify our presence there, I spent part of June and July traveling 2,000 kilometers up and down Highway 3 to track down witnesses who could describe the ambush near Baing Kasey and the disappearance of Ishii, Sakai and our NBC colleagues.

Sharing the grim task with us was Jim Sturdevant, an NBC cameraman whose drive and concern energized our efforts.

By this time, we knew for certain that everyone in the Jeep had been killed. Shortly after Syvertsen's body was discovered, the remains of Gerry Miller, Lekhi and Sam Leng were also found and positively identified. Kurt Hoefle had returned to Cambodia to help in their recovery.

During this period, CBS gave me a free hand to do whatever I thought necessary to discover the fate of Ishii and Sakai. For the past year their families' emotions had swung between hope and despair. Now I owed it to them to find answers.

Cambodian peasants we questioned confirmed the hostility that the Viet Cong and Khmer Rouge held toward foreigners, especially Americans. The Viet Cong insisted that all foreigners be driven from

Cambodia. In some villages, they even announced that all foreigners should be killed.

The Khmer Rouge were little more than murderous bandits throughout the war. They had no organization, and the North Vietnamese wanted it that way. A strong Cambodian Communist movement could have restricted their activities in the sanctuaries along the Cambodian border. According to villagers, many of the Khmer Rouge were social misfits, robbers and murderers who thought nothing of mistreating people. Under the influence of the North Vietnamese, they became willing tools to assist in the killing of foreigners. Later, as we know, they raised the level to genocide.

Time and again, the Cambodian peasants confirmed how eager the North Vietnamese and the Viet Cong were to uphold the secrecy of their presence in Cambodia. They had no patience for nosy foreign journalists, whom they considered CIA agents.

None of this gave us much hope of finding our friends alive and well. Sturdevant proved to be a tireless pathfinder, leaving nothing untried if it might have offered the slightest chance of getting us more information. An ex-Marine, his code was not to leave a buddy behind. This motto drove him until death caught up with him one day on a mountain road in Hawaii when his car spun off a cliff. The missing in Cambodia could not have had a more loyal friend.

After weeks of traveling, searching, interviewing witnesses, chasing false leads and even enlisting the help of people like Deputy Prime Minister Sirik Matak and Information Minister Long Boret, Sturdevant and I composed the following report and sent it off to our networks in New York:

REPORT:
  At about 10 a.m. on the 31st of May, 1970, Syvertsen, driving a Jeep with Miller in the front seat, closely followed by a CBS-hired blue Mercedes driven by Cambodian Sam Leng and occupied by

Ishii, Sakai and Lekhi, came upon the destroyed bridge at Baing Kasey (1).

Syvertsen decided to take the Jeep around a rugged bypass and to look at what was up ahead on Highway 3 (2). He took with him Miller, Sam Leng as an interpreter and Lekhi maybe to have a cameraman with him. Sakai and Ishii stayed behind near the blue Mercedes (3).

Minutes after they had heard a sharp explosion but no other firing ahead, the NBC Opel pulled up behind the Mercedes and all occupants got out (4). After a short talk between the two crews, a group of three Viet Cong came near them and started firing, hitting the Opel. NBC driver Leng jumped under the gray Opel and was struck by a bullet that also punctured one of the tires.

A Japanese, maybe Waku, helped to pull him out. Just minutes before these events, the CBS Jeep was struck by a Viet Cong B-40 rocket, hit a mango tree and burst into flames (5). All in the Jeep died. The NBC crew and the remaining CBS crew were taken prisoner (6) and led for about 1 1/2 kilometers on a path running 300 meters east of and parallel to Highway 3, heading toward the village of Thnal Bot (7) about 6 kilometers from the scene of the Jeep crash in the village of Baing Kasey at km 54.

The NBC crew and our two Japanese did not see the Jeep again. After the march from the scene of capture, the latter part on Highway 3 itself, the entire group, accompanied by about eight Viet Cong, arrived at Thnal Bot around 3 p.m. and were put into the village teacher's house (8), which served the Viet Cong and Khmer Rouge as a prison.

At that time all valuables, money, watches, were taken from the prisoners as the Viet Cong demanded to see all and any kind of identification papers. At this point, Ishii and Waku were able to get rid of some compromising U.S. military and Cambodian

ID cards that were later found. Also at about this time, NBC's Cambodian driver was separated from the rest of the journalists who were kept upstairs with a Cambodian prisoner named Ben Phun from Thnal Bot village.

In the evening they were allowed to move about the house. The Viet Cong were not too threatening to the journalists, they even fed them dinner and told them that they would be released if indeed they were genuine journalists. The group spent the night at the teacher's house.

The next day, Monday, June 1, the Viet Cong became much more threatening to the journalists. They seemed very upset; they thought that they were agents or spies. At about 5 p.m. Hangen, Ishii and Sakai, with rifles pointed at them but unfettered, were herded into the NBC Opel by four Viet Cong and two Khmer Rouge named Ngon and Hoy and driven in the direction of Slakou village four kilometers south on Highway 3 (9). Then the car turned off onto a small road to the west (10) and stopped between two bridges (11) about 500 meters east of the temple called Wat Po.

They were led to a bamboo thicket about 10 meters off to the right (12) and beaten and shot to death. The Viet Cong and the Khmer Rouge then returned to the teacher's house, herded Colne and Waku into the Opel, drove them to the bridge, marched them to the wooded area and put them to death. Our men and the NBC crew minus their driver, who was released, were buried in three graves in the bamboo thicket near a canal (12).

The Viet Cong allowed no villagers to witness the killings and probably killed the Khmer Rouge for disclosing the murders. Two other prisoners were probably put to death on May 30 with shovels in Thnal Bot (13). They were buried in two graves near a pond (14). One of them could be a Cambodian government employee connected with agriculture, the other one a Japanese newsman captured earlier.

There are still some holes in the report: The NBC driver and Cambodian soldier Phun (see interview with him in appendix) claimed that they witnessed the journalists being driven off. However, their accounts differ. I went along with Phun's. The times and days of the stay at the teacher's house and of the executions are correct. It seems likely that the Khmer Rouge guerrilla called Ngon (or Noon, as told to me by a Tram Khnar detective and another Ngon from Baing Kasey) is the same Khmer Rouge who rallied to the government side and was killed around June 20.

I also find it curious that all bodies found or reported to us were deliberately buried near water. (The reason for this, as I found out later, was that graves were dug much easier in the soft ground near or in a body of water.) This would make it easier for us to find them, should we ever get near Wat Po. Again, despite the obvious flaws of my account, no one ever mentioned that the journalists' lives were spared.

After returning to Japan, I met Ishii's and Sakai's families in a small restaurant near the CBS office in Akasaka. Also there were my wife, Gisela, our new Tokyo bureau chief, Clarence Cross, Thanong Hiransi, and our office secretary, Suzuki Hashimoto. She gently translated to the families the words that robbed them of all their hopes.

The fact remained that Ishii and Sakai's bodies still had to be found.

Little did I know how accurate this report proved to be or how help-ful it would be in recovering the remains of Hangen, Colne, Waku and Sakai 22 years later (See attached maps).

CHAPTER 3

Cambodia, 22 Years Later

It has taken nearly a generation for what passes for peace in these parts to come to Cambodia. Now the search, near the village of Wat Po, could be resumed. A U.S. Army team came, this time not on a mission of war but of humanity, an attempt to give the missing men a resting place in their homelands and provide a sort of tranquility for their families. With them was CBS producer Kurt Volkert.

> *Bert Quint, CBS News*
> *April 1992*

Diary

February 24, 1992, aboard SA28 from Rome to Bangkok

I can't believe I'm returning to Cambodia after almost 20 years. The U.S. Army is going to look for five of my colleagues: three from NBC and our Japanese camera team, Ishii and Sakai, who were captured and murdered while on an assignment that had a purpose few can remember.

Ishii and Sakai. Not forgotten but nearly overtaken by the passage of time. The ghosts of Cambodia aren't with me yet. Sitting in business class doesn't help to bring them back.

Since their death, there have been other wars, other tragic moments. I never wanted the war in Southeast Asia to be the most important part of my life. But this trip will make it important once again, even if I don't now realize it.

At 600 miles an hour, the past draws closer.

It's been a strange day. Leaving my home in Rome, I felt blue in the mellow Italian sunlight. A day like Indian summer, and it isn't even spring. But it's behind me now. I am on my way.

February 25, 1992, Bangkok

In the 20 years since I lived here, Bangkok is dramatically different. There is more of everything: cars, tall buildings and ugliness. The trip from the airport to the hotel fills a charmless two hours.

Disappointments don't wait long. I talk to Peter Chuun, the NBC representative covering the U.S. Army's search for the missing. I get the feeling that CBS is running on the outside track of this recovery operation. Feel a little bit like an outsider. Peter is busy with his preparations for the upcoming operation. I have to be patient.

The legal basis for the Army's involvement, with the U.S. taxpayer footing the bill, is that out of the five missing newsmen, one, NBC correspondent Welles Hangen, was a U.S. citizen.

The Pentagon organized the search and will field the force to do the job. Our dead will be searched for as well, even though they are Japanese, because they were captured and killed along with Hangen.

I discover that I can't fly with the Army search team on its military aircraft to Phnom Penh. CBS New York seems to have failed to send a fax to the Pacific Command as requested. So I get myself a commercial ticket and should be on my way to Phnom Penh day after tomorrow.

I feel let down, but the show is getting on the road. I know there are anxious families waiting in Japan and elsewhere, waiting for what's left of their loved ones to be returned after so long a time.

I also meet Derek Williams, an old friend and former CBS camera-man, who has just been fired by CBS but is still very much one of us. He tells me that the Army team searching for MIAs collects only bones. None has been found alive.

After the bones are recovered, they are shipped to Hawaii for final identification at a high-tech military lab. This process can take four weeks. It's a little discouraging for someone who wants to get the whole thing over with as quickly as possible.

I call Ms. Hashimoto in Tokyo, the CBS secretary who was with me when I met Ishii and Sakai's families over 20 years ago, and tell her how long it might take. She gives me a very wise Japanese answer: "Mr. Volkert, we have waited for more than 20 years. A few extra weeks will not make any difference now."

Jet lag gets to me, fatigue sets in, and I retire early.

February 27, 1992, Bangkok to Phnom Penh

An old CBS driver named Suwon drives me through the nearly empty streets of Bangkok. It is an early tropical morning with a pungent mix of smells in the air: garbage and tropical flowers, car exhaust and cooking fires. Vendors and street cleaners are at work. Slowly, I feel I'm getting back into the spirit of Asia.

Asia for me was youth, adventure and war. A long parade of people, many long gone, who were at that time terribly important. Memories flood back. I need time to sort out a past that I, at times, have undoubt-edly tried to push away.

The airport is still dark. I board a prop plane from Bangkok Air, a fly-by-night outfit whose birds carry a checkered bunch of passengers to Cambodia. Many look like carpetbaggers out to make a fast buck in Phnom Penh: fancy suits, gold necklaces, carefully handled attaché cases, probably filled with money.

I feel tense as our plane bursts through the thin clouds over the flat, water lined countryside near Phnom Penh. Because of a postponement in the trip, my visa ran out a week ago, so I am glad I had faxed the Cambodian Foreign Ministry from Bangkok for help on arrival.

Bun Wat, a minder from the Foreign Ministry's press department, meets me at Pochentong Airport. The place looks the same as it did when I left after the killings of our colleagues 20 years ago: rundown and provincial. Maybe I would call it cozy if not for the memory of our last departure.

Bun Wat gets me through the formalities. I check into the old Monorom Hotel where a long time ago I went through the belongings of our missing, looking for the owner of a charred bunch of keys.

As I walk to my room, I still hear the lock of Ramnik Lekhi's suitcase spring open. That click had pronounced him dead.

My room is cool, bright and large. An efficient ceiling fan keeps the air moving. My fifth floor balcony looks away from the city in the direction of the mighty Mekong and the rich green foliage beside it. Over the palms and banyan trees, I see the red gabled roofs of the Hotel Le Royal, unofficial press center during the Cambodian war. The heavy, sweet smell of tropical flowers rides on the oppressive air. I love it. In the street below are cyclos and motorcycles and a few cars.

The small brown men pedaling the cyclos strain to transport overweight European or American clients. An old memory of this scene suddenly strikes me: Saigon in the mid-60s when, as a young GI, I went there for the first time.

Despite the beggars, the amputated children and the war veterans, I prefer Phnom Penh to Bangkok. It is an Asian city dealing with itself and its colonial past. Old two-story French villas throughout the city enhance my impression. Feeling at home, I slowly realize how much I missed Asia, how much it was a part of me.

I cross the city to Phnom Penh's only so-called luxury hotel, the Cambodiana, situated along the banks of the Mekong. Here I will make contact with the recovery team. I remember the Cambodiana. I sighted it first from a South Vietnamese gunboat 21 years ago. (Everything seems to be 21 years ago.) We arrived after a dangerous night trip up from Can Tho in the Delta while escorting small merchant vessels through territory controlled by the Viet Cong.

It was then an unfinished ruin in the shape of a Buddhist temple. It loomed on the shore, ominous and empty, signaling that our trip was over.

The Cambodiana is filled with tourists here to see the ancient ruins of Angkor Wat. I doubt they know the risks involved. Blessed are the ignorant. Most are grinning, elderly, small Japanese and large Germans. It is strange to see tourists in a country still reeling from war, where shooting, killing and maiming continue less than 100 kilometers up the road.

In the lobby, I meet Peter Chuun and Cmdr. Ken Patterson, a regular U.S. Navy officer attached to the search team as a press officer. He is a cool professional who lifts my sagging spirits just by being friendly and helpful.

I tell him that Kazuyoshi Sakai, the missing soundman's son, had originally wanted to come with me, but his family forbade him to go, thinking it was too risky. Patterson is glad that he didn't come. He says, "It's not good for his spirit to watch the remains of his father being dug up." Patterson later tells horrible stories about the business that has cropped up around the bones of missing U.S. soldiers. So-called respectable people present falsified photographs or parts of a skeleton to relatives of the missing, playing on their emotions and raising unjustified hopes. Then they string them along, prolonging their agony and drawing big sums of money out of them in the process. A despicable game.

This chicanery helped foster the political climate that led to the creation of the military search teams. At great expense, parts of Southeast Asia are now being turned over in search of missing American servicemen, just to prove to doubting relatives that their family member is no longer alive.

In a way, we are reaping the benefits of these sordid dealings. Neither CBS nor NBC has the resources to support a recovery operation on its own.

Yes, the world is full of sleazes. I remember a little Asian story that'll make your skin crawl. Some Thai women cut off the penises of their unfaithful husbands and threw them into duck ponds.

In the meantime, a Bangkok police clinic said it had the technology to sew them back onto their rightful owners, but only if the organs were recovered before the ducks got to them.

To prevent that from succeeding, one Thai lady tied her husband's severed penis to a helium balloon. The former family jewel was last seen soaring away above the golden spires of Bangkok's pagodas. The story is too good to verify.

Today I meet the leader of the search team, Maj. Jim Moye. He's a tough, athletic-looking infantry officer with all the right credentials, including paratrooper wings and a ranger tab.

He has a lot of digging experience, uncovering MIA remains in Laos, Cambodia and Vietnam. I'm surprised by how much he knows about the missing newsmen. It's all in his computer files. He is reassuring and hopes for a successful mission and a relatively quick identification.

But he warns me that the prospect of finding remains after all these years isn't very good. Twenty years in shallow graves, exposed to heat, rain and human and animal scavengers can cause a lot of damage.

Moye hopes to have his team complete by Saturday. The first step is to survey the burial site near a river. The team then will construct sandbag dams so that the river can be drained. The American soldiers plan to search until March 9.

I am back on my bed in the Monorom. High on the wall, my friend the gecko chases flies while the ceiling fan blows a stream of air over my sweating face. Directly above me is the hotel's roof garden where earlier I had dinner.

Sitting on the dimly lit terrace, looking over the dark city, I watch the dancing girls crowd around the bar. They are pathetic-looking creatures in search of an American or U.N. guy who will buy them drinks so they can make a living. Shades of Saigon. I fled the noise of a small band only to be harassed by its sound now filtering through the ceiling. Maybe a sleeping pill will help.

My thoughts drift to the upcoming operation. The complete search team will include forensic pathologists, an anthropologist, ordnance experts, a photographer, gravediggers and a chopper crew. Almost 40 people in all.

I think of the Cambodians who stayed behind when the Khmer Rouge took over: Sophan, our faithful fixer, and Joe Puy, our driver. Both had done so much for us and gotten us out of more than a few dangerous situations. Both dead. Murdered. We know of no grave in which to search for them.

Sophan did not survive the first Khmer Rouge roadblock. Asked whom he worked for, he just couldn't lie. For CBS, for American television, he said. Guards took him behind a shed and murdered him.

Four years later, Joe Puy also lost his life because he worked for us, murdered by the Khmer Rouge.

I will never forget Sophan, a gentle soul who once picked a red tropical flower with great care for my little daughter, Danika. She took it and smiled at him. Then Gisela and I and Danika got on a plane to Tokyo and never saw him again.

February 28, 1992, Phnom Penh

Today we finally go to Wat Po with Bun Wat and see the gravesite for the first time. Rice paddies, brown and dry, stretch away on either side of us. Wat Po, the Buddhist temple, stands in the distance beside the river. Still farther are the blue mountains held by the Khmer Rouge. They are the same mountains I had seen during my adventures on Highway 3.

The gravesite and environs look surprisingly similar to the sketches I made from witnesses' descriptions 20 years ago. Of course, there are some errors. A villager leads us to where he thinks the graves are. They are partially under water. It means the engineers will have to sandbag the river and drain the dammed-up area, which measures about 10 by 5 meters.

It's going to be a tough digging operation. An error by a half-meter and we'll never find our friends.

Once under way, the operation leaves little room for improvisation and no room for mistakes. Too much dirt has to be moved. Every step must be carefully planned and executed. Moving earth, mainly by hand in the scorching heat, can sap the energy of the strongest among us. Looking at the huge site that has to be excavated, I ask myself, will we ever find anything?

We're going on the best information available: witnesses from the village and notes taken so long ago. But there's a difference between the gravesite in sketches and in reality. What if my notes are wrong, or the memories of the villagers faulty? Too late now. The plan is in control.

On the drive from Phnom Penh to Wat Po, we traverse familiar ground. In 1971, a year after the killings, I drove 2,000 kilometers back and forth on this 60 kilometer stretch of road between Phnom Penh and the ambush site while gathering information from Cambodian troopers and villagers. Quite a few skirmishes, nasty and violent, took place on this short stretch of Highway 3.

We drive through the village of Tran Khnar, halfway between Phnom Penh and Wat Po. It is a collection of wooden shacks dotted with a few stone buildings still scarred with bullet holes. It was here that the young government flag carrier took a burst of AK fire in his face.

Twenty-two years ago, he lay sprawled on the asphalt, shrouded in his flag in the midday sun. Now, Tran Khnar is a bustling peasant village with no sign of war.

I also see the bridge where George Syvertsen made his fateful decision to push on, and the spot beside the stream below where Ishii and Sakai stayed behind. I sense the fear they must have felt after Syvertsen's Jeep was hit by the rocket grenade and when the North Vietnamese and Khmer Rouge captured them with the NBC crew.

The shooting has stopped, but many of the bridges are still blown. And if you look closely at the Cambodian villagers, you will notice that a whole generation of men is missing. Where are all the 40-year-olds? Gone. You see cripples begging in the streets, seeking some gratitude from their country. Bullshit.

At Wat Po I turn off Highway 3 onto a dirt road and drive down near the river. Here, in what used to be a bamboo grove, is where my Japanese friends and the NBC crew met their fate. They were all beaten to death by the village idiot on orders from the Vietnamese officers. The man, demented and mean, reportedly didn't mind. He has since died, possibly killed by the North Vietnamese to get rid of the witness.

A company of about 100 Cambodians, ragged and lightly armed, secure the place. Mostly they sit around, doing little more than trying to protect themselves from the ever-present heat. I don't expect much from them in case of trouble from the Khmer Rouge.

This peaceful second American invasion into their forgotten corner of the world entices the villagers to come to the site, to crowd around the GIs and their chopper. Now they can just enjoy the show.

I think of Sophan again as we pass the spot near Highway 3 where, on that day in May 1970, we got stuck in a vicious Viet Cong mortar barrage for several hours. We knew nothing definite about the fates of the NBC and CBS crews, but we were full of dread, somehow sensing that something horrendous had occurred. As the mortar shells got closer and closer, Sophan put his Buddhist amulet into his mouth, hoping it would protect him. It did that day. I remembered dropping my camera as I hit the ground and dragging it toward me by the battery cable, like a little dog on a leash.

We laughed about it later.

At the gravesite, a Bangkok-based correspondent for Fuji TV interviews me. He keeps shaking his head, barely able to check his tears as he hears how his countrymen, with their European and American colleagues, were put to death. Each was forced to his knees, hands bound, blindfolded, listening to the death screams of the man killed before him.

What were those horror-filled moments like? Staring into the darkness, far from home, knowing they hadn't done anything to warrant death. They had done nothing except follow their correspondent.

Ishii was then about 55 years old. My age now. In 1970, I thought of him as an old man.

Sakai was younger, with a cruel face. He boasted that, as a Japanese soldier in Singapore, he used to slap the faces of the Allied prisoners. We all know what the Japanese did in Singapore. Now, Allied soldiers will have to put up with considerable hardship to search for him. If they only knew.

The fact remains that he died while on assignment for CBS. For the moment, only this counts.

I always liked Ishii. For all I know, his war record was clean. He was a gentle soul, quiet and frail, with only part of his stomach. He should never have been sent to a war zone. Worse, he took my place when the teams were switched at the last minute. I have never forgotten that.

After the Army team finishes surveying the Wat Po gravesite, I go with Cmdr. Patterson to Pol Pot's killing fields. They are about 16 kilometers north of Phnom Penh. A shrine houses the broken skulls and bones of countless victims murdered by the Khmer Rouge after their victory in 1975.

Ironically, the site of the shrine is serene and beautiful, a tropical Eden. Eerie, silent, yet deafening. You think you hear the skulls scream.

I write in the visitors book "In Tyrannos." Patterson writes "Rest in peace." I find this less pompous. There's a time for rage and time for resignation, and a time to feel both.

February 29, 1992, Phnom Penh

The search operation is now under way. The team, with lots of local help, starts to sandbag 5 by 10 meters of a winding riverbed. A tough and tedious job. Wat Po villagers help fill the sandbags and carry them 40 meters to the dam site. The whole search team pitches in regardless of rank.

The civilian anthropologist and the pathologist, both women, stack sandbags. The commander, Maj. Moye, sets an example by working waist-deep in the muddy river. Other troopers operate water pumps to drain the enclosed river section. It looks like they'll need more pumps. About 1 million liters of muddy water must be pumped out to dry out the probable gravesite.

The team's chopper makes three runs today, carrying men and supplies. Ground transportation brings in tools, MREs (Meals Ready to Eat, the new version of the old C-rations) and lots of bottled water. The chopper ferries the soldiers to the site early in the morning and then back to Phnom Penh after work.

Across the fields, the temple at Wat Po appears to float on the waves of morning heat. Nearby it is a rickety wooden schoolhouse that looks more like a large tool shed. It may have been where our men were held before they were marched to the dried-out riverbed covered by a bamboo grove. I'm not sure. More questions must be answered to confirm it.

The bamboo grove is long gone. Pol Pot's troops forced the villagers to build a dam and inundate the surrounding flat fields so that rice could be planted. The bamboo grove was chopped down as the villagers cultivated the land.

Our people were killed at the end of the dry season, when the river was dry as well. Now it's again the end of the dry season, yet the river still carries water. Pol Pot's dam has permanently changed the landscape.

Not much press around today, except a Japanese reporter from a Tokyo Communist newspaper who says something that angers Cmdr. Patterson. I guess word hasn't quite reached the Navy that the Cold War is over. Old ideologies die hard. Patterson will have to report this incident to his bosses back in Hawaii.

I take pictures with a still camera and a small video camera. Whatever the results of the search, I intend to go to Japan to show the families the scope of this operation.

How many years I've waited for this moment. Members of the team constantly remind us how minute the chances are of finding the remains of the newsmen. My maps and drawings confirmed the general area of the gravesite, but nothing more.

Witnesses from Wat Po and the neighboring village of Kandaol are our main hope of pinpointing the exact sites. My apprehension becomes stronger with all the soil to be moved. Miss by a meter, miss by a mile.

Peter Chuun, NBC editor and a native Cambodian, puts all his skill and drive behind the enterprise. NBC's Welles Hangen is the star among the missing. This fact, being an American, got the ball rolling with the Pentagon. The four Japanese and French remains are merely incidental.

But the members of the search team, to their eternal credit, do not differentiate. For them, all the missing are equal. Their concern for the relatives is touching and quite real.

Peter Chuun is invaluable. He is our main contact to the villagers and the witnesses. There are two main witnesses: Mr. Chaak and "the fisherman." Mr. Chaak, from Kandaol, dug the last grave, probably Ishii's, and claims he passed the other empty holes on his way out of the bamboo grove.

The other, "the fisherman," is in his 40s, like Chaak. He saw what we think were Ishii's remains as they emerged from a shallow grave. He says he was attracted by the smell and heaped earth on the body because some animals had started to burrow into the grave.

Others, like a farmer named Gnan who owned a rice field on the other side of the road connecting Po with Highway 3, saw either some of the events or some of the newsmen and now come up with second-hand information.

The team's Sgt. Cabrera, a tough ranger, gathers all this information and stores it in his computer.

The heat becomes almost unbearable as the hours pass. I tire easily. The Army medic, "Doc," warns me to drink lots of water; otherwise dehydration will quickly set in. Good advice.

Maj. Moye, the unit commander, believes that it's going to take three more days to complete the draining phase.

Wat Po is a traditional Khmer Rouge area, and some of the villagers' eyes are cold and hateful. But many others, hundreds of them, watch in fascination as the Americans and their local help, with equal effort and pain, stand waist-deep in the water, hour after hour, piling sandbag on sandbag.

I am still a stranger to most of the team, which prides itself on its elite qualities. It will take time to be accepted.

March 1, 1992, Phnom Penh

The troopers, with continued help from the villagers, have now built a third dam. The idea is to divide the drained riverbed into two sections. One contains the assumed gravesite. The other, downstream, covers the river bend. That area will be spot-checked for remains in the event that at least some of the bodies were swept away by the current. Each section is about 35 by 45 meters. Two pumps work day and night to drain them.

The presumed gravesite, a wide, indented sandy stretch, is just about dry. Some of the troopers lay out a grid scale with tape, marking five possible graves where Mr. Chaak and the fisherman remembered seeing them. Others call Mr. Chaak "the gravedigger." We all hope the graves are shallow, but 20 years of current have deposited a lot of mud on top of the original riverbed.

This grid scale gives the site the appearance of an archeological site, as well as a formality that exudes a confidence that all will go well. The fact is that nothing is certain and the chances still are very slim.

The grid will help the troopers keep an accurate record of the excavation. The mood is professional and matter-of-fact.

I pass Ishii and Sakai's dental records to Dr. Schroeder, one of the anthropologists. She accepts them gratefully.

Capt. Bill Hudson, the lean and mean site commander, tells me today that he was 20 when the incident with the newsmen happened. He remembers it from watching TV Hudson is cut from the same mold as those young, hard paratroopers from two decades ago. It all seems so far away.

Flashback: Saigon, the day after Thanksgiving, 1967

Memories of Hill 885 and Thanksgiving 1967. With fearful losses, U.S. paratroopers of the 173rd Airborne Brigade had finally taken the hill against fierce opposition. We got to the top after the battle the easy way, by chopper.

I didn't feel we deserved to be there. Felt like a gawker at a traffic accident. There were more press than soldiers. The troops looked haggard and tired. I had the impression that there were more dead soldiers in body bags than live ones.

A young lieutenant shouted into his radio, "No more KIAs on the next choppers. Get the press out."

Then a sergeant yelled at the impatient press, "Just hold it, guys. You'll have time to file your stories." Not as much time as the guys in the bags. We had filmed the aftermath of one of the bitterest battles of the war and were clambering to get out to ship or file or whatever. Then our choppers lifted off the moonscape called Hill 885. A body bag, defying the lieutenant's orders, was sneaked aboard a chopper that carried an ABC crew.

Around us more hills, many of them higher than 885. Surely, they had to be occupied by the enemy. Fear welled up. My chopper carried a wounded paratrooper. A female correspondent had also jumped on my ship. She had on dirty fatigues and looked tired, but she still found time to apply makeup on Hill 885.

Wind gusts jolted the bird, throwing her against the wounded man. Big round eyes. "Does it hurt?" she asked. My God, lady.

We reached the valley where press, dead and wounded soldiers were unloaded from the choppers that then disappeared into the mountains for more.

Farther down the valley we reached the Pleiku Press Center. Suddenly a different world, full of life, laughter, drinks and easy chatter.

Among the correspondents was a French woman famous from another war. No smile there. She listened with some interest to a drunken discussion about the big Texan who was president of all the men on that hill on Thanksgiving Day. How did he enjoy his turkey today?

The discussions dragged on, getting louder but ending nowhere. Up there on the hill were so many still figures; down here in the valley, so much frolicking. Our worst casualty was a drunken newsman who fell into an irrigation ditch and broke his leg.

Wat Po Temple, March 2, 1992

Ishii would be 75 now. Today, the dead stay young and the young of today look for the dead. I go to the temple of Wat Po that villagers built on a small earthen mound overlooking their homes. It has snake ornaments on its triple roofs, and inside it is gaudy.

Nearby is a pond ringed with palm trees and covered with lotus leaves. Ducks and small brown children swim in the murky, greenish water. The whole atmosphere is dreamy. Village life hasn't changed in centuries. Thatched huts, a wooden schoolhouse and, the most modern building for miles, a simple brick meeting hall with a loudspeaker. One of the concessions to our time.

The hall was probably used by Khmer Rouge to assemble the villagers for indoctrination. These villagers hadn't much to fear from the Khmer Rouge, whose fury was turned mostly against the "decadent and corrupt city population."

Among the huts, cows rest while women hustle, carrying water, fruit or vegetables. Again, the 40-year-old men are missing, victims of the war. I don't see as many amputated children as in Phnom Penh. There are no cars or motorcycles. Only once in a while do I see a bicycle. Saffron-robed monks round out the picture of a sleepy, tropical village.

More press people are showing up. The search team shies away from them. Ever since Vietnam, the military has been indoctrinated to see in us, if not an enemy, then someone to avoid. After all, many argue, we caused them to lose the war. When in doubt, kill the messenger. Capt. Hudson, normally a very polite hombre, is especially suspicious and cautions Sgt. Cabrera not to speak to the press directly but to let him do the talking.

Cmdr. Patterson is cool. He questions the system and is forthcoming. The U.S. Armed Forces are facing sizable reductions with the end of the Cold War. Nobody wants to make a mistake and risk his job. Motivation through fear has always been part of Army life.

The primitive schoolhouse at Wat Po, where the captured newsmen might have been held after they were driven from Thnal Bot, is quiet. Outside, an old bicycle rim hangs from a banyan tree. Inside, after being momentarily blinded by the darkness, I see simple benches, a couple of chairs and a blackboard. The school hell. The floor is the naked earth. The only sunlight seeps in through ill-fitting boards.

The medical men from the search team pass the time treating villagers. Sick call is held in the assembly hall. Many villagers, especially mothers with their children in their arms, wait patiently for their turn. Dysentery is the main problem.

Few doctors have ever been to this village. The team's doctor and Sergio, the medic, a Special Forces sergeant, pass out pills, give shots, listen through stethoscopes and peer into ears, throats and eyes.

There's one welcome collateral effect from the deaths of the newsmen. Once we're gone, the curtain of time will drop again and no sign of our presence will remain.

Capt. Hudson poses with a bunch of village kids for a teammate's camera. You can almost watch as trust grows between the villagers and the Americans. There is a purpose behind it all, however. The village's friendly attitude is crucially important. Our safety could well depend on it.

The task force gives almost all of the village men jobs on a rotating basis. As many as 35 villagers a day find work and income. They help man the shovels and, later, the bucket brigades.

Now the chopper comes in for landing, throwing up clouds of dust. The entire village, except for those receiving medical treatment, streams toward the landing zone. The hovering chopper is probably the biggest event in their lives since the war went away.

At times I find it impossible to penetrate the wall of silence and empty looks. Here we are, trying to find five people who died 20 years ago. Strangers, agents in their eyes, of a country that brought them so much misery. That idea just doesn't go away.

Cambodia lost millions, and tens of millions of individual bones are now strewn across the countryside. There are no dental records, no photographs or passport information to help in identifying them.

Most of the time there isn't even a grave. Anyone who cares to look can find human bones bleaching in the sun or sticking out from scorched patches of earth, or skulls stacked in the Holocaust Museum. This country reeks of death.

For a moment I feel ashamed. All the time, effort and money spent on a search for our missing few, a pittance compared to their losses. Still, there are two old women and their families in Japan, waiting, who have lived through their own personal horror.

If this search effort brings peace of mind to them, so be it. The operation will cost about a million dollars. There can be no price tag attached to it.

Electrifying words: The digging will start soon. The two anthropologists, Dr. Madeleine Hinkes and Dr. Schroeder, confirm this even though the clay soil is tough. Worse, the stream, driven by 22 rainy seasons, has thickened the layers of earth covering the bodies, should they be there.

Now I am in Cambodia, body and soul. Everything else seems far away.

It rains during the night and the pumps go at it again. Not a good start.

A few hours later, we are on schedule once more. The owner of the land containing the graves comes forward as another witness with second-hand information. Chuun leads him to the river. The old man, almost bald and very shaky, walks gingerly along the riverbank.

He roughly confirms the spots that the gravedigger and the fisherman have pointed out as the possible graves. Some of the troopers start digging so-called test pits in the downstream section of the excavation site. These will reveal the soil consistency, as well as possibly turning up evidence of remains: small bones, a tooth, a button, anything that may have been swept into the bend of the river.

Maj. Moye isn't the only team member with digging experience in Southeast Asia. Capt. Hudson braved hardships in search of pilots missing in the Solomon Islands and New Guinea, downed during the Pacific campaigns of World War II. In those places, none of the searchers ever found a whole body. Blown apart with the impact of crashing planes or artillery fire, often only small bone fragments, pieces of clothing and teeth are all that's left.

Corpses swept away by currents also disintegrate. So, to miss nothing, the Cambodian workers carefully fill buckets of clay and sand from the test pits and dump them on huge screens. A team of locals, supervised by an American, hose the wet clay through the screens. Locals using trowels check the clay carefully for anything unusual as it is washed away. Dry sand is also put on screens. These are rocked by two locals while a third person, usually a team member, checks for any trace of the bodies.

The work is slow and hard. The original riverbed, as it was at the time of the murders, is covered by about 3 feet of sediment. The soil is heavy, sticky and wet. Watching the operation and the backup, I have little doubt that it could cost a million dollars. Most team members came by special military flights from Hawaii via Bangkok. One came from as far away as Alaska. Helicopter landing fees alone will cost about $100,000.

Good business for the Cambodian government. Local workers, drivers and their cars, hotels and even coffins, should remains be found, have to be paid for. Our Cambodian guards, all government soldiers, are also on the U.S. payroll. And then there is the special flight back to

Hawaii on huge C-141 Starlifters, while turboprop Hercules C-30s fly the short hop to and from Bangkok.

The sun seems especially hot today. My face and arms are as red as a lobster. Can't stand the heat without a hat. The work pace is slow but very steady. Our team is in good spirits. The troopers are finally doing what they came here for. They are truly dedicated. There's no banter; talk is all business-like. For the moment it looks like just another mission. But it is more. It's the spirit of adventure combined with a true concern for the families of the missing, professionalism and the closeness of an elite Army team now doing the only useful work of a military that's lost much of its reason for being.

A recurring thought is that all this sweat, all this organization, is only to recover dead people. Each day, as Peter Chuun finds more witnesses corroborating earlier statements by other villagers, I appreciate how lucky we are to have him. Without his diplomacy and language skills, the operation would suffer greatly.

CBS New York advises me today that I should go to Tokyo after the search is finished, regardless of the outcome. As if I hadn't planned to do so. If the desk jockeys in New York only knew the scope of this operation. I wish they could feel the heat, inhale the dust, drive the bumpy roads, feel the aching muscles, live through the endless days. I bet most of them don't even know or care about the CBS people we're looking for. To them, it's something that has to be done because NBC is doing it.

But, to be fair, a lot of time has passed and a new generation of executives now runs the company. And the fact remains that I am here in Cambodia and CBS is spending money to find two Japanese techs who were mere foot soldiers in the ranks of electronic journalism. My anger eases.

Actions and reactions back home would certainly be different if Cronkite were among the missing. Fact is also that the current president of CBS News, a guy called Eric Ober, has not contacted me once to inquire personally about the state of the search. People who know him say he has other priorities than worrying about a couple of low ranking Japanese technicians who died so long ago. Such is life.

During the past years I had not thought much about the war in Vietnam. Other events were more immediate. Now, suddenly, I remember events that are not even directly related to what I am doing.

Flashback: Near Saigon, 1967

Inside a U.S. Army chopper going on a combat assault. Ours is the first lift in. Five birds total. The choppers trail across the sky like a string of pearls in the morning sun.

Don Webster is in the second chopper; I'm with my camera in the first. The soundman, my Vietnamese friend Duong Van Ri, is in the third.

We're circling high over the landing zone. From below, the muffled sound of bursting artillery shells. Big guns are softening up the landing zone.

Our fleet of choppers descends, sweeps the treetops and settles into a hover just above the murky green and watery surface.

We jump out of our choppers, which had come in almost simultaneously, link up and head with the infantry for the tree line.

We struggle onward, almost hip-deep in the stinking brew. So far it looks like a "cold" landing zone. That's fine with us. Camera and batteries are getting wet, but we film the landing operation as well as we can.

A GI machine gunner knows we're filming and grins, his helmet at a rakish angle. A little posing for the camera. Good for the folks back home.

Looks like another hot walk in the sun. Maybe the troops will discover yet another Viet Cong tunnel complex. Christ, they must get sick and tired of seeing this on their screens back in the States.

This is not a battle; it's more like a maneuver. The troops move by the book. Someone described the war in Vietnam as stretches of utter boredom interrupted by moments of sheer terror.

Then the terror comes. Carefully planted Claymore mines tear into the forward element of the advance. The lead had run into an ambush. One of the dead is a man named Terry Allen, son of a U.S. World War II general and hero of the Normandy landings. The troops pull back, waiting for the Air Force to hit the Viet Cong.

The colonel running the show is less than pleased when he sees us. Not good to have press around when the enemy gets the better of you. He's still his shiny and polished self, but he doesn't play soldier anymore.

He doesn't like the camera pointing at him.

The next day the advance resumes. The troops take the same route through the jungle as yesterday. Same pictures as yesterday, too. The unit's Vietnamese scout urges the colonel not to make the same mistake twice. The colonel just ignores him with an icy stare. The scout looks away, calmly pulls out a fried chicken and starts to eat it.

The battalion creeps very slowly into the jungle. Yesterday isn't forgotten. There's fear at the head of the column as boredom sets in at the rear. Then, without apparent reason, the colonel breaks off the operation. The tally: several U.S. dead, no known enemy dead. A pall of smoke hangs over the jungle. Two days in the bush and no story.

We get a chopper back to Saigon just in time for a shower and a late dinner.

I wake up and am in the real world again.

May 2, 1992, Phnom Penh

Moved to Hotel Le Royal today to escape the incessant bad music from the bar. The sound of the drummer came through the ceiling every night from 7 to 11. However, I will my miss airy and cool room.

The Royal houses all the specters of my Cambodian past. Here is where I saw our crew for the last time, when it left for its ride to hell on May 31, 1970, at about 9 a.m.

Not much has changed at the Royal, and I easily slip back in time. Any moment now I expect all of our people to reappear, but know they won't. I remember Ishii's sad and anxious face as he handed me cookies for my daughter. And I thought that this would be an uneventful visit for her and my wife, a diversion from life in Saigon and Tokyo.

I take a swim in the hotel pool at night and think of all my press colleagues who used to lounge around, drink in hand, after returning from the fighting down the dangerous highways. We were a boisterous crowd, living high and hard.

Beside the pool is a little bungalow that used to be a hotel restaurant, the Cyrene, I believe. Newsmen ate and drank there, not knowing what the next day would bring. Yes, we were young. Life was dangerous, adventurous and at times full of horrors. Alcohol, ambition and the pride of being part of a tough group of newsmen on a dangerous but important assignment kept us going. Now the restaurant is some kind of United Nations headquarters. U.N. employees have their own bar next to it. Just for them. Must be a rough war.

The swim is refreshing, the sunset spectacular, a rich tropical yellow, deep and warm. Palm trees sway gently. On the hotel roof, three monkeys jump from one gable to the next. Disco music mixes with the mournful sounds of tropical animals, geckos, birds and cicadas.

I swim alone, again seeing Syvertsen and Miller in the small gazebo near the pool. I still hear myself arguing with Syvertsen about his recklessness in the field. Here he was, I thought, talented, ambitious and bent on saving a sagging career at the expense of his crew. I still feel the old resentment.

It was Syvertsen and Miller's last evening on earth. Miller recognized the tension. Maybe this made him change crews and assignments. I still get bitter when I think how avoidable the whole affair could have been.

Tomorrow we continue looking for the dead we left behind. Wish we were looking for the living. I leave the pool shivering. This place gives me the creeps. I eat dinner in the Royal beer garden but it is ruined by more loud disco music. The place is crowded with young prostitutes. About a hundred or so are waiting for foreign customers. Most of them were probably not even born when I was here the last time. Most of them, despite their youth, have experienced war and death in the family.

Their voices are loud, their heavily made-up faces are expressionless masks.

March 3, 1992, Phnom Penh

Are we at the right site? I trust my sketches and maps. Another small surprise. I am startled by how unfamiliar Peter Chuun is with his missing NBC folks. He knows next to nothing about the cameraman, Roger Colne, or the soundman, Waku. Disturbing. Even the team's anthropologist has few records of them, making an eventual identification very difficult. I am angry but will cool off.

Two Cambodians from another village provided cause for confusion today. They told Peter that one of them helped dig the graves and that the location is about 100 meters east of where we are digging. This is a very unlikely location because it doesn't match any of the information we gathered in 1972 or any we are currently receiving.

The team surveyed the new site but decided to continue digging where we are now. The troopers may decide to dig test pits at the new location just to be sure.

In the muddy riverbed, troopers laying out marking tapes sink up to their knees. We all hope and pray that it doesn't rain anymore. Digging at the test pit site downriver continues, while digging at the assumed gravesite hasn't started yet. Felt a bit blue tonight and hit the sack early.

March 4, 1992, Phnom Penh

Leave the Royal early. Morning shadows are blue and cool, but the warm air promises another hot day. A press chopper is available but I want to get a driver and go by car to recheck Highway 3. Bun Wat comes along in a separate car. I believe I went to the wrong bridge. Our people must have been captured and killed on the north side of Baing Kasey.

The vegetation and the topography, under the relentless sun and monsoons, has changed. No permanent structures remain to be used as a guide. I remember no landmarks. My notes simply say that the CBS Jeep was hit at km 54 or so. We find an old milestone near Pochentong Airport and, by resetting our mileage gauge, we retrace the road until our old Toyota dies of a failed gas pump.

I wait three and a half hours for Bun Wat to return with a new pump. It is now 1 p.m. Not much shade and the boiling heat is doing its usual job of producing sweat and fatigue. The press chopper passes overhead. I wave frantically but the distance is too great. I feel a bit lonely out here. Just parched rice fields in the unrelenting sun. A few kids, a few skinny cows, all trying to make a living off the dry earth.

The heat bounces off the asphalt and blurs distant images. I know it's supposed to be peaceful in this region, but it is still Khmer Rouge controlled. Some strange characters drive their Hondas up and down the road, wearing balloon caps, a Khmer Rouge trademark. Some carry AK-47s. None are in uniform. Shots in the distance. Maybe hunters. All harmless I know, but sure wish Bun Wat and the car would return soon. I wonder what is happening at the gravesite. Thinking about assignments in other places, cooler climes. Remember Colombo Kelley? Sure do.

Fall '89 in Botswana. CBS Rome correspondent Bert Quint and I were there, waiting for Pope John Paul II to land. Father Colombo Kelley, a young priest, had a special surprise waiting for the Holy Father. About 40 or so native girls singing and dancing, swaying their ample hips to the direction of Colombo. Nothing wrong with that. Should really give some joy to the pope. The girls' breasts were bare, firm and bouncing in rhythm to the soft music. A happy little group.

Then came the press, and the pope. If looks could kill. Camera crews and photographers, without the benefit of a police line protecting Colombo and his bouncing beauties, just walked all over his show, photographing a very angry pope who had just turned on his heel. JP2 didn't bother to hide his anger over what Father Colombo had believed would be an especially thoughtful presentation.

Later Quint and I hitched a ride with the father to a downtown hotel. After noticing that we were part of the press gang that had shambled his show, he said in his deep Irish voice he would forgive us nonetheless. After 10 minutes he stopped and let us off, telling us our hotel was just five minutes away. An hour and half later we got there.

God bless Father Colombo Kelley. Wonder what he's doing now. Getting interrupted in my thoughts. The heat is bearing down on us. Bun Wat is still not in sight. The driver and I push the car into the skimpy shade of a mango tree, little more than a bush. Then a car stops beside us. Its drunken driver, wearing the balloon cap of the Khmer Rouge, staggers out, gives me a hard look, utters some unfriendly sounds, gets back into the car and drives off.

Finally, Bun Wat returns. The new gas pump is installed and we are on our way to Wat Po.

At the site, Capt. Bill Hudson and three troopers are up to their waists in mud, probing two of the five prospective gravesites. The muck is gooey and repulsive. The smell of decay clings to the men and the mud and follows all who come near the site.

Slowly, ever so slowly, but at a steady pace, the diggers fill bucket after bucket. Another group of soldiers and natives carries them, two at a time, to narrow-mesh sieves. This work goes on through the rest of the day. Exhaustion and sweat mark the faces of the men. There is little talk. All try to preserve their strength to do their jobs.

Gallons of water are drunk to ward off dehydration. No soft breeze brings relief. The men toil on without complaint. Several tons of earth are moved by the diggers and the bucket brigade. Each shovel and bucket of soil is treated as if it held the key to the search for the bodies. Archeologists couldn't be more diligent.

I feel very down. Before getting to Cambodia, I had the dumb notion we'd pull out the old maps, point to a spot on the ground and start digging, get the job done and be on our way home with all the bodies. Standing there at the edge of the grave pits, dead tired from the heat, it sinks in for the first time that the whole effort could be in vain. I realize just how big the job is and how small the prospects are of finding anyone or anything. I fear that the newsmen may be part of this Cambodian earth forever.

Madeleine, the anthropologist, tells me that 1,500 cubic meters of water had to be pumped to drain the part of the riverbed where the graves are believed to be.

The men of the Joint Task Force continue to go about their job professionally. They just keep slogging on, unimpressed that their physical endurance is being pushed to the limit. All of them chip in, taking turns at the shovels or the screens or in the bucket brigades. Doctors, scientists, photographers, an explosives expert all work shoulder to shoulder with the grunts and gravediggers.

I hear no laughter, little banter, only once in a while a funny remark to relieve the tension and break up the boredom of the long working hours with no results in sight.Late afternoon. Capt. Hudson calls it a day. Tools are cleaned. The Cambodian guards take over. The team piles into the chopper heading for Phnom Penh and dinner, a few hours of rest and the prospect of another long day in the field tomorrow.

Back at the Royal, a shower. Then the beer garden for a quick meal. Loud music. About 200 young Cambodian hookers, as always, crowd the garden, waiting in the blaring music for customers. There are plenty: U.N. soldiers, civilian aid workers, businessmen hungry for profits and prostitutes.

The girls are small, very young, very pretty. I become more aware of just how bored, disinterested and in a strange way lifeless they are, like puppets on a string waiting for their master to make them move. Cambodian men entering the beer garden are checked for weapons or grenades. Westerners pass freely. Shades of Saigon.

I finish my meal and head for my bungalow to sleep, hoping that the electricity for the air conditioner doesn't conk out during the night. Checking my old notes again, I decide I still have more faith in an old diary than a new witness. Old diaries have fresh memories, fresh witnesses have old memories. I believe we are at the right place. The land around Wat Po has changed since Pol Pot took power. Dams were built, bridges as well. Perspectives changed, but there is still the first bridge, the bend in the river and the short path to the old bamboo thicket that stands no more. Yes, we are at the right place.

But digging is hard and missing by a foot is missing by a mile. It would be impossible to jump all over the countryside. Strength should be concentrated on our prime spot. Of course, there is always a lingering doubt about the reliability of witnesses and the accuracy of our maps. Of course, the remains could be in a different place. Anything is possible. I believe they are near Wat Po.

March 5, 1992, Phnom Penh

Digging and probing is especially tough today. It is not just the heat. Maj. Moye feels that if the diggers were ever close to any possible remains, it is now. So the men put down their shovels and remove the sludge with their bare hands. Hour after hour. Wish I could find other words than merciless, unrelenting, punishing or broiling to describe what the sun is doing to us all.

Moye takes the lead, standing in his pit sucked hip-deep into the mud. He orders his troopers to dig till they reach sand, which would indicate the original riverbed. Twenty years of sediment will have to be penetrated. Then they have to go another 2 feet, the depth of a shallow grave.

Water seeps into the pits and has to be drained. A frustrating task. I hear no complaints. Again, no banter, and only what is necessary to be said in low tones. Again, only once in a while a funny remark to relieve the drudgery in the overpowering heat. Not a twig or even a leaf is moving. The routine of carrying bucket after bucket of mud to the screens continues with only short breaks and a pause for lunch, from morning until late. The men at the screens check the mud with trowels, eyes staring, looking for any trace of the missing men.

Nothing changes. The hours trickle by. It is slow, tedious, plodding, backbreaking work that cannot be done faster or any other way.

The anthropologist sits near the pits, watching, taking notes, waiting for her time to come. After a while it becomes obvious that it is she who calls the shots, determining, along with Hudson and Moye, the strategy of where and how to dig.

She doesn't say much and is hardly noticed, but nothing happens without her OK.

Our chopper stays on the ground all day today. I'm told the flyboys don't feel appreciated. They're not the center of attention, just a bunch of flying bus drivers hauling men and supplies. Actually, no one is the center of attention. Only the job.

Capt. Hudson, during a rare break, gets talking about his digs in New Guinea and the Solomons, looking for pilots lost during MacArthur's Pacific Campaign. He talks about the rough Stanley Owens range, bringing back a war we know only from books. He has searched for lost pilots and planes near Port Moresby and other famous World War II battle sites. These experiences taught him to trust native witnesses with caution. A predicted two-hour walk often turned into five arduous days.

Maj. Moye reminisces about dead buddies at Sepone in Laos, lost during the South Vietnamese invasion of that country some 20 years ago.

He then decides to dig some test pits at the alternate site. There is no other choice. Everybody saw the Cambodian witnesses point out the site, and the team is under orders to follow up any and all leads. Let's hope our witnesses are prudent and rare, or the team will have to dig up a sizable portion of the country.

Today I count 40 U.S. and native workers going at it in the pits, schlepping buckets and sifting sand. About 80 Cambodian soldiers secure the immediate surroundings. Yesterday the hacks were here again. Bored. The story is, after all, 20 years old and for them as dead as the men we're looking for.

"Maybe if you find Errol Flynn's boy," one press guy said, "then maybe we'd have a good story."

He's right. Anything for a good news story. But on this trip I'm not one of them. How obnoxious and even ugly they (we) can be. Unfortunately, however, the hacks are right.

My Cambodian government minder likes to speak German with me. He studied political science at Humboldt University in East Berlin. I guess the Communist regime sent him there. Once he clicked his heels and threw me a military salute.

Villain or survivor? Not important anymore. He's a nice guy. His main determination is not to get his hands dirty. Bun Wat doesn't join me in the physical work.

Bun Wat lost a sister in the holocaust, as well as his brother-in-law, who was a captain in Lon Nol's army. Their children were also killed. They were just in the way.

No one knows where their graves are. Just a few of more than a million murdered. Bun Wat approves of the operation near Wat Po. Poor guy, he has to support his family on 60 bucks a week.

The troopers drudge on. How young they are. Some of them were barely born when our people were killed. Since then peace has yet to come to Cambodia, and don't forget that the killing in Southeast Asia started long before that. How's that for continuity?

This passage of time makes the troopers' dedication to the job almost mysterious. I hope the CBS brass will take the time and trouble to find out what this recovery operation is all about. (I don't think they fully understand. Stories narrated by Bert Quint and Tokyo bureau chief Bruce Dunning were buried in a broadcast called "Up to the Minute," with a minimum audience and broadcast at an ungodly early hour.)

Having dinner again at the Royal beer garden. Do not see anyone from the Joint Task Force. Their general is in town. Again, the usual parade of young hookers. Bits of French conversation at the next table. German military medics in military uniforms, drinking beer, perhaps dreaming of the cool March weather back home. In the bushes, the cicadas chirping, monkeys jumping in banyan trees. The entire scene is drenched in loud, bad music.

It's almost a blessing when the electricity breaks down, killing the music. Then the juice returns. Lights illuminate the old colonial facade of the Royal. It reminds me of other great hotels in the Orient: the Raffles in Singapore with its incomparable palm tree garden, or the romantic Oriental in Bangkok near the Chao Phraya River, boasting great cuisine and a good wine cellar.

The Royal is a bit shabbier. Despite what the war years have done to the place, though it still retains some of its former class.

Prostitutes chatter on, eyeing customers. Their beautiful faces do not quite match the cacophony of their language. Looking at them, I cannot forget that their men folk can be real killers. Many of the girls look terribly sad.

The satellite phone is out tonight. Feeling isolated.

March 6, 1992, Phnom Penh

This will be a short entry. Digging and probing at both the main and alternate sites is now in full swing. No results so far. The patience of the troopers is remarkable. When the team feels it has dug deeply enough into the riverbed at the first site, they call Peter Chuun to get the fisherman, one of our two main witnesses. He gestures and chatters. Peter translates it into "Dig just a little deeper, it is the right spot."

This "just a little deeper" is repeated throughout the day.

Only the troopers' professionalism keeps them from throwing down their shovels and shouting, "Enough is enough."

Today is the usual hot day and by mid-afternoon the diggers are digging even deeper but find nothing.

We assume that the graves were shallow. After all, Mr. Chaak had seen Ishii's body pop out of his grave before he covered him with earth. Nevertheless, the team does go "just a little bit deeper." Frustration deepens as well.

Peter is getting restless. For him a lot is at stake. The pressure from the NBC brass hasn't let up, it seems. He looks like a man with promises to keep.

I play bucket man at the second site. My job is to pass buckets full of clayish mud from the pits, where the troopers search for bones, up to the screening team. The screening team hoses the mud through large sieves and looks for the smallest particles, teeth or small human bones.

This is hard work for all of us toiling in the humid heat. Hour after hour passes. The men in the pit and manning the screens hardly take a break as the sun passes its highest point in the white sky.

Capt. John and three troopers dig a straight trench across two suspected gravesites. The soil is dry and very hard. The sun beats down as the men slowly reach a depth of about 50 centimeters. Digging in the relentless heat is without doubt the hardest job. The Army men are in top physical shape and their sweaty faces rarely show fatigue. The trench is about 10 meters long and 75 centimeters wide. Digging gets harder the deeper they go as the dry, crumbling soil turns to clay.

Again, we screen each bucket carefully and find nothing. No one has much hope. This cannot be the right site. A lot of energy is wasted on "just in case" probing. There's no choice. Once a probable gravesite is identified, the troopers must check it out and treat it like a real one, even if the chances are nil. Lots of water and soft drinks are consumed today. Dehydration can come fast and must be avoided. By now, most of the villagers have disappeared. They are now used to us. Just another hot day near Wat Po and little else.

I should talk about Gnan, the farmer, who owned the rice field across the road leading from Highway 3 to Wat Po. It seems that my trusted original report also has its flaws. Nothing is right in this changing landscape, where in the course of 20 years, bridges, roads and dams appear and just as suddenly disappear.

Current and rain, wind and sun and the passage of time shape the land. Most structures, even bridges, are flimsy and can be easily changed.

The only constant things are our old diagrams, and nature often makes them obsolete. Gnan, whom I first met 20 years ago, tells me today that he saw an Opel and a second car between the two bridges near Wat Po the day the newsmen were killed. He also remembers armed Viet Cong nearby and the closed graves, but further upriver, a good hundred meters from our primary site. He says he saw the graves again three months after the killings.

He says Gen. Lon Non, President Lon Nol's brother, conducted an operation to clear Wat Po the day after our people were murdered.

An impending advance by government forces could explain the nervousness among the Khmer Rouge and the Viet Cong, and the hasty killings. It could also explain Ishii's shallow grave, which was obviously dug in a hurry. Only his information about the gravesite doesn't jibe with what the fisherman and Mr. Chaak told us with such conviction.

I speculate that maybe Gnan is right, but the bodies were swept into the deeper part of the river where we are digging now. No, that doesn't make much sense either. Talked to Peter Chuun about it and we decided to stick with what the fisherman and Mr. Chaak told us.

What we don't need is another major gravesite the troopers will have to check out, further diverting manpower from our main effort. Right or wrong, "The Plan" is still in charge. I don't believe we will ever find our friends. I talk to Kikuchi-san, our Tokyo bureau office manager, and give him my daily (or almost daily) progress report. Mrs. Sakai wants some rocks and earth from the gravesite. No problem. We are all quite exhausted by the end of the day.

March 7, 1992, Phnom Penh

Today I begin to lose faith in Peter and feel badly about it. Right now, in his eagerness to succeed, he is like a loose cannon on the quarterdeck. Guess what: He has found another "eyewitness" with yet another sure thing grave about six kilometers east of here, on the other side of Highway 3. The witness told Peter the grave contains one of our Japanese newsmen.

What does that mean for all the other eyewitnesses from Wat Po? We've come to trust them so much. We should have the courage to ignore it. Nothing sounds right about it. The location is absurd. We are virtually certain that our people were killed at Wat Po and only there. There is just too much evidence for this to be ignored. Anyway, it's now too late. The news is out, and U.S. Army regulations demand the site be checked out.

We are now probing three sites: one promising, two useless. Our manpower is spread very thin. I got a little angry, which I shouldn't have shown, but at times I believe it is best to restrain overeagerness. It will cost us two precious days and at least six or seven people to dig another futile hole in the sand.

After Peter informed Capt. Hudson about the new site, he privately admits to me that it is most likely useless. What else is new?

Again, the plan has taken over. Madeleine Hinkes, the civilian anthropologist who is technically in charge of the excavations, pulls rank on Capt. Hudson today, forcing him to dig to the required depth at the second site. Hudson had wanted to close the site and stop the digging after his experience and common sense told him that it was a waste of time.

Cmdr. Patterson informs me that even Madeleine doesn't think the site will get us anywhere. Must be some kind of petty power struggle going on inside the team. Everyone wants to defend his or her turf. Pecking order and rank are the essence of military life. To think this nonsense goes on in the field so far from HQ back in Hawaii.

Several of the digs at the primary site have reached the required depth plus and yielded nothing. They are being closed down. The test pits further downriver are like pinpricks in the hard, often clayish riverbed. Remains could be just inches away and we would never know it. Peter and I mused it would take an excavator to turn our portion of the riverbed upside down. Maj. Moye announces today he wants to do just that.

I join the workforce again as bucket man. Good for body and spirit even in the 100 degree heat. It helps to pass the time and feel a bit useful. Therapy for the bored and frustrated.

One of the men tells me he doesn't mind "moving dirt" as long as it makes sense. Good that he doesn't know his bosses' thoughts about the two alternate sites. There is no open bickering among the leaders. The major doesn't look like a man who'd condone it. He wants to get on with the job, but even he has to listen to the "anthro" and follow regulations.

The team plans to meet tonight to discuss further strategy now that none of the sites have turned up even the smallest, most minute indications that our people are buried there. All we have are our notes, our witnesses, our sunburns, our frustration and our disappointments. And heaps of soil and muck. Using an excavator is a last ditch effort. If nothing is found, all sites will be closed down.

Peter Chuun is obviously worried about the prospect of failure. He mentioned almost prayerfully how grateful he would be if only a tiny bone fragment would turn up. My feelings are different.

Let us find all or none. What will you tell the family whose loved one could not be found? A nightmarish thought. I applaud the search effort and all the sweat and backbreaking that went into it. But I begin to detest the purpose of the mission if it instills a fear of failure or becomes a contest for success, a chance to move up the career ladder.

How long does it take for it to sink in that we are not looking for survivors? We know the men are dead. We've known that for 20 long years. Having tried is the most important thing. Nothing else counts as we stand here on the eve of failure.

March 8, 1992, Phnom Penh

All the sites have been closed down, including the one 6 kilometers east from Highway 3. All that earth and all that water were moved for nothing. Really for nothing? I keep telling myself that the effort will always count. Reliving the past counts.

Recounting the incident of 1970, I relearned how unimportant and temporal the products of my profession can be. No one remembers the story our people died for. Is it only the continuity of our reporting that counts, as if our daily stories were bricks in a huge wall? Would this wall, representing the total information of our lifetime, collapse if the Cambodian stones were missing?

I feel both frustration and relief. Frustration that we walk away empty handed; relief that the job is almost done. Relief that rather than having found some remains we found none, so that the disappointment will be evenly shared. Relief also that the effort was made, after all these years, to recover the bodies.

The team doesn't share my feelings. Capt. John, tireless mover of earth, is disappointed. It's not only because he has to tell his general back in Hawaii that the mission failed. He's also thinking of the families' peace of mind. He wanted to help remove the last bit of doubt that their father or husband could still be alive. We all know they aren't. But…

Tomorrow the excavator will make the final try. Then we go home. I plan to go to Tokyo and tell the families all I know. So tomorrow the excavator will plow through the riverbed and probably nothing will be found.

March 9, 1992, Phnom Penh

I go to Wat Po early in the morning. Hardly a soul is there. Just piles of sand and muck. Capt. Hudson and a few others stand around in the heat, talking about the operation. What went wrong, if anything? Could they have done it differently? The team had dug up the gravesites as the witnesses had pointed them out. They had dug deeper and far beyond the confines of the gravesites. They had followed up every bit of information, probed two extra gravesites, opened test pits, moved and screened tons of earth, allowed for margins of error. Now, there is nothing else to do but wait for the excavator.

Maj. Moye takes the day off to show the gravesites to some VIPs. Later he expresses his amazement that nothing was found, not even a button. He is very keen on turning the riverbed upside down.

An obnoxious female journalist corners me during lunch back at the Cambodiana Hotel. Tries to get me to say something critical about the search team and the recovery effort. Even though I may have my own private reservations, I don't tell her anything.

She implies that the Defense Department looks for the missing newsmen only because Welles Hangen, the NBC correspondent, is an American. Undoubtedly true. Welles Hangen justified the search operation in the first place. But it is also true that the team looks for all the missing with all its strength.

She keeps talking about wasted taxpayers' money. Money that could be used for better purposes. I believe a great country like the United States can and must have the ability to do several things simultaneously. Not one less school or hospital will be built in Southeast Asia because of efforts to recover the war dead. There is a human dimension to be considered.

Families have the right to know what happened to their relatives and to have at least the remains returned from a war that ended up as a useless affair. Recovering bodies is first and foremost a physical effort, designed to ease pain, not a financial investment for dividends to be reaped later. If the relatives want this effort to be undertaken, then it must be done. Families who lost a father, husband or son in this failed adventure called the Vietnam War want a full accounting of what happened.

March 10, 1992, Phnom Penh

Today is supposed to be the day of the excavator. When I get to Wat Po I find, instead of the excavator operation going full blast, just a token force of locals. Heading back to Phnom Penh, I come across a relic of a Russian-made wheeled excavator broken down because of faulty hydraulic pumps. The puzzled Cambodian operator just stares at this contraption. When I ask if I could help he just shrugs and gives me a smirk that says everything.

A few moments later, a shiny Toyota stops and a feisty little man smelling just too good for the occasion gets out with his pretty

Cambodian interpreter. He introduces himself as a retired U.S. Army Colonel. I will call Jeb Glume, veteran of the Vietnam War and proud master of this wreck of a machine.

His bowlegged, perfumed, well dressed and, despite everything, quite acceptable-looking girlfriend-interpreter, of course, stands next to him, expecting her hero to take charge and get the show going.

Neither had bargained for a very angry Capt. Bill Hudson who, disregarding the exalted former rank of the retired carpetbagger, tears right into him. He tells Col. Glume (Peter calls him "Doom") in no uncertain terms what he thinks of him, of the excavator, and of his whole operation. The excavator is certainly too big for what Hudson thinks the colonel should do with it. I have the feeling the unhappy colonel appears quite a bit smaller to his girlfriend than he did just a few minutes before.

Hudson is a hard paratrooper and though usually unfailingly polite, he is not the type to take a "can't do" for an answer. He leaves the good colonel and his friend standing in the heat, drives off and hires another machine from one of the outfits improving roads just outside the capital.

Col. "Doom" even wants to keep Hudson's down payment until threatened with arrest by one of Peter's friends in the Cambodian government. The country is steadily filling up with Col. Glumes, eager to make a fast buck before Cambodia goes under.

Later in the day, Mr. Al Pitkin, assistant secretary of defense for MIA and POW affairs, gave a presser in Phnom Penh. Bud Pratty, an NBC producer, and I thanked him for the job his men were doing looking for our people. Patterson was pleased. The little people usually get little praise.

March 11, 1992, Phnom Penh

Today is the last day of the search. Hurrah, there is the new excavator churning through the riverbed. How fast the shovel moves, digging much deeper and quicker than the men ever could. The danger is, of course, that the mighty shovel may easily break up any remains and rebury them in the big heaps of soil it piles up so rapidly.

Therefore, Maj. Moye orders a team of natives led by two of his troops to go carefully through the clumps of soil, checking for the usual things. The excavator moves about 150 cubic meters of earth. Despite a careful search by the shovel team nothing is found. Not a trace. Nothing, nothing. All that could have been done has been done. The search is over.

The fisherman and the elder of the pagoda just can't believe that the site is closed and we are leaving. They keep pointing at one of the graves and motion to dig deeper. The troopers have done that.

We think the villagers want us to stay indefinitely. After all, it was good for their economy. We just shrug off their pleas. Nothing left to be done.

Peter and I talk about asking the villagers to keep looking for any sign of our people after our departure. It is important to us, to assuage any nagging doubts and not to burn all our bridges behind us. The anthropologist believes what we all believe: The bodies have been swept away. Maj. Moye rationalizes that the bodies, if they were indeed buried where we had dug, were recovered by natives and the bones sold by bone merchants. He recalls that in Laos not a single grave he and his team found was undisturbed.

Mike Eagle, one of the team members, said he went to the outskirts of Kampong Thom a few days ago on a hot tip about the remains of a U.S. pilot. A local farmer led them straight to the gravesite after a long, arduous march. He and his men started digging and after a while found a jawbone. Their joy was great. Then one of the men cried, "Wait a minute, isn't that thing a bit too big?"

As they continued, they found the rest of a cow buried several feet in the earth. They are still wondering what the farmer who took them there had on his mind. Well, we all had a good laugh.

The entire team openly shows its disappointment over not having been able to finish what it had set out to do. Not because it means failure to the general back in Hawaii, a mark against him that he'll pass down the line. No, the guys really voice regrets about not having been able to help the families of our missing. I try my best to dispel their dark thoughts, assuring them how much I appreciate their concern. I promise them to relay their thoughts to the relatives of the missing.

Peter and I throw a party for them tonight: small reward for heavy work. Maj. Moye promises the team that the sites may be closed but not the case. They all hope a reason can be found to return and finish the job.

Moye tells me I am in the brotherhood. It's a reason to feel proud. This is a very tight group of soldiers, almost impossible for an outsider to get in, especially a newsman. Shades of Vietnam. Jay Steed, the ordnance man, even calls the press "scum of the earth." He promises to make an exception with me. That's nice of him.

I leave the restaurant and get into a cab when a one-legged kid begs for money. I am about to give him some when suddenly my cab pulls out, leaving him empty handed. A nasty feeling. What is Cambodia today? A broken nation, a nation of the maimed and missing. A dead body that miraculously came back to life, only to be pounced on by the Glumes and Dooms of this world who'll leave it even more dead after they're through.

It'll feel good to get out of here. Strange to have traveled Highway 3 for the last time. So much has happened there. Reminders of the war are everywhere: bullet-scarred buildings, broken bridges, torn-up roads and cripples, everywhere begging cripples and the invisible faces of a missing generation.

I hope I don't have to come back again.

March 12, 1992, Bangkok

Now I really believe our mission is finished. A military C-130 waits at Pochentong Airport to carry us to Bangkok.

On board, a footlocker covered with a U.S. flag in a plastic cover holds remains of doubtful origin that were found someplace else in Cambodia. Maybe one of the Marines who died when his chopper crashed off the coast during the attempt to free the Mayaguez, a U.S. merchant ship captured by the Cambodians during the Ford administration.

All U.S. presidents seem to need one act of war to satisfy their hero image or to distract from troubles at home, no matter how ludicrous this may be. So the U.S. government made a big affair out of using military force to free the ship. I remember a disproportionate number of U.S. servicemen were killed.

The footlocker, almost lost in the huge plane, rests there, one of the men sitting on it unceremoniously. So the output of this mission is a footlocker containing remains of what is assumed an unidentified American military man, nothing from Wat Po and a dug-up cow from Kampong Tom. The general in Hawaii will not be pleased. After all, he wants to get promoted too.

Eleven days of this [search operation) and nothing....It looked as though 22 years of mud and monsoons had swept away the bodies. The team packed up and left.

But the villagers kept at it and found...human remains.

The Americans rushed back to continue the search in a land where life is cheap.

Bert Quint, CBS News Correspondent
April 1992

CHAPTER 4

Partial Success

March 13, 1992, Bangkok

I relax in the cool hotel. No cockroaches, no mosquitoes, only air-conditioned splendor, and then the phone rings. The ring even sounds strange. It is a disturbing call from Bud Pratt, the NBC producer.

Wat Po villagers reportedly found bones and teeth. They then contacted Peter Chuun, who had remained in Cambodia to bury his mother. She had died years ago when the Khmer Rouge were still in power and Peter couldn't enter the country.

March 14, 1992, Phnom Penh

Slept fitfully last night. Spent the evening at a typically sleazy Bangkok bar near the hotel where the boys of the team had laid out a Thai buffet with all the trimmings. They needed to let off steam before returning to Hawaii and other recovery operations.

The men have heard that some of them will have to return to Cambodia and check out what the villagers have found. I hear self-recriminations for not having listened enough to the villagers. I tell them they did all they could on the information available. Also, the villagers are part of the team.

Nothing wrong with going back to Wat Po and continuing where we left off. Imagine if the news reached us 24 hours later, with the troopers already on a plane to Hawaii and me on my way to Tokyo. Let's count our blessings—and never mind what the big general in Hawaii thinks.

Moye is sad that he cannot return. Capt. Robert John is going to be in charge, with Capt. Hudson as site commander. Madeleine, the anthro, will also go back to Wat Po with a handful others.

Morale is high. All the troopers assigned to the new effort are eager to go.

I go back to bed for a few hours of sleep. Wake up early. It is before dawn. I catch a cab and head for the airport through empty streets. At the airport, I meet the team. Madeleine is bitter about going back. She has doubts about the villagers' findings. Maybe they just want to get the economic prosperity to return to their village.

To be honest, I also have serious doubts about their findings. Are they playing some sort of game? Producing bits of remains, then stringing us along for money? How is it that only a few hours after our departure, miraculously, bones were found after the best professionals the Army could muster had to shut down the site?

Or had we underestimated the honesty and expertise of our village friends? Peter Chuun always believed in them. After all, the team's medics had treated them, and many of them showed us friendship through little gestures, leading us to a shady spot or bringing us pieces of fruit. Only our inability to speak with them in their own language bred distrust on our part. Peter speaks Khmer, so he understands them better than any of us. Maybe we are just tired and grumpy. After all it is too early in the morning.

I get bumped off the first flight to Phnom Penh. On arrival at Phnom Penh airport, a friendly press lady from the Foreign Ministry smuggles me through Cambodian passport control. I hire a car and look for Bun

Wat, my steadfast Cambodian escort. I find him at the Foreign Ministry and head straight for Wat Po without looking for the rest of the team.

The scene at Wat Po has changed. Gone is the thatched shelter under which the team would rest during its short breaks. No chopper waits nearby. The operation is considerably scaled down. There are only about half the men as before. No doctor, just one medic, Sergio. But he knows his stuff. The men on the team, about seven, look extremely fit. They're highly motivated after the perceived "failure" of the first attempt.

Part of the motivation is embarrassment. Some try to hide it for not having trusted the villagers. They also assume the big general is not pleased—in the Army only success counts. Now everyone is raring to go. Capt. John, overall commander, Capt. Hudson, site commander, and Madeleine, the anthropologist, huddle and decide on strategy.

The plan is to plow systematically through the entire dammed-up portion of the riverbed—excluding the test pit section—to a total depth of 2 meters. The work is to be done with shovels and bare hands, with each bucket carefully screened. This second operation makes the first one look like kid's play. And kid's play it wasn't. The estimate is that it will take about a week. But, with the reputation of the entire project at stake, I'm sure it will take as long as necessary to complete the second stage.

Secretly, all of us wish we had taken the villagers' insistence that we stay a bit longer more seriously. Whatever, the show's going on.

March 15, 1992, Phnom Penh

Today the probing starts again. The men, deep in the stinking mud, use their hands to feed the insatiable bucket brigades. I work with the men hauling up bucket after bucket containing smelly muck. The sun is burning hot as ever.

Suddenly, Sgt. Cabrera probing deep into the muddy water pulls out a human skull. He holds it up triumphantly as a shout of joy reverberates through the ranks of the troopers and native workers. Peter's face shows relief.

Later we are told that a villager had reburied the skull yesterday to let us do the finding. It doesn't matter to Sgt. Cabrera or us. As long as it kept us going. There is nothing like success, even if it needed a little help.

Other bones follow. The wet screening yields a tooth with good dental work, a rib and a vertebra. Finally we are going places. The heat and pain of the last weeks are forgotten. The tempo quickens, but the treasure hunting atmosphere is tempered by the troopers' professional digging techniques. They probe as carefully as archeologists at an Egyptian burial site.

The team recovers the rest of the skeleton, the lower part still stuck in blue jeans and shoes. It is somewhat gruesome to see the leg bones being pulled from the pants. There is no shirt. Twenty years in the mud destroy anything made of cotton. Only pants, shoes and belt survive. The jaw is smashed, maybe caused by a heavy blow from a club or handle. A horrible death. I am trying not to think about it. Obviously, the body was just heaved into the grave. It twisted during the fall.

Time to reassess the state of affairs before getting carried away. What do we know, where do we stand? All we know is that a skeleton—can't really call it a '"body"—has been found. Cause of death: blow to the face. Time of death: unknown. All this will have to be determined later in a high-tech Army lab in Hawaii by forensic experts.

Our anthropologist's role in this operation has really started now. She is very serious and very concentrated, examining each bone, taking notes. Clyde, the grave registration soldier, takes pictures for the record. The whole process is very professional, very scientific and very slow. Nothing personal creeps into the team's conversations.

Obviously, this is a prepared gravesite. Four more to go. The villagers have been vindicated. The fisherman and Mr. Chaak, who led the village protest against our departure, beam satisfaction.

Neither has made any mistakes. Their memories, after all these years, are remarkable. Chaak points out other probable gravesites spread across the riverbed.

Capt. Hudson and his assistant, Sgt. Williams, or Sgt. "Will" for short, translate their information about the possible location of the other bodies into a floating grid of tape covering the entire excavation site. Our fisherman, buoyed with pride, squats silently in the shade and watches the scene from a distance. After all, these big Americans came back on information he had tried to convey to them before their departure. And now they have returned. He obviously enjoys the growing respect they are paying him.

The head priest of the pagoda erects a small altar made out of tropical fruit and decorated with joss sticks. He sits there and stares into the distance, his deeply lined face fixed in a frozen expression but fully aware of the foreign intrusion into his world. More and more, our suspicion is ebbing that the villagers planted the body to get the economy of the village going again. None of them talks money so far, even though their needs are obvious: a new dike, a school or a simple bridge.

Eventually $15,000 in wages were paid to the villagers for helping us dig for the bodies.

Spirits are high. We're certain the other four remains will soon be found. Forgotten are the heat, the smell, the desolation of the place. Forgotten is the fact that the prizes we seek are dead men's bones. We all hope to find the next skeleton later in the day, oblivious for the moment of how dry and unforgiving the earth was that held our friends. Capt. Hudson brings the team back to reality. He cautions us not to believe in patterns, that one grave will be placed neatly next to the other just for our convenience.

The entire section of the riverbed to the last inch will probably have to be turned upside down before the job is finished.

As to the identity of the remains, Madeleine is very cagey. She doesn't want to commit herself. Seems to be a Caucasian: the bones are larger than Asian ones. Could be either Welles Hangen, the NBC correspondent, or Roger Colne, his cameraman. Doesn't matter at the moment. The lab in Hawaii is better equipped to make the final judgment.

Dinner again at the Royal beer garden. For dessert, "la Paloma": steamed bananas wrapped in pancakes. The same group of dancing girls crowds the garden. The young ladies seem to look especially sad this evening.

Maybe it's the lack of customers. Many of the girls are Vietnamese, attracted by the influx of new, fast money from the hordes of rich tourists, businessmen and U.N. people now in Phnom Penh. The Cambodians put a lot of faith in the U.N. people. Especially those who own property or businesses.

Meet Derek Williams at the beer garden, the old Asia hand and former CBS cameraman I bumped into last month in Bangkok. He got the CBS boot a little while ago in the usual shabby manner. His talents are without question. An old warhorse famous for his sense of humor and no-bullshit attitude, he's covered combat from the Middle East to Southeast Asia. We reminisce over drinks—soft drinks on my part. (Shouldn't reminisce without booze; it's only half as sad.) Talk about our dead colleagues and all the wars since Vietnam. The roll call is long. Not only armies are decimated. Yugoslavia even now eats up journalists. The Croats and Serbs seem to be gunning for them.

My home at the Royal is Bungalow Two. It looks familiar. Was it the one I stayed at more than 20 years ago? If only the walls could talk. The U.N. folks usually arrive in a country when there is a cease-fire, and when the cease-fire holds, the carpetbaggers come. This country is going to be corrupted just like Vietnam when the U.S. forces were there in strength. There are already too many rich foreigners, troops, pimps and speculators around.

I'm not so sure the Cambodians have the cockroach characteristics of their unloved neighbors, the Vietnamese, which would allow them to survive almost anything. The Cambodians survived their holocaust. Barely. I hope they survive what is called peace in this part of the world. Right now the country's timber is targeted for a fast buck. The Khmer Rouge, of all people, play the role of the Green Party. Only in their territory are forests protected, I'm told.

Strangely enough, the murderers of the past are presently the least corrupt. That doesn't help their victims. Their victims, including my colleagues, are still dead. But human memory is often like a hangover—gone the next morning.

There is fear that the Cambodians, mainly those in the rural areas, may turn to the Khmer Rouge for help. Many simple folks here believe that Sihanouk and his crowd, as well as some of the other factions, are interested only in looting the country.

March 16, 1992 Phnom Penh

We come up empty today. Again, bare hands and shovels turn over muck and mire. Innumerable buckets of earth are carefully checked. Talking every day about the hellish heat just gets boring. The elder of Wat Po burns joss sticks and prays silently at the small altar he erected near the gravesite. He stares into the distance. Maybe he's praying for us.

The troopers plow systematically through the riverbed. Looks like a miniature Panama Canal construction site. They aren't in a hurry, they take no shortcuts. After prayers, the Wat Po elder hit me up for money. Bun Wat explained to me that he needs it for food. This is the first time the question of money has come up. The old reservations about the first remains come back. Were they planted after all? I feel ashamed to be so suspicious. The legacy of the bone merchants has poisoned a lot of minds around here. Right now I am getting skeptical about finding the other remains.

The digging continues and may last until everyone in Wat Po is a rich man. Workers come in shifts, giving each able-bodied villager a chance to earn some money. Most of them are very strong. Their diet of fruit, vegetables, fish and chicken doesn't put much fat on them, and daily hard work in the fields keeps them fit. Many are barefoot, pushing shovels into the earth with their naked heels.

The anthropologist is still silent as to whose remains have been found. I exclude our Japanese. Some U.S. military big shot from Hawaii got the VIP tour today. Pale and self-important, he inspected "his gravesite," hands on hips, assuming command posture.

Our captains defer to him. They take him very seriously. Humanitarian the effort may be, but it is still a military operation waiting to be crowned by success.

Wonder if the brass in Hawaii or the Pentagon took offense because we closed the site too early. Well, one body has been found so far and that is a success of sorts. So the day ends without another find but with a lot of earth turned over and piled up.

March 17, 1992, Phnom Penh

I believe we found Welles Hangen today. It started with a shout from Capt. Hudson who, knee-deep in the mud, recovered something round and black: "Look here, a coconut."

Again, shouts of joy and relief can be heard, just like the last time. When the anthropologist declares it a human skull, it is as if the home team had scored a victory.

Like magic, at that very moment a runty, shifty-eyed Cambodian major general arrives. He seems to be the regional military commander or something to that effect. Capts. John and Hudson treat him with respect befitting his rank. His main concern is not to check on the progress of the search but to make sure his soldiers, who are responsible for the security of the gravesite, have been paid properly. Fair enough. I guess it takes a general to do that in this country.

When he sees the skull, he cries, "Now there can be smiles on our faces. I am sure you will find the others."

Capt. John replies, straight-faced, "Our general will be very happy with our success."

As the probing continues, the spirit of competition drives the men spearheading the search. Usually three do the archeological work with the rest clearing away the mud, tidying up or filling buckets.

Capt. John pulls rank. "I want to be the one who digs. I like that. It's great to find something."

John is a very decent and serious officer, but at this moment he looks like a little boy waiting to grab his favorite toy. It is all done in good spirits and for a good purpose.

Jay Steed, the explosives expert and a strong digger, adds, "Let's do it. I like to find 'em. It's a great feeling."

Peter Chuun speaks up, "Now I know we will find all of them."

The anthro says the skull is Caucasian. Whoever it is, we now have Colne and Hangen. Three Japanese to go: CBS's Ishii and Sakai and NBC's Waku.

Peter and I shake hands. My earlier doubts feel very cheap now. I want to join the optimism of the moment. One more find and a pattern will develop. After the midget general leaves, a lively argument starts among the "spearheaders."

Who will be the one to retrieve the next skeleton? In the troika of diggers only one can do it, just like in a surgical team where the head surgeon does the actual carving job assisted by his most qualified doctors. Shortly after the discovery of the second skull, Capt. John and

Capt. Hudson burrow their way, with much gentle probing, through a wall of clay leading to the rest of the skeleton.

It is almost sitting up, both hands tied behind its back. Again, belt, shoes and trousers are perfectly preserved. The shirt, probably cotton, is rotted away. The skull again appears to have been smashed in the mouth. Another horrible death.

A Wat Po villager tells Peter how the Viet Cong used the village idiot to carry out the killings with a club. Of course, he came from the neighboring village of Kandaol. After all, a local boy just would not do things like that. Of course not. The skeleton looks tall. To me that could make it Hangen. Now what's left of him fits into two buckets.

The diggers seem to have an almost erotic relationship with their job and the bodies they're finding. They retrieve bone after bone with loving care, naming them by their anatomical descriptions. It's almost like stripping a woman of her clothes, bit by bit.

Peter Chuun joins the celebration marking our progress. Has his fear of failure disappeared? Has the pressure eased? I am still surprised by how little he knows about the NBC missing.

I have the impression the mission to recover Hangen is more for cosmetic reasons, to make the network look good, than to help the families of the missing. There is an almost total lack of information concerning Colne and Waku. Even the officers of the team notice that and complain about it. However, there is no doubt that it was NBC that got the ball rolling. In the end it won't matter much. What counts is that we find all the bodies.

All in all, it's a good day. The big general should be pleased. The troops end the day on a high note.

Capt. Hudson, thoughtful as ever, gives me a small stone he found in the muddy riverbed. For some reason there are not many rocks in the mud. The one he offers me is just about the only one I've seen up to now. He wants to cut it so both our Japanese families have a memento of the operation.

Sgt. Williams, Hudson's closest assistant, a big black man from Atlanta, directly supervises the workforce, both local and American. He's a quiet man who doesn't have to raise his voice to have people do what he wants them to.

His face is good-natured. He's physically very strong, always there where the digging is tough, sometimes exhorting, more often leading by example as he slugs away, covered with mud. Will, as he's called, is one of the few on the team who's not overcome by the treasure-hunting mood. For him it's a job that needs to be done. He sticks out from the more exuberant crowd, taking care of loose ends and calming down his buddies when nerves get frayed.

If the next body found is that of Waku, the NBC soundman, I plan to go to Wat Po village and Thnal Bot, where our people were kept prisoner before being led to their death. Just curious if anyone is still alive who remembers what happened, maybe to plug some gaps in the story I recorded so long ago.

Tomorrow, the team plans to dig between the last two confirmed gravesites. Mr. Chaak believes we could find another body there. I continue to admire the stamina and dedication of the troopers. They've smelled success and are obviously ready for more. I understand their sportsmanlike spirit and enthusiasm, which doesn't obscure their great concern for the families. Only once in a while do they get carried away. Who could blame them?

There is a little more banter and laughter today. We are getting used to each other. One thing we are not getting used to is the oppressive heat. Seems to get hotter each day. We all drink a lot and eat Army rations. The troopers call the MRE combat rations "meals rejected by Ethiopians."

The troops, as is Army tradition, make fun of the food, but some of it, like tuna and noodles, is tasty if you're hungry enough. "Chicken a la king" is universally disliked. The troops generously share food and water with Peter and me. I usually bring lots of bananas and paper-backs. The soldiers are straightforward and grateful. I feel a part of this tightly knit brotherhood and the soldiers let me know I'm welcome.

I am by far the oldest guy on the block. Sergio, the medic, and Capt. Hudson look after the "old man" so that he doesn't overexert himself at the wet screen or the bucket brigade. I take a lot of pictures so the relatives of the missing will know how hard everyone worked.

Hudson, always very much aware of propriety, tries to prevent anyone from taking pictures except for the record whenever remains are found, but he has gotten used to my cameras and me. I believe I am gathering an unusual pictorial document of an unusual operation. The Wat Po elder keeps his lonely vigil, praying silently and burning joss sticks, hour after hour. A strange and somehow disquieting sight. His prayers are especially intensive when a camera is on him.

When the operation started, I thought I knew a lot about the whole episode of 20 years ago. But now, the closer I get to it in my search for details, the less I seem to know. At times it is like the process of developing a photographic print, only in reverse.

Instead of sharpening images, contours blur and finally disappear. I have doubts about my original research, the same research I was so certain of only a few weeks ago. Did Sakai and Ishii stay together till the end or were they separated? Villagers report different sightings. Different combinations of men who could be ours were seen in a variety of places. The question dogs me.

I want to believe my original research that all five men met the same fate at the same time in the same place. The next few days should tell us.

March 18, 1992, Phnom Penh

The team lets loose another collective shout of pure joy today when Jay, the explosive ordnance man, hit the third set of remains. Could be Waku. I have Ishii and Sakai's dental records, and the teeth of this body bear no resemblance to them. The anthropologist mumbles something about Hangen. That's a surprise. Is there an error? Only a thorough identification at the lab in Hawaii will give us the final answer.

Capts. John and Hudson, Jay and Maj. John Sovocool from the U.S. mission in Phnom Penh, who joined us for the day, proceed carefully. Very slowly, very gently.

Jay says, "Never pull bones from the soil. Dig them out and never jab your trowel into the earth."

"There may be exceptions," answered the anthropologist.

She didn't elaborate.

Madeleine never joins the actual digging. She sits there wearing pants and a wide brimmed hat. She rests on her haunches, scrutinizing the progress of the work, taking notes, only rarely offering a remark. Her strength is remarkable, but she's distant and not very sociable. There is no doubt about her overall competence.

Carefully the men recover what remains of what was once a living, breathing human being. Gingerly Capt. John pulls the socks off bare leg bones after stuffing shoes and pants into a bucket. Everything helps to identify remains. The cotton shorts are gone, but the waist rubber is still in place. It even has some pull left.

Waku's bones, if they are his, fit into one bucket, including the skull.

"A perfect specimen. Good for demonstration purposes back at the lab," cried the anthropologist. When you see the lower part of the remains freed from the covering soil, dressed in boots and pants, you almost expect a person to get up and walk out of the grave. But only for a fleeting moment.

Then, as shoes and pants are pulled off to reveal fleshless bones, when you see the smashed skull, you realize that murder was done and the earth has eaten up the flesh a long, long time ago. After having recovered the smashed skull and jaw, a thoughtful Capt. Hudson said, "Kurt, I know what you must feel right now. They switched teams at the last minute, right?"

Right, Captain. Ishii took my place. But have we found Ishii yet? Who is this man? What of the horror of his last moments on earth? Alone in his blindfolded hell. Tortured, with broken ribs. Hearing the death cries of his companions as they were systematically murdered by the village idiot before his turn came to have his face smashed by the handle of a hoe.

Today the men feel proud—and they should. All the suspicions I had about the villagers' motives have been swept away. Peter shook my hand and gave me the "thumbs up" sign. We were all very emotional.

All the toil, all the worry of the last weeks are now paying off. Chaak points out another possible gravesite. The men remove the earth around it to have a clear approach. Sgt. Cabrera, whose hobby is body-building and who can do 100 push-ups just for fun, does his day's work, digging away for hours.

Mr. Chaak, on whom none of us would probably have wasted a second glance should we have met him anywhere else but here, is now our hero, a towering giant. We rely on his memory. He has pointed out three graves so far and his margin of error is slim.

The locations of the graves are roughly the same he had shown us the last time, but now the men dig much deeper, and instead of making pinpricks in the mud, the whole riverbed is being churned up.

Chaak is a man in his early 40s, wiry and strong. His calls have been right and he's confident we will find Ishii and Sakai. I hope he is right. Pray he is right. I know should have more confidence. But it could be that our folks were separated from the rest of the crew in Thnal Bot and marched to their deaths someplace else.

I've spoken to several villagers, and they seem to support that. But the "gravedigger," Mr. Chaak, insists he saw all five in Kandaol shortly before he says they were murdered. I want to keep the faith and trust my notes. I want to trust Jim Sturdevant, the NBC cameraman who was with me up and down Highway 3 in 1971.

God bless that old, tough soldier who died on a mountain road in Hawaii shortly thereafter. His last letter to me is still in my file. A depressing message, as if he knew the end was near. I feel as if he is still around, still part of the team.

In a TV spot on the NBC evening news, Peter is almost euphoric. At the end of the first attempt, his correspondent in Los Angeles had called the search a failure. That still angers him. Now Peter is vindicated.

The general back in Hawaii should also be relieved. After all, he has to answer to an even bigger boss in the Pentagon. I heard that the secretary of defense is behind the operation, and it's costing a lot of money. But now it's already a success by any measure.

I invite the team to dinner at the Pacific Restaurant in Phnom Penh. New place, built by some Taiwanese or Thai to rake in lots of money before the roof caves in. Food's so-so, but for the troopers, who are an unspoiled lot, the restaurant is a place of luxury and comfort.

At the next table sit a busload of French tourists. Their happy chatter and laughter dominate the room. They probably came to see the ruins at Angkor Wat after a goose pimple dinner in dangerous downtown Phnom Penh. All included in the price.

There is something obscene about it all. Outside, groups of amputees wait to beg enough to survive; inside, a bunch of tourists out for a quick thrill, most likely ignorant of the suffering this country is still going through. Life goes on.

Sgt. Williams leaves the dinner table early to get water for the next day. The rest stay a bit longer even though the wake-up call comes early, about 5 in the morning. The atmosphere is very congenial. Even the anthropologist relaxes and is friendly. Only a press guy who came along is a nuisance. Endless war stories no one is in the mood to hear. Looks like a burnt-out case. Too much booze and too much war.

Peter Chuun tells me during dinner that the Khmer Rouge are stirring up trouble in Wat Po. "The Americans make you work for them like slaves," they insist. Some of the villagers are so intimidated they don't sleep in the village anymore. Others even carry arms. In practical terms, the Khmer Rouge threaten to mine the road to Wat Po and generally promise to get even with the villagers after we've left. I believe that. For the moment, the Khmer Rouge are happier than they pretend to be simply because they also profit from the influx of money, most likely taking their share of the wages the villagers earn working for us.

There is one hard-eyed guy out there everyday, carrying a gun and never joining in the fun and card games of the drivers and villagers who have a day off. The Khmer Rouge, old murderers that they are, pretend that they haven't killed over a million people.

But it's also true that Nixon and Kissinger helped to lay the foundation for the Cambodian holocaust. Again the villagers are caught in the middle. They have to live in Wat Po long after we are gone.

Most of the troopers, mainly the older ones, disapprove of the Vietnam War but several of them continue to blame the press for having lost it. Especially Jay Steed, the explosives expert, who still thinks the press are the scum of the earth, despite the exception he makes for me.

The streets of Phnom Penh remind me more and more of Saigon in the 1960s when I was there as a young GI. A mix of cyclos loaded down with overweight foreigners, busy natives selling black market goods or running small souvenir shops, uniformed men blending into the crowd and, everywhere you look, amputees, mostly kids.

New buildings and hotels shoot up as a lot of foreign money streams into town, invested for a quick profit. The city is nervous, lively, smelly and rundown. Bright sunshine, tropical flowers and vegetation detract only for a moment from the sight of a land and people still smarting from the war.

For Westerners, prices are cheap, but on the eve of the arrival of well-paid U.N. troop contingents, you can sense that all this will change soon.

Talk to citizens in the streets and the countryside and you can sense how fed up they are with war and death. Now they put their faith in the U.N. There is little other hope left. In the meantime, the country will become, or is already, a playground for carpetbaggers, soldiers, whores and pimps who will bleed it dry as long as the peace lasts. An impression that grows by the day.

March 19, 1992 Phnom Penh

Today I believe we found Ishii. Body No. 4 must be him or Sakai. He suffered the same horrible death as all the others. Mouth and skull smashed by brutal blows, hands tied behind the back.

His teeth were found exactly where Mr. Chaak said they'd be, about four meters down river from the last grave. Jay, the explosives guy, proceeds with infinite care.

"You have to treat bones just like grenades," he shouts as he probes the skeleton's spine and rib cage. "You don't want explosives to go off and you don't want to break bones."

The moment of triumph is gone. No more banter now, just work in the unbearable heat.

As these bones are found, work on a grave further upriver continues. Sgt. Cabrera and his helpers work long hours and go deep, deeper than necessary. This should yield body number five, but nothing so far.

Just what I was afraid of—not enough bodies to go around for all the families of the missing. We speculate that the fifth body, hastily buried in a shallower grave because of the approaching government troops, was swept away by 22 years of rainy seasons, rising tides and rapid currents. We believe it was Ishii's body the fisherman saw and covered up, so this means that we had not found him but Sakai, his soundman.

I am wondering how my friend Kurt Hoefle, my old teammate during those weeks in Cambodia, must feel. He's now a cameraman in Bonn. I thought of his hair-raising experience in 1970, when an overly ambitious correspondent drove past the last government checkpoint deep into Viet Cong and Khmer Rouge territory. If not for the courage Kurt showed in insisting to the mean-looking Viet Cong that they were all Germans, we could just as easily be looking for their bones as well.

So now we have four bodies. Mr. Chaak stares at where Ishii was supposed to be, poking around in the mud. Even he seems to have run out of ideas. Capt. Hudson collects sand from all over the excavation site—along with the stone he found earlier—to pass on to the families in Tokyo. Today, for the first time, after so much work and sweat, a crack appears in the united front of our troopers. Capt. Hudson and Sgt. "Will" want to close down the site for good.

The riverbed had been turned over by shovels and hands almost from the beginning to the end of the dammed-up section. All that was humanly possible had been done. There is no more sand to screen. "Lay down all tools," is Capt. Hudson's order. That's when Capt. John, of equal rank but second in command behind Maj. Moye, steps in.

"I'm working for the general and he wants more of this river dug up."

Bitter exchanges follow. Rank is pulled. The debate gets heated. Everybody can hear it.

The anthropologist sides with Capt. John, implying Hudson isn't thorough enough and reminding him that the site was closed down too soon the last time. All these arguments are carried out before a crowd. I am embarrassed and walked away. I feel sad seeing these people who had toiled so hard as a team fall apart.

Now all the tension and frustration just explodes. After much shouting and arguing, Capt. John lays down the law: The work continues, not only tomorrow, but until every square foot of earth is turned over—even where Ishii's grave could not be by any stretch of logic—

to a depth of two meters into the riverbed and four meters from the edge of the riverbank.

"It ain't over till it's over. It's only over when the fat lady sings. And the fat lady hasn't sung yet," Capt. John mumbles.

"As long as we don't move the same dirt twice, it's OK by me," says Jay. "That's against the rules."

The others agree with him.

Sgt. Cabrera must have seen that Peter and I witnessed the altercation among the officers and the anthropologist. He apologizes for it. We calm him down: "You should see how we go after each other at CBS and NBC. No holds barred."

It is better to have it all out in the open. It's preferable to reach decisions this way than to have military yes-men just following orders. Yet, the fact remains that now the team is split wide open.

I get the first inkling of just how serious it is later in the evening when Capt. Hudson knocks on my bungalow door and asks me to come to dinner at the Pacific Restaurant.

When I arrive, there is a free chair next to Madeleine, with Hudson sitting as far away from her as possible. Not a word is exchanged between them. Capt. John isn't there. Hudson is a natural leader but now John stops him in his tracks, knowing the general in Hawaii will back him up. So much for natural leadership if you don't have the rank to go with it.

It's very clear to everyone that the uncanny memory of the man from neighboring Kandaol, Mr. Chaak, proved to be the key to finding the bodies. We always called him Mr. Chaak as a sign of our respect.

He'd often been staring at the ground as if his eyes could penetrate the earth and see our men beneath it. Considering so much time has passed, his errors were indeed negligible. He was the last to leave the bamboo grove 22 years ago. The sight of Ishii's grave must have burned into his memory as he left, shovel on his shoulder, following the gentle bend of the river past the four other open graves.

He, the fisherman and other villagers always insisted that we dig deeper. But the work of the excavator convinced us that the bodies just weren't there. I remember how Peter and I stood at the riverbank, staring into the mud and saying, "Somewhere down there in the muck are our friends." Only we didn't say it loud enough.

We did, almost as an afterthought, ask the villagers to keep looking. Then, on the morning of our departure, they found what we now think are Waku's remains only 40 centimeters from the edge of a presumed gravesite.

Maj. Moye had dug there and moved heavy, clayish soil with his bare hands for hours. He couldn't possibly know that he was within an arm's length from hitting pay dirt—in the true sense of the word.

Capt. Hudson, with typical candor, said, "Hell, we didn't find a single body. The villagers did it all."

But the officers, the anthropologist and Sgt. Will did decide on the successful strategy, and they inspired the workforce to get on with the job.

Even after their success the team still has a nagging bad conscience for having pulled out too soon. They did well and the first part should be forgotten. I know how unforgiving the Army can be. Hudson seems to be the least concerned. He made his decisions based on the best knowledge he had at the time and his conscience is as clear as it should be. Excavations for him are not a science but a tactical military problem. You assess it and then employ the necessary assets and skills. After you decide that your position is untenable (i.e., you can't find the bodies after all your means are exhausted),you break off the engagement and regroup for the next fight.

For John, Hudson and the anthropologist to carry out their fight in the open is a good indication of the unseen presence of the general. Against all tradition, they forgot the officer's code never to show differences in front of common soldiers and strangers. These soldiers believe in what they're doing, no doubt, but they can't afford to make their general look bad.

Men like Sgt. "Will," who kept calm during the officers' fight, have no further career goals. He has risen as high as an enlisted man can go. His dream is retirement in a few weeks. He plans to join his sister's dump truck business, so moving earth will still be part of his life. So Will takes it in stride, minds his own business and keeps filling enough buckets with his bare hands to keep most of the local workforce going single handedly.

March 20, 1992, Phnom Penh

Well, the big general back in the happy isle of Hawaii laid down the law: "Find the fifth newsman or tell me a good reason why not—and it won't be good enough."

My guess is that the affair is getting some play in the press and the issue has now become political within the State Department. It is a good public relations move. It also means there is a lot of pressure on the general and he is passing it down the line to the men at Wat Po.

And so the guys keep digging, digging, silently in the heat. They take short water breaks and then dig some more. Not a trace of No. 5. Mr. Chaak, the gravedigger, runs back and forth, straining his 20-year-old memory, pointing out a new possible site. Peter Chuun translates that Chaak remembers how a Viet Cong marched him all the way to the end of the riverbed to dig a grave.

Then Chaak changes his mind and walks downriver about 15 meters beyond Waku's grave and points to the ground. This is our last hope. In the meantime, some of the team probe the bend of the river in case the body was swept there. Nothing is found. It is another heavy day at the screens, looking for anything. Again, nothing. Nothing to show at the end of the day.

My partners at the wet screen today were Cabrera and Clyde. Cabrera likes to jump out of airplanes. He is a cheerful guy, strong as an ox. After a short stint in civilian life, he rejoined the Army and is at home there. Clyde, the other black man on the team, is different. He is a professional gravedigger. He spent his time during the Persian Gulf War bagging and tagging U.S. war dead. He is very quiet, always friendly, but there are shadows in his face.

Sergio, the airborne medic, replaces Clyde for a while at the screen. He likes to talk about the human body and how intelligently it deals with the abuses we inflict upon it. Besides working in the pits or at the screens, he keeps an eye out in case sun or stress get to any of us. Outwardly at least, the team now displays its usual unity.

Their boss in Hawaii has spoken and they concentrate on the task even if it means digging where it doesn't make any sense at all. The soldiers keep moving and screening earth by the ton.

More than ever before the site looks like the Panama Canal, without the mosquitoes, thank God, but with plenty of leeches populating the mud we screen. Fat, greenish and very slimy. The Cambodians, seeing our discomfort, simply pick them up with their fingers and, laughing, fling them into the river.

Buddhist monks from Wat Po in saffron robes squat near the "canal." Led by the elder of Wat Po, the one with the sly and pious face, they chant their prayers for the dead into the morning sun.

Scrawny village dogs parade in front of the monks, mixing their barks with the chants. Peter, a devout Buddhist, joins in the prayers. Only a few meters away, in the shade of one of the minibuses, drivers play cards, laughing and shouting. The cold-eyed Khmer Rouge with his gun on his belt watches silently, contempt and suspicion on his face.

The air is filled with the sounds of shovels, buckets and prayers. Later, the heat swallows all sounds. The promising morning becomes just another day in the mud. Nothing to show. Now the feeling is that whatever work is done is done for the general. Frustrating for a civilian, but I too have done my share of useless chores to satisfy my CBS bosses. Today is another long, miserable day. Ishii is not found.

Each day before the pumps are turned off, we finish up by hosing ourselves down with muddy river water. We look awful but it gives us the illusion of cleanliness.

On the way back to Phnom Penh on Highway 3, I drive through the villages I now know so well, Thnal Bot, Baing Kasey and Tran Khnar.

Bullet-scarred walls are reminders of our adventures there during the war. While driving along I muse about the men in the team, their lives and prospects.

They do feel like elites, elites in an Army with little to do outside of routine security jobs in various parts of the world. Now, the most attractive job for a soldier is to look for the missing in action from past conflicts. What a commentary on the usefulness of an armed force in these days of a world without a Cold War.

But, again, our men must be driven by something more to this job; not even a cynic could deny them their sense of duty and responsibility. Even after all these days of physical hardship, they still have a sense of sportsmanlike competition: who works the hardest, who moves the most earth and who goes after the body when one shows up.

Especially the younger ones, like Steed and John, are full of zest tempered by a touchingly serious professionalism they never shed.

The villagers from Wat Po and Kandaol actually like the soldiers. The U.S. troopers deal with them not as their French colonial masters did, but in a curiously easy egalitarian spirit. They take their turns at the shovels, buckets or screens, working shoulder-to-shoulder with the villagers. They also share with them food, water and shade from the blazing heat. The soldiers have invented a kind of pidgin English combined with body language to get their ideas across, all done gently and with humor.

The troopers pick up Khmer words for cigarettes, fruits and a few other things. The villagers get a kick out of it. They all have a good time trying to talk to each other. It shortens the hours of a long, hot day.

I ask Peter Chuun today what keeps him going. He recounts how he started with my old friend Jim Sturdevant around 1971, when Jim sent him to Cambodian refugee camps to interview people there, trying to get information about the missing newsmen. Peter used his remarkable skills as a native Cambodian and his good connections with the Cambodian government to get the job done.

Peter's big moment came in June 1971 when he went to Thnal Bot, just off Highway 3 and, with the help of a farmer, dug up two Japanese bodies buried near a pond. He had about 20 minutes between Viet Cong patrols to get the smelly, decaying cargo into a burlap bag and tie it to his motorcycle. Dodging enemy patrols, he rode his bike to Phnom Penh to deliver the bodies. He had reason to believe they were part of the NBC or CBS teams.

As it turned out, they were two Japanese agricultural experts working for the Cambodian government who were murdered by the Viet Cong or Khmer Rouge forces. I remember that they wound up in the U.S. Army morgue at Saigon's Tanh Son Nhut airbase for identification. I still have texts describing their injuries.

March 21, 1992 Phnom Penh

Today is the first day of spring. It passes unnoticed in the 110 degree heat. Every day is a summer day. The monotony of screening buckets of sand and clay makes me drowsy. But the routine goes on mechanically. At times I am daydreaming, going through the sand with my trowel as if in a trance.

I dream about sand being washed through a screen. I hear the trowel scratching the wire mesh. The hours just drag on and the sun doesn't want to join the horizon. Some of the guys slog upstream to look at another possible gravesite. Desperation drives them now. Let's just fin-ish the job, get the ordeal over with. Maybe it is not so much of an ordeal for the troopers. Many of them are 30 years younger and in top physical condition, but even they show the strain at the end of the day.

Today, the gravedigger's fertile mind finally gives out. Even he has no more new ideas what to do next. We've come to a dead end. After a tenuous peace, the unity of the team's leadership is again showing cracks. Again there is an ugly confrontation between Hudson and John. The project is no longer to find Ishii but to prove who runs the show.

Today John, usually a hardworking, quiet officer who does more than his part of the physical labor, shows his hard side.

Again he dresses down Hudson and Will in front of Peter and me. John curses and orders Hudson and Will to continue digging downstream tomorrow, well beyond where any of our witnesses believe remains can be found.

We are now south of Sakai's grave. John forces the troopers to disregard the pattern that has emerged so far. He also ignores the fisherman's and gravedigger's testimony that Ishii's grave should be the last one upstream. Army fear and protocol dominate these last efforts to find our fifth body. Presently there is not much left of the officer and gentleman in Capt. John.

Will, a mere sergeant, stays quiet, his face inscrutable. He is caught between his loyalty to Capt. Hudson and the orders of his superior, Capt. John. Now he does what he is told, not with subservience, but like a man who shows what he thinks of a dumb order without saying it out loud.

The rest of the team stays out of today's fight. The lines are pretty clear now. It is Hudson, Will and the rest of the team versus John and the anthropologist. The team uses two buses to get to work and carry supplies since the helicopter was taken away from us. One bus is ostensibly for nonsmokers. Now each feuding faction uses its own bus and to hell with the smoke. I feel sad when I watch the two vehicles disappear toward Highway 3, throwing up dust, traveling so close together and yet so far apart.

All this tension and feuding is so unnecessary. The team is doing a splendid job not just because the general wants it done, but also out of an innate sense of duty combined with decency and a constant awareness that there are families in the United States, Japan and France who wait for definitive answers.

We miss Maj. Moye very much at this point. His rank along with his natural authority would have nipped in the bud the kind of infighting now demeaning our common cause.

One reason for this ugly confrontation is certainly the meddling of faraway higher-ups. But the strain of the last three weeks also has something to do with it. The physical and emotional commitment has been awesome.

We all are tired of looking for graves. We all believe that we know who the missing person is: Ishii. And this belief is not very pleasant. What do I tell the Ishii family in Tokyo? Exactly what I was afraid of at the beginning has happened. We didn't find all of them.

I am tired of seeing Madeleine naming the bones of my colleagues as she puts them into a bucket, one by one. Her detached voice will stay in my ear for a long time as she identifies the tibia, the femur, pelvic bones, clavicle, mandibles and others. Buckets full of them.

I am tired of seeing these buckets carried to a water hose to have their contents washed down. Cracked skulls cleaned as you would a watermelon.

"Perfect specimen, the best the team ever found," Madeleine says.

I envy the security guards and drivers. They sit in the shade of the team buses and play cards. The Wat Po elder still stares, unsmiling, into the distance, while the local Khmer Rouge boss watches the whole scene with the same cold eyes. The drivers and guards are oblivious to the little human drama before them. They shout and laugh, losing or winning money as the days drag on.

Later in the day, I desert my screening job and drive to Thnal Bot. I almost get dizzy in the heat, as if my brain is being fried.

My plan is to visit the teacher's house where all of our missing were held before they were driven to Wat Po and killed. The house is gone. Only a few holes in the ground, where the foundation once rested, are all that's left.

Maybe I am lucky and will find someone who saw all five being driven off. Or just four. Will has just told me that some villagers spoke of only four persons being seen together. But reliable Mr. Chaak has said time and again that he saw all five of them in his village on the road to Wat Po.

What happened to Ishii? Was he really swept from his shallow grave? We all want to believe it except Capt. John, who keeps digging with a persistence I have to admire. "It ain't over till it's over, said the fat lady," he shouts with more confidence than I could ever have. He will dig to the bitter end like a driven man.

Peter stands at the edge of the river, focuses on the muddy water that has collected in the grave pits and mumbles loud enough for me to hear: "Ishii, Ishii, don't you want to come home?" I am deeply touched.

Bun Wat, my guide and interpreter, tells me now why the excavator didn't find any bodies. "The shovel of the machine stopped just a few centimeters from Waku's head. The head made it stop." Land of superstition.

Peter is increasingly worried about the Khmer Rouge stirring up the Wat Po villagers against us. They still intimidate some of the people on the workforce. The agitators play on the ugly face of capitalism. They charge that the Americans pay big money to the fisherman from Kandaol and other witnesses. Peter wants to walk over to Wat Po tomorrow, bring gifts and try to calm down the people there.

We have disrupted village life and I feel it is time to get out and let things go back to normal.

The ride to the hotel in Phnom Penh on Highway 3 takes about 90 minutes and gives me ample time to think about what we felt on this fateful stretch of highway so long ago. I still see George Syvertsen wearing a khaki shirt driving the navy gray CBS Jeep down this very road.

George was then a man in his 30s, tall, slender and scholarly looking. He was an accomplished writer and correspondent who had his prior experiences with communist regimes in Poland and the Soviet Union. He was especially impressed by what the communists were doing to Poland, a country he had fallen in love with.

Poland was also the home of his wife, Gusta. After his experience with communism in Eastern Europe, I think George believed that the United States should take a stand against communism in Southeast Asia. His stories reflected his convictions. Not in any propagandistic way, but you could read them between the lines.

This attitude did not necessarily go with the general attitude felt in the States at the time. The country was tired of the war and didn't want another one in Cambodia. Consequently, the network shared this antiwar mood. George once told me during one of our long discussions about the war that some people probably considered him a reactionary.

My feeling is that George felt the company's disapproval. The bosses in New York probably never voiced this openly. They certainly had very subtle methods to let a correspondent know how they felt about his reporting. They just make it very hard for him to get on the air.

And so Cambodia, caught in the vice between communist and Vietnamese forces, seemed a perfect place to do meaningful reporting and regain some of the good standing George deserved. He decided to recoup in Cambodia, taking chances in the field with almost suicidal abandon. He went further than any newsman, putting himself and his colleagues in mortal danger.

I saw George Syvertsen at his best during the Tet offensive. Right up to the end of January 1968, the war in Vietnam had been sufficiently eventful to last a normal person a lifetime. Then the war really blew up.

Tet tore the place apart from the so-called Demilitarized Zone in the North to the delta in the South.

Everything that happened before Tet seems now, by comparison, to represent the good old times, when it was possible to cover combat in the rice paddies during daytime, then chopper back to Saigon for the cocktail hour before dinner in a good French restaurant. Our motto was to make Cronkite (our name for his evening newscast) during the day and everything else during the night.

Tet changed all that when it started with a bang nobody really had expected.

Most of the press gang were sitting on the patio of the Marine press camp in Danang to watch a traditional Vietnamese fireworks display light up the Danang River. The noise of the fireworks reminded some of us of a firefight, but the mood among us was happy, apprehension calmed by drinks.

Shortly after midnight most newsmen, among them George, my Vietnamese soundman, Boom-Boom Ri, and I left to get a good night's sleep. At about 3:15 in the morning we were awakened by the unmistakable sound of exploding rocket shells. We rushed outside. The sky in the direction of the Danang air base was as bright as daylight.

Syvertsen and I ignored the protests of the Marine guards at the press camp and talked our way past Vietnamese soldiers to film a report on the damage caused by rockets. We thought this had just been another attack and nothing more. It had happened before. When the sound of firing continued we thought that the Tet celebrations were still going on.

A Marine officer told George that a battle royal was under way just a few blocks from the press camp. George shouted to my soundman and me to leave our ham and eggs breakfast and join him.

We commandeered the services of a civilian pacification worker and his Jeep and rushed to the headquarters of the South Vietnamese First Corps, the military and political command center for the five northern provinces. We were alone; our competition was either still asleep or didn't get the word.

A Vietnamese policeman tried to stop us as we ran past him. "No can go, no can go. Dangerous!" George gave him his answer, "Get out, bao chi, bao chi," Vietnamese for press.

We got through several roadblocks and saw civilian refugees streaming from the area around the First Corps compound.

George released our involuntary chauffeur and remarked calmly, "It's the first time I hitchhiked into combat."

The firefight in the cluster of houses next to the Vietnamese compound was bloody. Bodies lay in the streets. A Vietnamese army Jeep stood in the middle of the road, both occupants sitting in the front as if they were sleeping. Both were dead. We ran into a group of Vietnamese rangers charging through a cemetery. They attacked through the tombstones, killing Viet Cong on top of all the other dead who had been buried there for years.

All the time as they charged they urged us to run with them. We must have presented a strange sight: George, though crouched, still towering over the yelling helmeted Vietnamese troopers leading me and my soundman, Boom-Boom Ri, packed with our gear, running like hell to keep up with the front group of the rangers. The madness of heavy fighting seemed to continue forever. At the end of the day, George Syvertsen had scored a remarkable beat, as the following cable attests:

CRONKITERS SAY CONGRATULATIONS AND WELL DONE FOR ONE OF MOST MEMORABLE BEATS IN RECENT MONTHS STOP WE WERE ALONE VIA SATELLITE AND MILES AHEAD OF ALL OPPOSITION ON DANANG ATTACKS STOP BE CAREFUL CRONKITE

Unfortunately, these accolades have a short life in a profession where the desk jockeys in New York like to say, "I know how good you are, but what have you done for us lately?"

My thoughts go to Duong Van Ri, a short, very strong 40-year-old from Long Vinh in Vietnam's Mekong delta. He went with Syvertsen and me on many a military operation all over the country. Ri was called Boom-Boom. Not for his expertise with explosives or his love for a fire-fight but for his activities that gave a certain quarter of Cholon an abundance of seamstresses for a few years. Why so? Because Boom-Boom was a gentleman. Every time he grew tired of a girlfriend he didn't just dismiss her into the harsh world of Vietnamese life. First, he would send his former lover to a seamstress school to make sure she had an honest profession that gave her a chance to survive in the jungle of a big city.

Boom-Boom was also my friend. Though his English was about as good as my Vietnamese, we communicated very well. Boom-Boom took care of me in tough places. As a former trooper in the South Vietnamese army he had become an expert in the art of survival. He smelled danger, found shade in sun-drenched places, shelter during tropical rain storms, water where there seemed to be none and sometimes a coconut to enhance a dull meal in some awful place.

And Boom-Boom was brave. Needless to say, he was braver than I was. During the Tet offensive I noticed that Boom-Boom became even braver than usual as opposed to me during those hard days. It came to a climax at Phu Bai, a strategic Marine base serving as main supply point for the Marines manning outposts near the Demilitarized Zone separating the North from the South.

While waiting at the edge of the airstrip for transportation to somewhere, Boom-Boom, Syvertsen and I were straddled by a barrage of 122 mm rockets, a frightening experience as many know. The closest impact was a mere 5 meters away.

Boom-Boom barely took cover. He laughed and pointed at me while I tried to crawl even deeper into a slit trench. After the dust had settled, I asked him what he thought was so funny and why he didn't duck. He said, "No problem, Kurt, I go fortune teller and he tell me I die only when I am 75." Boom-Boom Ri was half right. He didn't reach 75, but he didn't die in war either. Boom-Boom wasn't yet 50 when he died in a tragic accident in Saigon. But maybe he passed some of the years he was promised but couldn't get to live on to me along with his cheerfulness. Boom-Boom was buried in his hometown on a day even the Viet Cong seemed to honor. They held their fire while watching silently along with CBS friends as he was put to rest in the rich soil of his beloved delta. I still miss him today.

The confrontation that arose between George and me the night before he was killed all those years ago was a lot like the one between Capts. John and Hudson today. Only the stakes were higher. Lives were at stake. Stories, reputation and career came second. Only George didn't see it that way. Welles Hangen, the NBC correspondent, was driven by fear of getting beaten by CBS. A battlefield is a lousy place for competition among newsman.

Hangen, based in Hong Kong since 1966 as NBC's "China watcher," had spent a year at Columbia University on a fellowship from the Council on Foreign Relations. He was an experienced and respected newsman.

Cameramen and sound technicians like Ishii and Sakai, having communication problems because of their limited language skills, had almost no chance to make their views or objections known. The correspondents were their overlords. They had no voice.

The murders of our friends was a hard way to learn that in life or death situations every man is his own free agent, and no story is worth a life. But where does calculated risk end and foolhardiness begin?

We've all been careless at times. Our profession demands it. It's a good feeling to take chances and survive. If you get away with it, it's more than good. It's exhilarating. But it can't become a steady diet and has to be done only when all team members are in agreement.

Peter's motives, I think, are clear: personal satisfaction, a feeling of accomplishment and a sense of honor as a native Cambodian to do the right thing for colleagues murdered in his country. His language skills and understanding of Khmer culture are essential to this operation.

What are my motives? I don't have an answer yet, but I'm looking for one.

March 22, 1992, Phnom Penh

The team has again found its unity and spirit. We all know the job is drawing to an end. Capt. John asserts his authority. The men now comb the fringes of the riverbed. They are just about reaching the southern and northern dams. A brief flurry of excitement goes through the ranks when a tooth is found downriver a short distance from the fourth grave. Maybe the fifth is downriver rather than upriver? Hudson warns that this find means little. It could belong to one of the bodies we've already recovered. The anthropologist agrees. Nothing else is recovered.

So where is Ishii? Where is Ishii? This is the question that haunts all of us.

The men voice their disappointment. We all need the hope for some progress. Something has to give. Soon!

Capt. John, Peter and I return to Thnal Bot to talk to the farmer who had helped Peter recover the bodies of the two Japanese agricultural workers in 1970.

Asking around, we get a few new answers concerning our people. Some are contradictory. But after sifting through them they all pointed squarely to Wat Po as the place of execution. John, Peter and I come more and more to the conclusion that Ishii's body was indeed carried away by the current, slowly disintegrating on its journey down the river to the South China Sea.

A villager claims to have seen some bones stuck in a bamboo grid used to catch fish, and good old reliable Mr. Chaak believes that the Viet Cong soldier charged with filling in the graves was surprised by approaching government forces, did a hasty job and ran away to stay out of trouble.

The government troops were Gen. Norodom Changtrangsay's 13th brigade. A relative of Norodom Sihanouk, he was charged with keeping the Communists away from the capital. I visited him during his father's funeral. I had brought flowers and deposited them at the bier with his father's coffin. He became quite friendly when one of his officers told him that I had carried one of his wounded troopers to safety.

Gen. Changtrangsay had considered it a point of honor to launch an operation in the Wat Po area and look for the missing newsmen. We didn't know until now how close he came to freeing our people. There was also the possibility that his offensive hastened their murder. We do know that the Vietnamese and their Khmer Rouge helpers were on the run and very nervous during the first phase of the U.S. and Vietnamese incursion.

Even the most eager among us are now ready to call it a day very soon. We are just looking for a plausible reason to end this torture.

Madeleine says that all the remains showed torture marks. The Caucasians, Hangen and Colne, were singled out for especially brutal treatment. As I head down Highway 3, I am again passing for the umpteenth time through Baing Kasey, Kandaol and Tran Khnar. Seeing how peaceful they now appear, it is hard to believe so many fateful events took place here.

I notice small temples in the countryside, scrawny cattle looking for food in the dried-up fields. We pass rickety buses loaded with people, chickens and furniture. Some passengers hang from the sides, others crowd the roof. Oxcarts slow traffic. These carts haven't changed in centuries and probably won't in the years ahead. They make their way slowly and undisturbed by modern traffic flowing past them. Anything goes.

The only traffic rule is the rule of survival. Cows are liable to come out of nowhere and jump in front of your car, forcing you to a sudden halt. One cynic claimed that the Khmer Rouge didn't just murder all the smart people, but also all the smart cows.

I pass through Tran Khnar, site of small but very vicious firefights. I remember the spot where the very young government flag carrier lay after taking a fusillade of Viet Cong bullets in the face. I remember how still he was on the hot asphalt road when we dared to raise our heads above the trench next to this highway. Can't find the exact spot, though.

I think I recognize the rice field where we spent three hours pinned down in the heat, tired, thirsty and scared. The combined mob of TV and other newsmen half submerged in a stinking rice paddy cheered a U.S. fighter coming in low, hoping the plane would strafe the Viet Cong and Khmer Rouge troops who had us pinned down. I still feel the disappointment and hear our collective groan of anger when the Phantom's belly exposed a camera, took some shots and flew away.

The heat that day was hellish, just before the rainy season. I crawled to a big clay container and drank from it, not caring if the water was OK or not.

Now the little towns and villages are peaceful, the markets filled with life. Fly-covered meat of uncertain origin hangs in small stalls lining the dusty highway. Bananas, coconuts and assorted black market goods beckon to be bought. Where the asphalt is gone completely, clouds of dust thrown up by passing cars envelop the lively scene.

Gas is sold in soft drink bottles. Hordes of little kids add to the confusion of village life.

Back in Phnom Penh I hit bed early.

March 23, 1992, Phnom Penh

The Japanese Embassy here wants the remains of Sakai and Waku, insisting it has the authority to demand them since these men were Japanese citizens.

"No dice," says Maj. Sovocool, the Joint Task Force's representative in Phnom Penh. While the digging was going on, I talked to an embassy official and informed him about our action. He just looked at me as if I had just come from Mars, listened more or less politely and, after a few noncommittal remarks ushered me out.

Later, after we really had gotten into the digging, the embassy didn't even bother to send someone to Wat Po.

Maybe they were simply annoyed or embarrassed that foreigners were meddling in Japanese affairs.

A Cambodian government doctor wants to inspect the remains before they leave the country. Wants to make sure no Cambodian remains are evacuated. Can't blame the Cambodians. We simply came to this country, got a government ok and started digging as if the country belonged to us. Bureaucracy and red tape will certainly get worse as the country tries to get back on its feet and assert its sovereignty.

I am relieved to see the team united again today. Madeleine bares her soul, talking caringly about the mission and what it must mean to the families. She says she gladly bore all the hardships. The whole affair certainly wasn't easy for her as the only woman and civilian on the team. Uncomplainingly, she spent endless hours in the sun, watching, checking, giving directions, methodically registering the remains as they were uncovered.

The search is over for good. Ishii will never be found. Hudson, Will, Peter and I say goodbye to Wat Po. The village headman assembles the villagers near the pagoda. Not many men aged 30-40 are among them. Hudson, Peter and I make short speeches expressing our thanks for all the help and protection. Peter translates for Bill Hudson and me. The applause is not exactly deafening. Peter and I, on behalf of our companies, donate money. Enough to make the villagers greedy—not enough to make them happy.

Then the Wat Po elder makes his little speech emphasizing that it was he who instigated the renewed search after our departure. We get the message. Members of the village militia guard the meeting.

A saffron-robed monk watches the whole ceremony in silence. He sits on an elevated mat. He is quite young, but the villagers treat him with respect. After the ceremony at Wat Po, we return to the excavation site. I deposit a huge bouquet of tropical flowers at the gravesite, where water, seeping up from the ground, is already covering the efforts of hard and deep digging. Soon all traces of our labors will have disappeared.

Peter and Hudson stand silently for a while and look into the riverbed in silence. I thank Hudson for all he has done. I shake hands with Peter. Again a long silence. Everyone seem lost in his own thoughts. There is just nothing more to be said. We leave the gravesite and Wat Po for the last time. As this place of murder disappears in the dust of our cars, I feel relief that it is finally over and sadness that we could not find Ishii.

Much remains puzzling and unresolved. Do we really know what happened between the village of Kandaol where Mr. Chaak saw two Westerners, fettered and blindfolded, and three Japanese, only blindfolded, and the bamboo grove where the killing took place?

Was the group first led to the schoolhouse in Wat Po, where the commander of the Viet Cong combat group, about 400 men, had his command post? Were only the Westerners taken there? The somewhat erratic scenario of the preparation of the graves suggests that all five were not condemned at the same time. What feelings of hope and despair did the prisoners go through?

I believe that they made the final walk together. They shared the horror of their last moments on earth.

As for Ishii, we will probably never know for sure what happened to his body. The Joint Task Force has closed the site but not the case. And so it is high time for us foreigners to leave Wat Po. We are upsetting the delicate balance of relative poverty, bringing too much money into a village without any prospect of keeping up the new standard of living our presence has brought them.

Some villagers do feel left out of the temporary prosperity. Suspicion and distrust among the villagers are growing by the day. Khmer Rouge agitators persist in their anti-American propaganda to the end. The village militia has to protect us until the last day. Peter believes that more than half of the workers are Khmer Rouge followers. Nevertheless, they did their jobs. Without them we couldn't have finished the mission.

In this primitive country, without good transportation or communication, these simple people probably never knew what horrors their ideological brothers inflicted on the city dwellers in the killing fields up north. They didn't tell us that the murder of the newsmen came as a shock to them. Most people saw it as an act alien to their moral code, their religion.

We feel safe in their midst. The only really sinister person we notice is the Khmer Rouge district chief, the man with the cold eyes who watches the card players and hardly ever speaks a word. The villagers tell us he keeps part of their pay as proper dues from the capitalists who brought war to his country. Yes, it is time to leave. Our welcome is wearing out quickly.

We are all in a good mood today. We have a little get-together in a downtown restaurant. Everyone shows up. The nasty interlude between Capts. John and Hudson is forgotten. The entire team looks happy and relaxed. I express my thanks.

Hudson says, "Hear, hear."

Madeleine speaks up and says how glad she is to have been part of the team. Now that we've all gotten to know each other well, it is time to part. We are all tired and drained.

I don't plan to return to Cambodia. There are too many bad memories in the streets, in the fields and on the highways. Long forgotten memories have come back. I never wanted Vietnam and Cambodia to dominate my life. There are other, more important things than war and violent death, but I have to admit that I doubt I'll ever forget the events of the past month.

March 24, 1992, Phnom Penh

We had all met at the team's hotel at 8:30 a.m. Most of the members appear worse for wear, with bloodshot eyes. They had gone out after our get-together and, tiredness notwithstanding, obviously had themselves a hell of a good time. They had surely worked for it.

The stubby coffins containing the bones are loaded into a van and driven to Pochentong Airport for the departure ceremony.

I help carry the coffins to the VIP room, where we line them up on a table. Hudson makes sure they are aligned head to head and toe to toe.

A whole lot of embassy and Cambodian brass arrive at the tarmac to say goodbye. Then word is passed from the tower that our plane is not going to come today. A flat tire is keeping it from leaving Bangkok. A flat tire keeps the Air Force from flying? Strange. Someone whispers that the dead don't want to leave Ishii behind. Bun

Wat blamed the delay on the fact that today is Tuesday—In Cambodia a bad day to do business.

After the cancellation of the flight we load the coffins back into the van and return them to the team's hotel. The coffins are now stacked in Clyde's room. I wonder how he will be sleeping tonight. But then he's used to being with the dead.

An armed Cambodian guard now sits in the lobby. Army regs require that remains be under guard at all times. The botched departure upsets the timetable. Departure from here, arrival and arrival ceremony in Hawaii now run one day late. It also delays my trip to Tokyo and my meeting with the families.

I call our bureau in Tokyo and tell Kikuchi-san, the CBS office manager, that the mission is finished and one man is still missing. He wants to know who it is but I choose not to tell him yet. I want Mrs. Ishii to get the news from me personally.

Tokyo is going to be the hard part. Looms like a big black concrete wall in the darkness.

I use the rest of the day to drive to Neak Leung, famous Mekong town and scene of many battles during the early days of the Cambodian war. The place was a key bastion contested by both sides. It is remembered best for a tragic miscalculation by the U.S. Air Force during the early days of the U.S.-Vietnamese incursion in 1970, when confusion was the order of the day. Bombs were dropped in the wrong place and more than 100 civilians lost their lives.

Neak Leung is also the town where Webster, Hoefle and I wanted to go to cover a combat operation that never came off the day George Syvertsen's group, followed by Hangen's, was killed and captured on Highway 3.

The drive on Highway 1 to Neak Leung is in sharp contrast to the parched, palm-dotted plains bordering Highway 3 south of the capital. There everything seems shabby, beaten-down and frying in the heat.

Highway 1 leads through a lush, fertile part of Cambodia, rich with well-irrigated rice paddies, tobacco fields, vegetable gardens, mango trees and coconut palms. Solid wooden houses decorated with the exploding colors of tropical flowers, quite unlike the drab and rickety dwellings south of Phnom Penh, hide behind banana trees and lush vegetation.

You can almost sense the liveliness and optimism in the air. The Mekong River is the great fertilizer and spring of life in this part of the country. At Neak Leung the mighty stream forms a powerful barrier across the road to and from Vietnam, the often hostile neighbor.

Bullet-scarred buildings are vivid reminders of the war years, but today peaceful ferry traffic carries a colorful, noisy crowd across the stream in both directions. Women with conical Vietnamese hats selling prawns and watermelons, soldiers in less than regulation uniforms, ragged-looking peasants and laborers, and trucks and cars stuffed with passengers with lots of kids, furniture and boxed-up electronic equipment all crowd the huge ferry boats.

On the far side of the river is the other part of Neak Leung. The first sight is a huge war monument honoring two brothers in arms, a Cambodian and a Vietnamese soldier. Wishful thinking must have been behind the sculptor's motives—or government orders. These two nations don't have "brotherly" feelings for each other. Swarms of cyclos and vendors selling everything from turtles to Tuborg beer await customers near the statue's base. Bun Wat doesn't believe the statue will have a long future.

After the debilitating heat of Wat Po and Phnom Penh, the fresh Mekong breeze adds to the mood of optimism. The town on both banks of the river exudes peace and prosperity. Brightly painted pagodas, more intricately designed than the ones down south, reflect the joy of life of the people here. Even the cattle look happy, well-fed and appetizing. Fishermen stand in rice fields trying their luck and nude kids bathe among lotus leaves in small ponds.

I often found the towns and villages along Highway 1 intimidating. But now, no danger lurks behind the distant tree lines or paddy dams. It is still the dry season with little to do but to get married, and so it is also the wedding season. We see wedding parties in progress as we press our way through a maze of oxcarts, pedestrians and motor traffic.

But, Bun Wat tells me, the weather is a little cooler than normal and so are the hearts of the young people. Fewer knots are being tied than during "normal" times. Who remembers "normal" times in this country, I wonder? For a few passing moments I feel the magic of this tropical country and I remember how much I had loved Southeast Asia.

The visit to Neak Leung helps to get Wat Po and the war out of my system. But not entirely.

My memory travels back 22 years. May 1, 1971. I had just arrived in Vietnam after a long and tiring flight from New York when David Miller, the Saigon bureau chief, asked me how I'd feel about joining Syvertsen and Hiransi at 5 the next morning.

"I reserved a place for you all on the fifth U.S. armored personnel carrier going into Cambodia," he smiled.

I was overjoyed. After all, it could have been the first. Bureau chiefs are all heart.

We met at 5 a.m., sleepy-eyed but in full gear: film, food, water and spare batteries for camera and amplifier.

We hopped a chopper ride to a U.S. staging area near the Cambodian border, found ourselves an armored personnel carrier, introduced ourselves to the crew and tried to control our apprehensions about going into Cambodia. The staging area was in the so-called fishhook area of South Vietnam. It borders Cambodia and was generally considered "Indian country," a place where the Viet Cong had the say, especially at night. The task force commander didn't waste any time and very soon the armored column was moving through thick bamboo toward the border.

The spearhead of our attack force was a column of five medium tanks followed by track mounted infantry armed to the teeth with rifles, machine guns, pistols, grenades and grenade launchers—in short, everything that could make life tough for anyone who tried to stop us.

The mood of the troopers was professional as they scanned in all directions, eager to be the first to spot any opposition. He who sees the enemy first fires first. And he who fires first usually wins. For them it was a job to be done—clean the North Vietnamese and Viet Cong out of their Cambodian sanctuaries, take no unnecessary chances, survive and go home.

I liked these troopers and no matter what I thought about this stupid war, I felt closer to them than to any of the protesters in the streets of America or Europe. Our track was the medical vehicle. It was to be full by the end of the day. The column made its way westward—very slowly. It stopped to give the scouts a chance to reconnoiter the front before the rest of the force followed. Suddenly, we noticed houses on stilts surrounded by beautiful, very bright and deeply colored tropical flowers. We were in Cambodia. And then the shooting started.

Our forward element received small arms fire from a small Cambodian village straddling the road of advance. The column came to a halt. The five "big boys," as the tanks were called, fanned out and pronounced a death sentence on the little village. Obviously, a clear case of overkill. But the troopers were in no mood to screw up their chances of coming out of this alive.

Only a few minutes after troops opened fire, the flimsy huts were a sea of flames. Troopers jumped off their tracks and advanced, firing at what, just moments before, had been a peaceful village.

They fired rifles and dropped grenades into burning houses and trenches and holes. An anti-tank rocket hit the carrier right behind us. We couldn't see very much. Smoke from the burning village and from the explosion stung our eyes. There were two wounded soldiers. Our medic friends helped their wounded buddies into our track and put them low inside to protect them from the dangers outside.

And outside, more happened than I could possibly film. What a limited view the people at home get of the battlefield. Ten cameras would not have been enough to show a fraction of what was happening there. I don't know all that I missed. I don't know how many times I changed film. The noise, the firing, the crackle of burning wood, the shouts of fighting and wounded men, and all around us a tropical paradise, or what was left of it.

Filming was like experiencing a horrible and at the same time incredibly beautiful dream. I had noticed before that often a cameraman believes he is on a Hollywood set, that death and injury are only for others, never for him. But we would live through other moments that taught us our own vulnerability.

The whole episode lasted only about 15 minutes. The few Viet Cong who had stopped the column melted deeper into the lush green. Obviously, they had fought only a delaying action—small consolation for those who got wounded fighting it. One of the wounded troopers needed to be evacuated by chopper, or so one of the medics thought. But the task force commander remained tough. His unit was on the move and the injury wasn't serious enough for him to stop the advance.

A rubber plantation swallowed up the column. Light rain and an ominous veil of fog made the trunks of the rubber trees look almost human. Tall, dark figures watched the passing column in silence. This looked like ambush country. The troopers held their weapons with easy grace and stared back into the burgeoning darkness.

All I remember is that the shooting started along the length of the column and didn't stop for hours. Tracers from the machine guns gave a weird glow to the foggy dusk. This was for the most part reconnaissance by fire. Most of it was outgoing. But I sensed the fear creeping along the tank columns as young men eyed the passing landscape, ready to fire first. It was clear on our moving armored personnel carrier that no one wanted to be the last to die in these waning days of a massive U.S. presence here.

The shooting, the sight of the soldiers crouching very low on their vehicles, the big guns firing, the movements among the rubber trees became so repetitious that I just stopped filming. My story was in the can and so I watched with fascination until complete darkness enveloped the countryside and only muzzle flashes could be seen.

A little later the column stopped for the night, forming a kind of circling of the wagons, like settlers in the Old West. Soldiers erected protective screens of wire mesh in front of their tracks and tanks to stop bazooka rounds. We newsmen got out that night on a chopper carrying wounded troopers and were dropped at a firebase in the middle of nowhere. When we finally reached Saigon it was night. Syvertsen wrote a beautiful piece about the spearhead of the U.S. incursion. New York loved it. They just loved bang-bang pieces.

Because of the Cambodian incursion, the tempo and scope of CBS's war coverage increased. We had crews from Tokyo, Saigon and Hong Kong all over the battlefield. Satellite points in Hong Kong and Tokyo processed, edited and transmitted more stories than the broadcasts in New York could put on the air. Generally, news shows devote limited time to overseas pieces. Our advantage was that Vietnam was considered a domestic story, but we still had to compete with urgent reports from America's home front. Students were on the march, protesting the war and were getting shot and killed on an American university campus.

So, we often lost out. Stories filmed at great peril never made it on the air. Sometimes producers in New York who didn't care for the war thought that a lighter story would better fit the spirit of a weekend newscast. Such attitudes didn't make the chances that crews took to get good pictures any less dangerous. Well, the job has its hazards and rewards.

Combat was nasty enough, but some things were even nastier. Syvertsen and I drove almost daily from Saigon to Svey Rieng inside Cambodia to film Vietnamese refugees fleeing the fury of their Cambodian hosts. These refugees were the lucky survivors of large-scale slaughter committed by Cambodians.

Massed bodies were seen floating down the Mekong, looking like human rafts. Once, in the Cambodian town of Svey Rieng, I tried to film burning houses that had belonged to Vietnamese and were intentionally set afire by Cambodian artillery. A shabbily dressed Cambodian soldier, known as the "cowboy" to his Vietnamese victims, stopped me with his rifle. I got my shots later under the protection of Vietnamese arms. The misery of these people was indescribable, but maybe the camera did it some justice.

We got to know South Vietnam's Lt. Gen. Co Dao Tri. He was dubbed by U.S. propaganda as the "Patton of Parrot's Peak" after the famous World War II general and a contested area near the Cambodian border. Vietnamization of the war needed a Vietnamese hero. The general fit the bill with his baseball cap, paratrooper wings, close-cropped gray hair and a cigar.

Co Dao Tri was undoubtedly brave and able, but he didn't have much competition in this respect inside South Vietnam's army. He was also a notorious and corrupt drug lord, but his charisma was legendary. Tri liked us. On several occasions he let our little Jeep follow his leading armor.

A day after Kampong Cham, the Cambodian provincial capital, was occupied, Tri arrived there to confer with his Cambodian counterpart commanding the northern front. He landed in his chopper after drawing fire from the opposite side of the Mekong River. A squad of well-armed, wiry Vietnamese Rangers jumped out after him, darting ugly, contemptuous looks at the raggedy Cambodian garrison, holding their rifles at the ready. The Vietnamese reminded me in turn of our

American GIs who showed the same contempt toward Vietnamese soldiers. Everybody needs a scapegoat.

Tri and his Cambodian counterpart were conferring over a map in a dilapidated French colonial building when Cambodian soldiers half-carried, half-dragged three Viet Cong prisoners into the hall. They were horribly wounded and obviously mistreated and had their hands tied behind their backs. Tri interrogated them calmly in their common language, his face betraying no emotion for his tortured countrymen.

He couldn't have missed the marks of brutality on their bodies and the terror in their eyes. Later I saw them dragged by their hair and thrown into an empty pig sty, their hands still tied behind their backs. Respect for the individual human being didn't count for much in this part of the world. Gen. Tri left shortly afterward in his chopper.

He shook our hands and said, "Be careful. Don't take too many chances."

Brutality and concern often live side by side. A few weeks later he was dead. His chopper was shot down.

Thinking about these faraway events, I'm glad I was allowed to join the search for the bodies. It was a frightening, depressing experience, but it was also a tribute to the human spirit by all who took part in it, a demonstration that for whatever reason, every single human being is important, even in death.

The villagers taught us this lesson.

Maybe it would have been different when the holocaust raged around them. Most of the team members believe that their support of our work was not just for the money.

They were impressed that Americans came from so far to look for only five men in a country that suffered more than a million dead, most of them unclaimed and unidentified. We Westerners at times felt embarrassed investing so much effort into finding and digging up our dead. How could we expect to get understanding and cooperation from a people who had suffered so much?

But the villagers of Wat Po, as Bun Wat and Peter tell me, see it differently. Mistreated and ignored for centuries by whomever ruled in Phnom Penh, they and their ancestors were used to being treated as a nameless mass of peasants barely worthy enough to set the tables of the rich and noble.

Respect for life and the dignity of the individual were never part of their lives. And then we came after 20 years to look for five people, showing that we care for the fate of every individual, a respect they were never accorded.

Bun Wat and Peter's views are a bit lofty for me, but there is a kernel of truth in them.

March 25, 1992, Bangkok

Will, not Clyde, sleeps with the remains in his room. But, like Clyde, he's used to sleeping with bodies under the same roof. His cousin owns a funeral home. I'm surprised the hotel let the coffins on the premises.

At the airport, the same procedure as the day before. Again we carry the coffins into the VIP room. We place them head to head on a table. A huge jet transport, a C-141 Starlifter, lands and disgorges a military honor guard led by a tough Marine gunnery sergeant.

This time the stubby coffins are laid into full-size metal coffins. One of the troopers covers them with a neutral white shroud. After identification, national flags will be placed on the lids for the long road home. For now, white will have to do. During the military departure ceremony the honor guard stands at attention.

Madeleine joins their ranks in civilian dress, blond hair blowing in the hot breeze. The honor guard sweats profusely as the U.S. Embassy representative makes a short speech, spouting something about these men dying as members of a free press trying to bring home the story of the horrors of war.

A short Cambodian official also makes a speech—the usual drivel about international cooperation that seems to be de rigueur at such occasions. Our sly-looking Cambodian major general in full uniform is also part of the brass. He looks satisfied. We probably overpaid him handsomely for providing the guards for Wat Po.

The American soldiers carry the coffins onto the U.S. military plane. The honor guard, at attention, salutes. Maybe some of the fathers of the soldiers and airmen honoring Sakai, or of those who found him and dug him out, had fought him during the long, brutal Pacific campaign.

I happen to glance over to Capt. Hudson's truck. A fifth stubby coffin lies in the back, empty. A grim reminder that one body will remain behind in Cambodia. I say goodbye to my faithful friend Bun Wat and climb aboard. Then the powerful plane lifts off. I have one last look at the brown landscape of Cambodia, and we are heading for Bangkok.

The plane is less than half full. The living sit in the front, the dead lie in the rear. In Bangkok, remains from Vietnam and their escorts will join the remains from Cambodia for the long journey to Hawaii. This jet transport is solely dedicated to carrying the dead.

The Army takes care of me to the end. In Bangkok, Hudson offers me a ride to his hotel, where the embassy has reserved a room for me. I enjoy the luxury of a Bangkok hotel but feel restless. I could use a few days off but something pushes me on. Talk to Joe Peyronnin, a CBS vice president. Looks as I've been elected to escort Sakai's remains once they're released for repatriation in a few weeks. This may very well mean a journey from Rome to Hawaii to Tokyo and back. A trip around the world.

CHAPTER 5

Mrs. Ishii and Sakai's Son

March 26, 1992, on board Thai 640

After a short night without much sleep, I get up early and decide on the spur of the moment to head for Tokyo. I had planned to take Will and Clyde out for lunch, but leave a note telling them of the need to push on.

Now I am sitting in business class enjoying a drink after months without booze. The captain has just announced in a lazy voice—we are about 30 minutes out of Bangkok—that he has to extend and retract the landing gear of the 747 a few times. He tells us not to worry if we see liquid spraying from the wings.

It's only gas, he says, that has to be dumped before landing in Bangkok again. So the huge plane turns around and heads back. Somebody up there doesn't want me to leave Ishii behind. The pilot is obviously Australian and his voice is calm and matter-of-fact. I haven't had much luck with landing gear lately. First the military plane and now this bird. At the moment I am just a little curious how the landing will turn out. Is this trip jinxed?

Our plane does not make a neat impression. It is the old version of the 747, and age is catching up with it. The stewardesses keep serving drinks and this occasion is as good as any to fall off the wagon. Everyone on board is calm.

With each drink my confidence grows that the Aussie captain knows what he's doing. We make a smooth landing. The landing gear doesn't collapse and we are all safe. As soon as we come to a halt, about five mechanics storm into the cockpit and spend five minutes doing the right thing because we then hear the captain announce our imminent departure.

The rest of the flight is alcoholic routine. I am back in Tokyo where I lived in the late 1960s and early 70s. Reach my hotel about midnight and fall fast asleep.

March 28, 1992, Tokyo

Tokyo feels as if I'd never left it. A sea of faceless buildings surrounded by traffic jams. Curiously, only some of the big international hotels preserve traditional Japanese houses, gardens and fish ponds. This is true with my hotel—its restaurant is a handsome Japanese house in a rock garden full of trees, its facade reflected in a lovely pond.

Young Japanese are taller these days. Must be the hamburgers and ice cream sodas. Otherwise they look just as busy and hurried as their parents did in the late-60s. I have always believed the Japanese shouldn't be allowed to wear Western-style clothes but should be urged to wear kimonos. It sure would slow 'em down, and we wouldn't have this economic mess to deal with.

Saw my old Thai friend Thanong Hiransi today for the first time in more than 20 years. Back in our halcyon days, when he was my soundman in Indochina, he used to be the best-looking young guy on the block, the envy of us all for his ways with the girls.

But now, time has painted his hair almost white and his once carefree face is lined and spotty. He is still a handsome devil. Love of good times is written all over his face. He is now the proud husband of a Japanese wife and the father of a beautiful daughter.

I meet Kikuchi-san, Tokyo bureau office manager. His forehead is much higher than it was in 1970, and he has given up trying to hide his bald spot, wearing the rest of his hair in a sorry fringe around it. His smile of welcome is sincere. He has been the main contact to the Ishii and Sakai families through the years. Kikuchi-san arranges meetings with Mrs. Ishii and Sakai's wife and son next week.

Go out with Thanong. Sushi, sake and bullshit time.

March 28, 1992, Tokyo

Mrs. Ishii called. She can see me on Wednesday. Kikuchi-san has the Cambodian stills processed and is now busy preparing a video Wat Bun and I shot of the excavation. He wants to leave in all the gruesome details, like close-ups of skulls and bones. But after checking with Miki Itasaka, another old CBS hand, we decide to clean it up. No sense making it harder for the families than it already is. Dinner at Mary Walsh's house tonight. She is the CBS producer in Tokyo.

She invited several people for dinner, including Charley, a man in his late 50s with gray hair and matching beard who presents a convincing philosophical appreciation of life. He startles me with his arguments that certain aspects of Italian and Japanese life are similar. I still find it hard to see similarities between peoples who live on this earth like two strangers in the same town, but he cited a similar sense of family and family honor, innovative food and strong roots in their history and culture.

We must see the Japanese, he says, in the context of their own past and not as a monolithic society per se. He sees them as a conglomeration of different hierarchies where every person has a firm place and knows where everyone stands regarding his fellow man. Heavy stuff to go with beer and sake.

For me that's where the Italian connection stops. Italy is a nation of individualists in a highly mobile society. Anyway, I don't pursue the argument. He seems fascinated with my tale about retrieving our dead in Cambodia. At times the mood becomes almost macabre. I have the feeling that I am telling more than I should. Suddenly the evening turned gloomy. Later, Mary tells me privately that Charley suffers from terminal cancer. Feel pretty stupid and sad.

At lunch today Ms. Hashimoto, the bureau's secretary for as long as I can remember, talks to me at length about Ishii and Sakai. Time has been very kind to Ms. Hashimoto. She is beautiful in an ageless way. She points out the differences between the two men, differences I had sensed but wasn't quite able to articulate.

I am surprised to hear that Ishii and Sakai didn't like each other. This happens quite often between cameraman and soundman. I knew that Sakai was hell on wheels—always ready for wine, women and song. He was strong, short, bowlegged, quite ugly and very loud. I remember the sly and at times brutal expression on his face.

Ishii was the opposite. Quite a few years older and frail, Ishii was a gentleman. He proved to be a superb professional, very conscientious but, as a child of his generation, in awe of his Western bosses. He was a devoted family man, always happy to be home.

I had always liked Ishii and had my reservations about Sakai. But I really did not know either of them very well. Now in death they are equal, to be treated as faithful CBS staffers who died in the service of their dumb company.

March 31, 1992, Tokyo

Sakai's son, Kazuyoshi, visits me at the office today. Mrs. Sakai is too ill to leave her house. Young Sakai is an unassuming young man, quite pleasant and very polite. He looks a bit like his father, the same slyness without the brutal touch. He tells me proudly the family left the house virtually untouched since Sakai's disappearance. Should Sakai ever return, he would find the place the way he left it. Also, by leaving the house the way it was, they would not offend the Buddhist spirits looking out for its safety.

Kikuchi-san, who acts as an interpreter, tells me with a straight face as the three of us sit there how he saw George Syvertsen's ghost in his old house and in the office. Kikuchi-san is a modern Japanese whom I thought I knew quite well. Oh, the Japanese. Will we ever understand them?

I show young Sakai the pictures and the video of the excavation. It is important for him to understand that American soldiers from halfway around the world came to look for his father. I try to explain the near superhuman effort it took to recover the remains while his own government showed scant interest in his father's fate.

Yes, I want him to be grateful to the soldiers from the JTF. After my little speech I present him with a silver box made in Cambodia, filled with the sand and pebbles from the gravesite that Capt. Hudson had given me. He seems to appreciate it very much. A shy but pleasant smile shows on his face. I tell him that his father's bones are now in Hawaii and that we must wait for their positive identification, even though the anthropologist at the scene believes they are Sakai's.

He is very insistent that his father's bones should not be cremated without his participation. He asks me to represent his family during repatriation and to escort the remains to Tokyo. After Kazu Sakai leaves, Kikuchi-san gets very angry, claiming Kazu didn't show the proper appreciation for all the hard work the troopers had done to find his dad.

I don't have that feeling. Kikuchi-san also tells me that both men dreaded going to Cambodia.

Trained to follow orders in the emperor's army, it was not in their nature to protest, and so they went to Cambodia out of a sense of duty.

Ishii, I believe, should not have been sent. I still don't know what was on the man's mind who ordered them to go.

So Ishii went with fear in his heart. I learned of his tearful goodbye and his promise to his family for an early return. And now even his bones will not be coming home. I still remember his eyes when he left the Hotel Royal to go on his last journey.

He didn't say much but he looked so sad. I still remember how relieved I was not to have to go with Syvertsen that day after our argument. I was also relieved that George's mission was to be a harmless look down the road. After Ishii's car left the hotel grounds and made the turn onto the main road, I never saw him again.

The time following his departure must have been an unrelieved horror for this sensitive man. The terror of his short imprisonment, the hope of an early release giving way to desperation, the muffled cries as the murderer struck his colleagues, the wait for his turn to die, the blindfolded fear and loneliness at the moment of death are all too imaginable.

Yes, it could have been me. Or could I have stopped the madness of Syvertsen's expedition that day? Probably not. Nobody wants to be called a coward, but we should remember that cowards often live longer.

Today I will meet Ishii's widow for the second time as a bearer of sad news. The first was when I told her of Ishii's death in 1971. This is going to be a rough meeting. Mrs. Ishii does not yet know that we haven't found her husband. Cmdr. Patterson just called from Hawaii to inform me it will take the Army lab months to identify the remains. Suddenly, there was Mrs. Ishii in the CBS office.

She is in her early 70s but doesn't show it. She stands very straight, with enormous dignity—an old, dainty Japanese lady of great poise.

Her face could almost be called girlish if it didn't hold such an expression of deep sorrow. She doesn't shake my hand but keeps bowing to Ms. Hashimoto and me in the old-fashioned Japanese way. I ask her to sit down in the back office and start carefully to prepare her for the news about her missing husband.

I am grateful Hashimoto-san interprets my stumbling remarks into coherent Japanese, leaving out or adding whatever is necessary to show compassion as I mean it to be shown. Mrs. Ishii hides her emotions well until I hand her the silver box with soil from the gravesite. Then she bends forward, hiding her face as her shoulders begin to heave. I can't hold back my own tears. I have to step out of the room, leaving her with Hashimoto-san.

I just stare out of a window and take my time joining the two again. Mrs. Ishii has calmed down, and she watches the video of the search with great interest. She is amazed to see American soldiers, men her husband had fought in World War II, work so hard. She is amazed that officers joined their men and the natives, standing in the mud, searching for Japanese remains.

She finds it hard to believe that the soldiers put in extra days under rough conditions to look for Ishii and gave up only after all possibilities had been exhausted. Mrs. Ishii had read in a Japanese paper that the newsmen were brutally beaten to death. She asks me if it is true. I tell her they were shot and that death was quick and painless.

She looks somewhat relieved. I will stand by this lie should she ask me again. She expresses her gratitude in simple words. She asks me to pass on her special thanks to the American soldiers. Nothing else needed to be said. She gets up, clutching the silver box, bows to Hashimoto-san and me and leaves quickly, a Japanese lady, a well brought-up child of her times, always aware that pain must not be shown. We all had felt her very special presence, the presence of a wife in mourning who somehow, after 20 years, is robbed of any hope of having her husband's bones returned to his family.

April 2, 1992, On board JAL to Frankfurt

It is time to leave. Thanong brings me to the city air terminal. Can't get Ishii and Sakai off my mind. Gentle Ishii and sly, cruel Sakai. We talk about Sakai's laughing boasts that he slapped Allied prisoners in the face. Brave little Sakai, barely 5 feet tall, with a big rifle and a bayonet.

I wonder what he might have done to terrified and helpless civilians if he was mean enough to mistreat prisoners. I can't shake the irony of it all. The tough Marine gunnery sergeant saluting Sakai's coffin in Phnom Penh, the same Marines who were Japan's deadly enemies in the Pacific, whose fortitude and losses in that campaign are legendary.

Ishii spent his time in the army as a cameraman. He probably saw little or no combat and mostly found himself at the receiving end of American bombing raids in occupied Bangkok.

I now face the prospect of traveling around the world escorting the bones of a man I sometimes wish would trade places with Ishii. If only I could have brought peace of mind to the Ishii family. Life is just not fair, not even in death. Cmdr. Patterson informed me of a wrinkle the Cambodian government has added to the repatriation of the bodies.

They insist that all remains be returned to Cambodia after identification. As a sovereign state, Cambodia must handle repatriation. God, there isn't even a direct flight from Cambodia to Tokyo. I already see them putting Sakai and the others into storage till their own anthropologist can identify them. Why take the word of the Americans? What if their anthropologist doesn't have the technical means to confirm the U.S.-made identification?

I see mountains of bureaucratic obstacles in front of me. The Japanese government's present disinterest in the case doesn't help. So far no assistance has been offered from those quarters. It can be a nightmare. Wish all these coming troubles would be for Ishii.

My hope was never to go back to Cambodia again. If I do, I will try to go to Wat Po again. Maybe the villagers, with their infinite patience, will have come up with something leading us to Ishii. I'll do it for Ishii's sake.

It's not good to return to the places of one's youth. They make you feel old and the ghosts never go away.

It took Kazuyoshi till now to return the remains of his father to the house he left 22 years ago...

Bruce Dunning, CBS News Correspondent
November 1992

Summer 1992, Rome

Summer comes with no news from Hawaii. In the meantime, TBS-TV in Tokyo finally gets interested in the story of the Japanese newsmen. I give a long-distance interview. T.B.S. insists on a black background behind me to emphasize the sadness of their story.

I tell them the tale from beginning to end without expressing my criticism of the Japanese government's lack of interest in the case. Maybe it will get somebody in the government moving. Turned out to be true.

Then one hot summer day Patterson calls from Honolulu. The Army lab there has had difficulty identifying the fourth set of remains, probably Hangen's from NBC.

His records are incomplete. Strange. Welles is an American, and Americans usually have records of the most insignificant medical or dental treatment.

Nevertheless, that is the present status of the identification process.

September 1992, Rome

Summer drags into September. My old colleague Hughes Rudd died in Provence in southern France a few days ago. I spoke often with his wife, Ann, as he lay in a coma for several weeks before he passed away. Depressing as his long agony was, we still had some lighter moments. Telling Hughes Rudd stories inevitably brought bursts of laughter that dispelled, however briefly, the dark clouds above our heads.

Rudd, in his time one of the great TV correspondents, was guided by a healthy distrust of his chosen medium.

Whatever lay outside the realm of this distrust he mastered in a convincing style, leaving the viewer with either a chuckle or the feeling that an important, poignant message had just been passed. Rudd was no plastic man, never a yes-man and never afraid to speak his mind. And he could write. Whatever he wanted to say virtually exploded out of his typewriter.

I spent time with him in Vietnam and Moscow. His drinking and temper were as legendary as his performance on the job. Ann asked me one day if Hughes didn't have a cruel streak. I told her certainly. But if Hughes treated someone with disdain that person usually deserved it. After his World War II experience, Hughes could not be called a friend of the Germans. Yet, showing his underlying fairness, he made an exception with Kurt Hoefle and me, calling us his favorite Krauts. He made sure nobody messed with us on assignment in Moscow during Nixon's visit in 1973.

One day Hughes said, "Let's do a story about all the places Nixon is going to see." Hoefle and I suggested we do pieces on the places Nixon would not be able to see. Rudd nodded, "That's right, boys. Let's do it."

After that we could do no wrong. Hughes' on-camera comments about life in the Soviet Union were often so funny that I had to let go of the tripod during shoots so that my laughing wouldn't shake the camera. There are two comments by Hughes that I will never forget. One was that he didn't believe a complicated story could be told on TV.

The other was when, as an anchorman during the waning days of the Vietnam War, he once described a B-52 raid as looking like the end of life when you watch it from a distance and being the end of life when you are under it. As a veteran, he knew what he was talking about. I hope someone who knew him well writes a book about him and his stories. It would be full of wisdom and laughter.

CHAPTER 6

Back to Cambodia

Fall 1993, Rome

Summer ends and still no word from Hawaii. Then, in October, the long-awaited call comes. A U.S. Air Force plane is scheduled to leave Hawaii on November 3 to make its way across the Pacific to Cambodia. I assume it will carry the coffins of Welles Hangen, Sakai, Waku and Roger Colne.

Cmdr. Patterson relays the message that I would be welcome onboard. My orders, approved by someone on the Joint Chiefs of Staff in Washington, had been given the nod. Peter Chuun cannot come along. He, who had done so much for the search and retrieval of the missing, cannot be spared by NBC. His services as an editor are needed on Election Day in Little Rock, Bill Clinton's hometown.

This comes as a bit of a shock. He deserves to be part of the final act.

October 30, 1992, New York

Make my way to New York. The final act is under way. CBS's foreign desk faxes a disturbing Associated Press story to my hotel. It reports that only three out of the four remains recovered in Cambodia in March have been identified. It lists the names of Sakai, Waku and Colne.

I call Patterson in Hawaii, who clears it up. Hangen's remains will stay behind. The Army lab in Hawaii still isn't satisfied that positive identification has been made. Still, there are medical records missing. Very strange.

David Miller was foreign editor of NBC when Welles Hangen's remains finally returned home. Since he had served as a lieutenant in the U.S. Army, he was entitled to a military funeral at Arlington National Cemetery. David witnessed the military funeral rites and heard a bugler play Taps. At the ceremony, he also met Hangen's son and many Vietnamese who had worked for NBC in Saigon. Miller recognized many of them who had come to pay their respects. They had been "the competition in the old days, and all the memories came back," David wrote in a letter.

In 1971, David Miller's mother went through a scare when she was told that Miller of CBS had been killed in Cambodia. She assumed it was her son David. Miller, far away in Southeast Asia, knew nothing about this mistake. Fortunately, one of his sisters called CBS and was told that it was Gerry Miller, not him.

November 3, 1992, Hawaii

Patterson meets me at the Honolulu airport with his little son. I spend the evening with him and his family. He invites me to spend the night at his place. Over sushi we talk about the coming days. He wants to be the escort officer for the trip but his boss has nixed it. Too bad. He is an unconventional military officer who gets things done. I am truly sorry he can't make it.

The day before my departure, Patterson shows me some of the sights of Hawaii. We don't have the time to see enough. The old truism still holds up: Newsmen have been everywhere but have seen next to nothing. Usually, we see the airport, our hotel, the local TV station and the action we came to report. Then we are off again. At least for a producer, this becomes more and more the reality of life.

But I did see Waikiki beach, Pearl Harbor and, from a distance at least, the Arizona monument. Where battleship row once shook under the bombardment of Sakai's contemporaries, destroyers from several nations line the anchorage. Even a Japanese warship has made port. I see at least five or six atomic submarines. The battleships of old are long gone.

Today, November 3, at Hickam Field, a military honor guard draws up near the C-141 military transport plane dedicated to carrying the newsmen back to Cambodia. Members of all branches of the U.S. military carry the three coffins into the huge plane as a Marine officer shouts the proper commands.

The Japanese coffins are covered with the Rising Sun, Colne's with the French Tricolor. The honor guard lowers flags laden with battle streamers as a row of high-ranking U.S. officers salute the coffins, paying their respects to the murdered newsmen.

It is a very moving ceremony. I imagine Sakai, proud conqueror of his little portion of Singapore, smiling in his dark box to see the sworn enemies of the former Imperial Army saluting him. I film the proceedings with my small video camera, intent on making a little story of the repatriation as I did with the excavation. Then it is time to say goodbye to Patterson, my reliable old friend who had done so much to make my participation on this trip possible. I climb into the nearly windowless whale of a plane.

On board with me, besides the crew, is an honor guard, the escort officer Maj. Overturf, three coffins and a couple of small pallets with supplies for search teams in Vietnam. Just as I make myself comfortable in one of the seats, the plane's crew chief invites me into the cockpit to sit behind the pilots. I gratefully accept. Then the plane rumbles down the runway. One last look at Diamond Head. At the end of the final loop, the pilot brought the plane on course for the 10-hour trip across the Pacific Ocean.

Guam is supposed to be the next stop. But the island is being lashed by a tropical storm and so our destination is changed to Okinawa. For the next 10 hours I watch the world pass beneath me. A civilian Boeing 747 flies past, slowly disappearing into the distance ahead.

The aircraft commander is a young black man, Capt. Hauston. He shows his co-pilot, also a young man, Capt. Browne, the finer points of handling a C-141. At no time do I feel uncomfortable. They both are serious professionals who have the situation well under control. The crew takes good care of me, offering food and soft drinks.

While the Pacific passes below, I think about the bureaucratic aspects of the trip. Here we are, flying to Okinawa, Japan, with the remains of two Japanese citizens on board. Their families have now waited for more than two decades to have them back, but we can't just unload them, hand them over to the Japanese and thus shorten the proceedings. No, we now have to drag them all the way back to Cambodia so that this two-bit country can show its sovereignty by doing the repatriation on its own.

Bad thoughts to have while flying. I should remember Ms. Hashimoto's admonition that after all these years of waiting, a few more days or weeks will not make any difference. Of course she's right.

Still, I secretly hope Japanese customs agents would just confiscate the coffins containing the Japanese. After all, the Rising Sun flags are still on the boxes. But it is not to be.

Okinawa's Kadena Airfield, one of the main bases for the U.S. Air Force in the Far East, is known as a big transit place for drugs. The Japanese customs officers there act accordingly.

Since I am a civilian, I have to go through customs. The officer eyes me suspiciously as he carefully goes through all of my bags. As a final token of distrust he glances at my watch, saying, "Very expensive." By this time I am sufficiently angry to yank my hand away with a gruff, "But not for me." After which we part as friends.

I take Overturf and the honor guard out for dinner. They are a good bunch. I am surprised how much interest these young troopers show in the social and economic problems of the United States. Many are concerned about the election. I find their comments about Clinton and Bush amusing and informed. Most of them are for Clinton.

But all of them worry about his plans to reduce the Armed Forces. Many could lose their jobs, but for the sake of the country they were willing to take the chance. The escort officer, however, does not hide his disappointment over Bush's loss. Will be interesting to know how they feel once Clinton's promises to let homosexuals serve in the military come into focus.

We all turn in early. Wake-up call is 5 a.m.

The next morning comes with the old Army game of hurry up and wait. At the Kadena air terminal, hundreds of soldiers mill around waiting for a plane. Thank God we have our own. Finally we are again under way, heading for Utapao, Thailand, where we will overnight and refuel for our last leg to Cambodia. I pass most of the six-hour trip in the cockpit again.

The pilots and crew are as hospitable as ever. But I also spend an hour or so in the rear of the plane with the coffins. It is dimly lit, and the sun, filtering in through two small portholes, casts a strange, melancholy light on the flags of Japan and France. One of the crew notices me on my perch and is thoughtful enough to bring me my personal oxygen bottle and mask, then he leaves me undisturbed. No human voice intrudes on my vigil.

Most of the honor guard sleeps as the plane drones on. The pilots and the loadmaster keep busy up front. I hear only the noise of the huge engines and the air stream rushing along the hull. I am with my thoughts as I stare at the coffins, praying for a speedy, uncomplicated repatriation.

Somehow, I lose a day crossing the international dateline. We spend the night in Pattaya, Thailand. No formalities here. Again the coffins stay on board under guard while the rest of us are taken to a fancy hotel. I knew Pattaya from 22 years ago. Then it was still bearable. Now it has turned into a maze of cheap bars, massage parlors, hotels, shops and restaurants.

I take the plane crew to a restaurant I knew when I lived in Bangkok. I warn them that the place would be "straight." They don't seem to mind. We have us a hell of a good time and a meal with all the required trimmings. I go to bed early and get ready for the last leg of the trip.

November 6, 1992, Phnom Penh

At the airport in Utapao, Capt. Hauston tells us that the Cambodians do not want an American-run arrival ceremony at Pochentong Airport. They want it to be low-key and the turnover quick.

They also do not want to see our honor guard in uniform. The Cambodians further insist that the stubby boxes containing the newsmen's remains be taken out of the huge metal caskets. They want the national flags folded. Only one U.S. serviceman in civvies will carry a box at a time to a small van while Cambodian and U.S. officials look on. All this has to take place within minutes of our arrival in Phnom Penh. This news is relayed to us from Hawaii.

Capts. Hauston and Browne are slightly worried about how to get to Phnom Penh airport, where there is an absolute lack of navigational aids on the ground. The pilots are hoping for clear weather so they can follow Highway 4 from Kampong Som to the capital. For technical reasons, they cannot raise Pochentong tower.

With all the U.N. and foreign aid air traffic in Pochentong, one wonders why some of the foreign support money could not be spent on improving air traffic conditions. We take off. The mood on board is tense, but the weather at least is fairly clear. It is the beginning of the cool season.

After a wide, lazy arc over the South China Sea, our pilots lock onto the Kampong Som road and follow it at a low altitude to Pochentong. I hear no chatter between the tower and the cockpit. It is all done by Kentucky windage. As our plane approaches the runway with wheels lowered, another plane suddenly appears on the strip, ready for takeoff. The pilots pour on power, fly another loop, and then set down safely on the bumpy runway.

A vehicle guides us to the main building, which is adorned with a gigantic and very flattering portrait of Prince Sihanouk.

I get off hoping to find Bun Wat, my interpreter and guide from excavation days. He isn't there. Capt. Rice and Mr. Underwood, representatives of the search team in Phnom Penh, welcome us. A fat, snide-looking Cambodian officer in an army uniform but without his military cap and someone I recognize as a representative of the foreign office round out the welcoming committee. I remember the fat officer from the digging operation at Wat Po. He was the uncouth, loud-mouthed slob sporting a gold Rolex with a gun strapped to his side who spent his time laughing and playing cards with the drivers.

The local press is kept away. I tape the turnover of the little boxes. Compared to Hawaii, it proves a pathetic little happening, but it is functional and quick. After all, how many ceremonies do you need? The fat Cambodian officer signs a receipt for the coffins and exchanges salutes with his American counterpart. With this transaction, the U.S. government's involvement with the search for my colleagues is officially over.

I feel a little lonely out there as I watch the big plane and, with it, my newfound friends roll down the runway and disappear into the sky. The Cambodian foreign office representative assures me the three coffins will be handled with respect. Turnover to the respective governments is scheduled to take place the following Monday, November 9, at the Ministry of Security. Sakai, Waku and Colne are now officially back in the country where they were murdered 22 years ago, after a journey to and from Hawaii. Their pilgrimage, involving about 10,000 miles by air, had started seven short months ago. Many miles are still ahead of them before they reach their final resting places. They probably traveled more as dead men than they did during their lifetimes.

Before that, more turnover ceremonies, paperwork and red tape. A smart soldier from the U.S. Embassy offers me a ride to my hotel. The Diamond is one of the new places that have shot up like mushrooms all over Phnom Penh. This is more than ever a boomtown in the old Saigon tradition. U.N. soldiers now crowd the streets. There are more bars, more beggars and more cripples than before. Some of the new hotels look so flimsy I wouldn't want to lean against them. Everybody is after the almighty dollar, the real currency of the country.

I call Mrs. Hashimoto in Tokyo. Someone must have read my mind. Just as I want to ask her about the possibility of young Sakai's coming to Cambodia, she informs me he would be arriving the day after tomorrow. Since the Japanese Embassy is now involved, his presence could help cut red tape.

Finally, outside the Cambodian Foreign Ministry I link up with Bun Wat. I am happy to see him. Tomorrow we plan to go to Wat Po. It is like a magnet.

November 7, 1992, Phnom Penh

The city is even seedier than I thought when I got here yesterday. The gulf between rich and poor grows. Most of the locals are left out of the fat business contracts. The aim is obviously to make the best out of this corpse called Cambodia. The overpaid U.N. troopers remind me of the

U.S. soldiers who once strutted the streets of Saigon. The difference is that the U.S. troops did a horrendous amount of fighting and dying in Vietnam. These U.N. troopers do nothing of the sort. All this money obviously upsets the economic balance of the country. The cyclo drivers earn a pittance. Their patience is incredible. How long will it last?

The initial euphoria over the U.N. presence is long gone. Khmer Rouge intransigence over being part of the peace process reminds me of a similar Viet Cong and North Vietnamese intransigence in 1975. In the end, it got them the whole country. The magical event that's supposed to end foreign and U.N. involvement and get all the troops home is elections next April. Then it was bye-bye Vietnam. Here it will be the same. Those left holding the bag are going to be the people. It matters little to anyone that they have suffered enough.

The social ladder has been reversed for years to come. Whores and soldiers lead the scale. The black marketeer and the racketeer have replaced the sage and the intellectual. Police have no clout and crime is the fastest-growing enterprise. Why do we never learn from history?

Bun Wat and I return to Wat Po after wending through traffic that must have tripled since March. Associated Press and Mainichi, a Japanese news service, come along. In Phnom Penh the heavy traffic sets a false sign of prosperity. Twenty dollars a month is still the average income for most of the population. Most cars are driven by the wrong people. Black marketeers and profiteers drive big European or American limousines.

At Wat Po, I meet one of the villagers I knew. He confirms what I had expected: no sign of Ishii. The gravesite looks as if it had never been touched by human hands. The forces of nature have wiped out all traces of our great earth-moving effort. Water left over from the rainy season covers the site. The dam leading to Wat Po is now a floodgate, and the gap once spanned by a footbridge can barely be managed on foot. A sharp wind ripples the water covering the empty graves. I look at the water and can't help feeling that somewhere down there is Ishii. Somewhere. But where? Futile thoughts.

November 8, 1992, Phnom Penh

Sakai's son, Kazuyoshi, arrives today. His plane lands in the middle of the departure of a large contingent of U.N. troops. He is dressed all in black and wears glasses. I almost miss him. Kazu, recognizing me first, sheds his Japanese upbringing and embraces me. I then lead him to two Japanese Embassy employees who welcome him and make an appointment to discuss further proceedings. After much bowing to the embassy people, I take him to Wat Po.

The Mainichi reporter comes along to get a story and to act as interpreter. I stop at all the landmarks along Highway 3. Sakai-san finally catches up with his father's fate and he seems relieved. He wants to retrace his father's last steps on earth. I show him the bridge where the newsmen were captured and what's left of the teacher's house in Thnal Bot, their one-night prison. Then Kazu arrives at Wat Po and the site of execution and burial. He is eager to know everything and I tell him everything. Catharsis.

Kazu is a man obsessed with the need to come to terms with his father's absence and death. I can see and feel that Wat Po is the only place where he can free himself from the burden of the past and start his own life. In Wat Po, Kazu tells me that for the past 22 years—he was 22 when his father disappeared—he had to take care of his ailing mother and his younger brother. Japanese tradition demands that the oldest surviving son is head of the family.

Neither he nor his brother had the time or desire to start families of their own. Now, Kazu hopes that this will be possible. His ailing mother, upon hearing that Sakai-san's remains were about to come home, has improved visibly. She is in high spirits now, he says. He looks almost serene, with a gentle smile on his face. Nothing is left of the slyness I thought I had noticed in Tokyo when I last met him. He behaves with great dignity and shows friendliness toward the villagers as he distributes small gifts.

We stay in Wat Po for a long while and leave just in time to return to Phnom Penh before dark.

November 9, 1992, Phnom Penh

Today the remains of the newsmen clear another bureaucratic hurdle. In a ceremony that was intended to be pompous but turns out a bit shabby, our Cambodian general, showing more braid than substance, hands the remains over to the representatives of Japan and France.

The general turns out to be the same officer who visited Wat Po back in March to make sure the U.S. Army paid his soldiers properly. Then he was only a major general. Today he sported three stars.

Inane speeches are made by the Cambodians. I am bored. The Americans, the French, even the inscrutable Japanese look bored.

The only one showing poise and dignity fitting the solemn occasion is young Sakai. I really start to like and admire him then. More importantly though, it is the first time the two Sakais meet again after 22 years. Kazu virtually embraces the pitiful little box containing what's left of his father. He lovingly touches its lid, reads his father's name on the label.

His face reveals satisfaction and, yes, happiness. The son, head of a small Japanese family, has now done his job. He joins up with his father and he is bringing him home, closing the circle between departure and return. It doesn't matter any more that old Sakai is dead, only that he is coming home at last. A few hours later, after a festive lunch, we return to the Ministry of Security.

The Japanese counselor, Shinohara, and his assistant are already there—but not the Cambodians. They came 15 minutes late. Maybe they also had a festive lunch. Shinohara is apologetic. Shouldn't be. After all, this is Cambodia. Finally we pick up the coffins of Waku and Sakai. Escorted by fellow newsmen who look more like they were bidding farewell to friends than doing a story, we drive to a local pagoda that serves as a crematory.

There, the Japanese counselor carries Sakai's little coffin to a small table near the huge enclosed oven used to cremate remains according to Buddhist rites. Someone pries open the lid and Kazu lays eyes on what used to be his father. The bright, hot sun lends an amiable appearance to the event. Death does not seem a distant and threatening phenomenon, but something conciliatory all men must eventually deal with.

Monks chant as a second funeral party arrives, bearing a multicolored coffin. There are flowers everywhere. Our coffin is then carried down from the larger crematory to another, where a monk prepares a sandalwood fire to burn Sakai's remains. Above us, the other party almost lustily shoves its coffin into a roaring fire.

Soon smoke appears from the ornate chimney and, mingling with the smoke from Sakai's fire, gently rises into the pleasant afternoon air. Sakai's remains take three hours to burn, the skull stubbornly resisting the flames.

His son stands by the fire, watching as still as a statue. Curious monks and bystanders from the other funeral join us. Many carry flowers. The monk handling Sakai's fire adds more wood. A cigarette dangles from a corner of his mouth. The informality is not at all offensive—just the opposite. I find it reassuring that the rites of death can be informal and serene.

After three hours it is over. We leave the charred bones at the temple overnight. Monks want to cleanse them with coconut milk and dry them. They use fresh coconut milk because it is pristine, untouched by human hands. We are to pick them up early the next morning.

As we leave the pagoda, another funeral cortege arrives. This time the gaudy coffin is decorated with twinkling electrical lights like we put on Christmas trees. The whole atmosphere is almost carnival-like, but not at all frivolous.

With the cremation behind us, we now plan to leave on the 11th and make it to Tokyo in time for Sakai's funeral ceremony, scheduled for Friday, November 13, 1992. I make the necessary travel arrangements. Since there is no direct flight, we have to go via Bangkok.

CHAPTER 7

Sakai Goes Home

November 10, 1992, Phnom Penh

As planned, Kazu and I pick up his father's remains at the pagoda. Kazu puts the charred pieces of bone into a silver urn. The ashes are unceremoniously packed into a carton previously used for a coffee machine.

Shinohara takes it all with him to the Japanese Embassy. There he transforms the package into a kind of diplomatic pouch. This guarantees that we'll get the remains through Cambodian and Japanese customs without any difficulty. Still, Bun Wat arranges export papers for them. Kazu wants to go to Wat Po once more, and so he and I go on what should be the last time for both of us. Kazu takes a large bouquet of tropical flowers.

When we get there he distributes some of the flowers to village children and gently tosses others into the water covering the gravesite. A young swimmer from the village takes the rest of the bouquet to the actual site and plants it on a little sandy knoll sticking out above the river.

Kazu and I stare at the water for a long time. I am thinking of Ishii, who is now part of this land, left behind forever. A gush of wind knocks over the flowers. After much shouting, the villagers get the young swimmer to plant the bouquet again. Then it stands firmly.

We meet Mr. Chaak. Back in March he looked almost like a super-man to us. He was a star. Today, with all the soldiers gone, he is just like any other Cambodian peasant you pass on the road. To me he is still a hero. It feels strange seeing him with the young Sakai. He is somehow the only living link between Kazu and his father after the capture of the newsmen. Kazu looks at him in wonderment. To him Chaak must have seemed like a man from another era, even though they are of the same age, just over 40.

Then we have one last look at Wat Po, the little village that occupied our minds for so many years. Sakai waves a final goodbye, turns and walks off into his new life. He grabs my arm and says in English, "It is finished, it is finished. Now we go home."

We drive back on Highway 3. For the 7,000 kilometers or more that I logged on this short stretch between Wat Po and Phnom Penh during 1970, 1971 and 1992, all I have to show is a bucket full of bones. But the troubles are worth it. All these years are worth the effort that went into getting the job done. Seeing the look on Kazu's face makes it all worth it.

Back in Phnom Penh at the Japanese Embassy, Kazu is handed his dad's remains, neatly packed up like a Christmas gift. The package is all signed and sealed, covered with Japanese writing. Very handy to carry. Tonight in his hotel room, Sakai will sleep with the remains of his father.

We spend our last night at a restaurant in Phnom Penh. It is besieged by little beggars, many of them missing limbs. High time to get out.

November 12, 1992, Tokyo

Sakai carries the box in his lap in the car on the way to the airport. My friend Bun Wat is with us on this final ride. When he tries to pass customs and immigration in order to come with us to the plane, he is suddenly stopped by a unrelenting guard. Kazu and I continue on alone, with no chance to thank Bun Wat and say farewell. This is an abrupt way to end our association.

On the plane Sakai's hand rests on the box until we land in Bangkok. At the airport, he and I take turns guarding it while each of us goes to have some food. After an interminable layover of about six hours, we head for Tokyo.

Thanong Hiransi is waiting for us. For him too the circle has closed. The last time he saw Sakai was more than 20 years ago when he left the hotel with Syvertsen and the others.

We drive to Uwara City where Kojiro Sakai, the late CBS soundman, finally comes home. Mrs. Sakai, a tiny, old Japanese woman with a deeply lined, friendly face welcomes us, bowing endlessly. Kazu's younger brother welcomes us too.

Then we enter the house Sakai senior has built. It's small but sturdy. "My father built, my father built," Sakai says with pride as he touches it. Mrs. Sakai showers me with rice at the door. I take off my shoes as is the custom and enter a tiny living room.

Raw poverty stares at me. A faded, out-of-date CBS sticker decorates an old closet. Many other odd items lie about in utter disarray. Nothing seems to have been touched for ages. The box with the ashes is placed on a family altar in one of the tiny rooms. A picture of Sakai stands on top of it, a retouched old photo. The old rogue looks at me kindly. Kazu says that his father played the guitar and doted on his sons. There are redeeming traits in all men, or so the saying goes.

Then, the oldest son, as head of the family, lights a joss stick, rings a small ceremonial bell and prays silently. He stands alone before the altar. The rest of the family takes turns. Thanong Hiransi and I do the same. Maybe Buddha listens to me as I pray for his soul.

Mrs. Sakai offers us food and drink. The mood turns cheerful. After all, Sakai is home. The long wait has come to an end. I think of Mrs. Ishii.

Finally, Thanong and I leave for Tokyo, where I go to my hotel room and crash.

November 13, 1992, Tokyo

As Capt. John would say, the fat lady has finally sung. Today is the last day of the drama that started on May 31, 1970, on a Cambodian high-way. Bruce Dunning, the Tokyo bureau chief, Ms. Hashimoto, Kikuchi, Thanong—all friends from the beginning of my CBS career—and I go to Uwara City just outside Tokyo for Sakai's funeral service. Sakai's remains, still in the sealed box provided by the Japanese Embassy, rest on a high altar in a Buddhist temple. An orchid-framed portrait of Sakai is again placed on top of it. Joss sticks, candles and Buddhist bells in the form of metal bowls decorated the lower part of the altar.

The Sakai clan, headed by Kazu, all attired in black and resting on small mats, occupy one side of the small prayer room. Guests sit on the other side with many more standing outside the temple.

As the mourners wait there, shoeless, two Buddhist priests, one in plain robes, the other colorfully dressed, enter and begin their chants and prayers.

Bells are rung, easing Kojiro Sakai's trip to heaven. Kazu's demeanor gives the funeral ceremony an added dignity. I turn to see if the Ishii family has been invited. I don't see Mrs. Ishii and find that strange. After all, Ishii and Sakai suffered the same fate. They were murdered only yards from each other, sharing the same killer, the same club.

Her absence more than anything else shows the great difference between the two men and their families. I had hoped the funeral would be a chance for reconciliation. Instead it became a symbol of an unbridgeable split between them. The Ishii family still considers itself a cut or so above the Sakais.

After Sakai's safe passage into heaven, the Buddhist priests leave the temple just as my knees are about to give out. Westerners are generally unused to sitting in the lotus position for any length of time.

Suddenly, Kazu gets up and starts to make an impassioned speech and then he breaks down, tears streaming down his face. His mother starts to move on her knees toward me. Ms. Hashimoto translates that they are uttering their profound thanks to me for helping them bring Sakai home. I am deeply embarrassed, thinking of the many people who were part of the effort: Sturdevant, Chuun, Cmdr. Patterson, Maj. Moye, Capts. Hudson and John, the tireless search team, the lab people, the flight crews and all the others.

Deeply moved, I accept the thanks on their behalf and leave.

I never saw Kazu Sakai again.

... and now the Sakai family, at last, was united again.
Bruce Dunning, CBS News Correspondent

During the following years, I often thought about Syvertsen and the others. When I had doubts about my profession, I liked to read from a letter my friend David Schoumacher, a reporter, wrote to me not long after the tragedy on Highway 3 near Wat Po:

"The trouble is that there is nothing more interesting to [us] than journalism. And it's also true that we are pretty good at what we do when we choose to do it. We don't kid ourselves that we can change the world, but every once in a while we do give it a small nudge in the right direction. And we also get a taste of all the triumphs and tragedies of mankind."

EPILOGUE

IN THE MONTHS following the 1970 coup, Cambodia steadily lost territory to the North Vietnamese and Viet Cong. At the same time, the Vietnamese communists increased the flow of supplies and training for the Khmer Rouge. On January 21, 1971, Vietnamese sapper teams launched a surprise assault on Pochentong Airport that destroyed most of the Cambodian air force, including 10 MiG jets and four helicopters. Losses among the Cambodian airport defenders were heavy. The brazen attack so close to Phnom Penh was a devastating psychological blow. Less than a month later, Lon Nol suffered a stroke and was air lifted to a hospital in Hawaii. Lon Nol returned two months later, leaning on a cane. Political and military events continued to move beyond his control.

With Lon Nol weakened, his younger brother, Lon Non, quickly assumed a high profile role. Before the coup, he was a little-known officer in the national security police. Within a year, he commanded several Army regiments surrounding Phnom Penh and was known as "Little Brother." Cloaked with a new status and his brother's protection, Lon Non surrounded himself with a coterie of men interested first and foremost in profiting from the war.

Shortly after returning from Hawaii, Lon Nol resigned in a move calculated to have himself returned to office with even greater powers. After Lon Nol accepted his renewed appointment as prime minister, Little Brother took every opportunity to undermine Sirik Matak's authority. Lon Non soon isolated Sirik Matak by ringing his house with army troops under the pretense of providing him protection.

Lon Nol, perhaps unduly influenced by his grasping brother, assumed more and more authority, as if grandiose titles would save Cambodia. He was named Marshal of the armed forces, a newly invented title. In addition, he then had himself named president, prime minister and defense minister. Meanwhile, Cambodia managed to survive largely because of massive U.S. military support. In 1971 alone, the military aid package jumped from $20 million to $180 million.

Ambassador Emory Swank, who had replaced Mike Rives in 1970, recognized that Lon Nol was incapable of halting the corruption and revitalizing the army. He urged the White House to put its full support behind Sirik Matak, but was ignored.

In the fall of 1971, the Cambodian army launched Chenla II, a major drive north to recapture the city of Kompong Thom. The North Vietnamese let them advance with only moderate opposition. When Cambodian troops finally entered the city, the government called it a great victory. Then, after waiting two months, Vietnamese Communist forces finally counter attacked. Kampong Thom was quickly isolated and the government reinforcements, strung out for miles along Highway 6, were cut to shreds. It was the government's worse loss of the war. Some 3,000 troops were killed, thousands more wounded, and thousands more deserted.

During the January 1973 Paris peace talks, the United States and Hanoi agreed to end their military activities in Cambodia. North Vietnam withdrew most of its troops and turned the war effort over to the Khmer Rouge. When the cease-fire agreement broke down a month later, the U.S. resumed intensive bombing throughout most of the kingdom. The civilian population took the brunt of the attacks in large part because Cambodian army commanders, claiming that the Khmer Rouge were hiding among the populace, called the air strikes on town after town. The effect on the innocent civilians was devastating.

Watching Cambodia's downward spiral, Sirik Matak no longer proclaimed support for Lon Nol. He expressed his beliefs that because of corruption and inefficiency, Lon Nol would lead the country straight to its final collapse. Sirik Matak hoped he might receive more support from newly arrived Ambassador John Gunther Dean, but that was not to be. Dean followed the White House line: regardless of its losses, keep Cambodia afloat as a partial shield for South Vietnam.

By 1974, the Khmer Rouge began randomly firing rockets and mortars into Phnom Penh from just across the Mekong. The capital was bursting with more than one million refugees who camped anywhere they could find space. Hundreds of civilians were killed in the streets, at the market or in their homes. The war-shattered people no longer had any faith in Lon Nol or the chance of victory. Several government officials wanted to begin negotiations with the Khmer Rouge, but Lon Nol rejected such plans.

In August 1974, President Nixon was forced out of office by the Watergate scandal. Washington now took even less interest in Cambodia's plight. The noose around Phnom Penh tightened perceptibly. For months, most of the city's food and ammunition needs had been supplied by old freighters making their way the Mekong despite being rocketed and machine-gunned much of the way. But by early 1975, the Khmer Rouge began floating Chinese-made mines down the river and this promptly halted to the river-born supplies. American airlifts began bringing in food and supplies, but the amounts were woefully short of needs. The situation in Phnom Penh was so grave that thousands of children began dying from starvation.

In March 1975, General Sosthene Fernandez, the cheery little former colonel, who was now commander of all Cambodian armies, abandoned his country by flying off to his villa in France. A few weeks later, on April 1, Lon Nol and his family also flew off, allegedly just for medical treatment in Hawaii. To encourage his departure so negotiations with the Khmer Rouge could begin, the government gave him approximately $1 million in cash in "recognition" of his deeds.

But it was all too late. On April 12, Ambassador Dean invited several senior government officials to accompany him on the last helicopters out of the besieged city. Curiously, the greedy Little Brother, Lon Non, declined. He had not accompanied his brother's entourage and now, remaining behind, he knew he faced certain death at the hands of the Khmer Rouge. Did he stay in hopes of carting away more loot? British journalist Jon Swain, who was in Cambodia during the hectic months following the 1970 coup, returned to Phnom Penh just as the city fell to the Khmer Rouge five years later. He recounted seeing the Khmer Rouge display Lon Non and several other officials—but not Sirik Matak—outside the Ministry of Information before leading them away for a brutal execution.

Sirik Matak also refused to accompany Ambassador Dean. In a poignantly bitter response to Ambassador Dean's invitation to fly away in the final hours, he wrote:

Dear Excellency and friend,

I thank you very sincerely for your letter and for your offer to transport me towards freedom. I cannot, alas, leave in such a cowardly fashion. As for you and in particular your great country, I never believed for a moment that you would have this sentiment of abandoning a people which has chosen liberty. You have refused us your protection and we can do nothing about it. You leave and it is my wish that you and your country will find happiness under the sky.

But mark it well that, if I shall die here on the spot and in my country that I love, it is too bad because we are all born and must die one day. I have only committed this mistake in believing in you, the Americans.

Please accept, Excellency, my dear friend, my faithful and friendly sentiments.

Sirik Matak

The Khmer Rouge entered Phnom Penh on April 17, 1975. The wide streets were eerily empty as the black-clad troops walked warily through the capital. They were young, many just barely teenagers. They did not smile. Refugees huddled everywhere throughout the shattered city must have asked themselves, can life be any worse now that what we have already suffered through? Nobody, except Pol Pot, could have surmised how much worse their existence would become.

In his fine book, River of Time, Jon Swain reported seeing Sirik Matak among a crowd of desperate refugees attempting to fight their way onto the grounds of Hotel Le Royal, which was wrongly believed to be neutral territory. Sirik Matak was later granted asylum in the French Embassy, where he was forced to hide in a dark closet for weeks. The French took a risk in harboring an "arch-enemy" of the Khmer Rouge, but kept him until they had to surrender him or risk a massacre of others on the grounds. With dignity and courage, Sirik Matak walked out of the embassy gates in an evening rainstorm and was driven away in the back of a truck. It is believed that he and other officials were then executed at the nearby sports stadium.

In the last, terrible hours as the Khmer Rouge entered Phnom Penh, Mean Leang, the Associated Press reporter there, sent his final cable: "I alone in post office. Losing contact with our guys. I have so numerous stories to cover. I feel rather trembling. Do not know how to file out stories. How quiet the streets. Every minute changes. At 1300 local my wife came and saying that [Red Khmer] threatened my family out of the house...Appreciate instructions. I, with a small typewriter, shuttle between the post office and home. May be last cable today and forever."

The Killing Fields had begun.

-TJW

About the Authors

Kurt Volkert lives near Bonn, Germany, with his wife Gisela, and has launched another career as an oil painter. T. Jeff Williams lives south of San Francisco with his wife Vera and two younger sons. He is currently surviving in a dot-com company.

APPENDIX

Journalists Killed or Missing in Cambodia, 1970*

Nationality	Affiliation	Disappeared	Location
American:			
Sean Flynn	Freelance	6 April 70	Svay Rieng
Dana Stone	CBS	6 April 70	Svay Rieng
Welles Hangen	NBC	31 May 70	Takeo
George Syvertsen	CBS	31 May 70	Takeo
Gerry Miller	CBS	31 May 70	Takeo
Frank Frosch	UPI	28October70	Takeo
French:			
Gilles Caron	Agence Gamma	5 April 70	Svay Rieng
Claude Arpin	Newsweek	6 April 70	Svay Rieng
Guy Hannoteaux	L'Express	6 April 70	Svay Rieng
Roger Colne	NBC	31 May 70	Takeo
Rene Puissesseau	ORTF	7 July 70	Siem Reap
Raymond Meyer	ORTF	7 July 70	Siem Reap
Japanese:			
Akira Kusaka	Fuji TV	6 April 70	Svay Rieng

Yujiro TakagiFuji	TV	6 April 70	Svay Rieng
TakeshiYanagisawa	Nippon Denpa	10 May 70	Kampot
Terro Nakajima	Omori Research	29 May 70	Unknown
Tomoharu Ishii	CBS	31 May 70	Takeo
Kojiro Sakai	CBS	31 May 70	Takeo
Yoshiniko Waku	NBC	31 May 70	Takeo
Kyoichi Sawada	UPI	28 October 70	Takeo

Austrian:
George Gensluckner	Freelance	8 April 70	Svay Rieng

German:
Dieter Bellendorf	NBC	8 April 70	Svay Rieng

Swiss:
Willy Mettler	Freelance	16 April 70	Kampot

Indian:
Ramnik Lekhi	CBS	31 May 70	Takeo

Dutch:
Johannes Duynisveld	Freelance	18 September 70	Unknown

*To the best of our knowledge. If any errors exist, the authors accept responsibility for them.

Map 1:

Based on interviews with Cambodians living in the area at the time the CBS and NBC crews were killed, Kurt Volkert put together three maps pinpointing the area where they were marched after being captured. This one shows where they were finally killed across from Farmer Gnan's rice field.

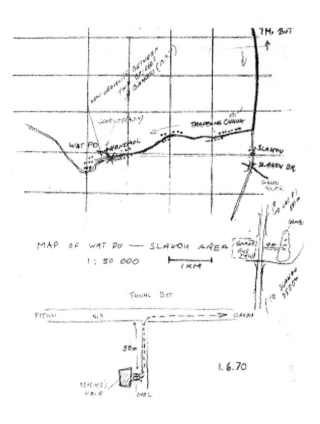

Map 2:

This map shows Highway 3 running north and south, and the village road running west to Wat Po. Below that is a close up sketch of the location of the bamboo thicket where the CBS and NBC crews were executed.

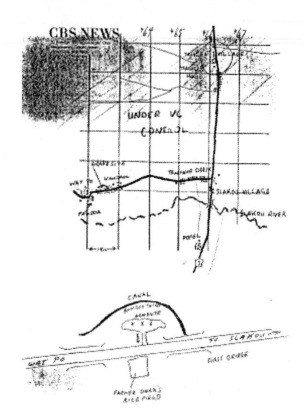

Map 3:

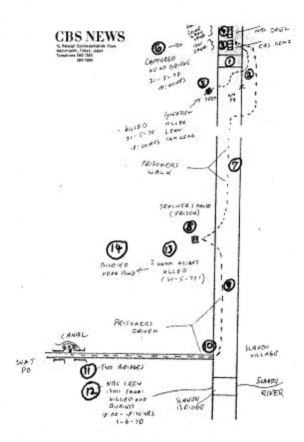

This map accompanied a first full report on the capture and killings of the CBS and NBC crews that Volkert sent to New York explaining the course of events. The numbers correspond to key points in the report.

REPORT:

At about 10 a.m. on the 31st of May, 1970, Syvertsen, driving a Jeep with Miller in the front seat, closely followed by a CBS-hired blue Mercedes driven by Cambodian Sam Leng and occupied by

Ishii, Sakai and Lekhi, came upon the destroyed bridge at Baing Kasey (1).

Syvertsen decided to take the Jeep around a rugged bypass and to look at what was up ahead on Highway 3 (2). He took with him Miller, Sam Leng as an interpreter and Lekhi maybe to have a cameraman with him. Sakai and Ishii stayed behind near the blue Mercedes (3).

Minutes after they had heard a sharp explosion but no other firing ahead, the NBC Opel pulled up behind the Mercedes and all occupants got out (4). After a short talk between the two crews, a group of three Viet Cong came near them and started firing, hitting the Opel. NBC driver Leng jumped under the gray Opel and was struck by a bullet that also punctured one of the tires.

A Japanese, maybe Waku, helped to pull him out. Just minutes before these events, the CBS Jeep was struck by a Viet Cong B-40 rocket, hit a mango tree and burst into flames (5). All in the Jeep died. The NBC crew and the remaining CBS crew were taken prisoner (6) and led for about 1 1/2 kilometers on a path running 300 meters east of and parallel to Highway 3, heading toward the village of Thnal Bot (7) about 6 kilometers from the scene of the Jeep crash in the village of Baing Kasey at km 54.

The NBC crew and our two Japanese did not see the Jeep again. After the march from the scene of capture, the latter part on Highway 3 itself, the entire group, accompanied by about eight Viet Cong, arrived at Thnal Bot around 3 p.m. and were put into the village teacher's house (8), which served the Viet Cong and Khmer Rouge as a prison.

At that time all valuables, money, watches, were taken from the prisoners as the Viet Cong demanded to see all and any kind of identification papers. At this point, Ishii and Waku were able to get rid of some compromising U.S. military and Cambodian ID cards that were later found. Also at about this time, NBC's

Cambodian driver was separated from the rest of the journalists who were kept upstairs with a Cambodian prisoner named Ben Phun from Thnal Bot village.

In the evening they were allowed to move about the house. The Viet Cong were not too threatening to the journalists, they even fed them dinner and told them that they would be released if indeed they were genuine journalists. The group spent the night at the teacher's house.

The next day, Monday, June 1, the Viet Cong became much more threatening to the journalists. They seemed very upset; they thought that they were agents or spies. At about 5 p.m. Hangen, Ishii and Sakai, with rifles pointed at them but unfettered, were herded into the NBC Opel by four Viet Cong and two Khmer Rouge named Ngon and Hoy and driven in the direction of Slakou village four kilometers south on Highway 3 (9). Then the car turned off onto a small road to the west (10) and stopped between two bridges (11) about 500 meters east of the temple called Wat Po.

They were led to a bamboo thicket about 10 meters off to the right (12) and beaten and shot to death. The Viet Cong and the Khmer Rouge then returned to the teacher's house, herded Colne and Waku into the Opel, drove them to the bridge, marched them to the wooded area and put them to death. Our men and the NBC crew minus their driver, who was released, were buried in three graves in the bamboo thicket near a canal (12).

The Viet Cong allowed no villagers to witness the killings and probably killed the Khmer Rouge for disclosing the murders. Two other prisoners were probably put to death on May 30 with shovels in Thnal Bot (13). They were buried in two graves near a pond (14). One of them could be a Cambodian government employee connected with agriculture, the other one a Japanese newsman captured earlier.

CBS's Kurt Volkert and NBC's Jim Sturdevant interviewed several people in 1971 who had information regarding the executions of the newsmen near Wat Po. The following are uncorrected copies of the transcripts as they were typed up.

Soldier Phun

Q. When were you captured by the VC?

A. I was captured in April, 1970, at Thnal Bat and was released in September.

Q. When did you first see the journalists and under what circumstances?

A. first time at the teacher's house in Thnal Bat named Seur.

Q. Was there another Cambodian with them?

A. No only five press.

Q. Do you know Leng the driver?

A. No.

Q. Did the government troops attack Thnal Bat the first day or two days after the pressmen were captured?

A. There was fighting after the pressmen were killed.

Q. Were you in the same room with the pressmen, all of them?

A. Yes, all of them.

Q. Were you kept in the stable of the house?

A. No, upstairs. In the evening they let them walk around inside house downstairs.

Q. Were the VC friendly to the journalists?

A. They were not threatening but kept asking questions.

Q. What was at Wat Po?

A. There were about 4 – 5 hundred VC near Wat Po and they had mortar and rocket positions 3 km west of Pagoda.

Q. What did the VC want to know from the journalists?

A. VC wanted to see ID card, all cards. I wasn't allowed to listen.

Q. Did the VC believe that they were journalists?

A. The VC did not trust the journalists. They thought that they were agents, spies.

Q. Is this because of the ambush of the jeep earlier?

A. I knew from the VC in the house that one jeep and three people got killed, one Amemrican, one Italian, one Filipino.

Q. Did they ever mention a fourth man getting killed near the jeep?

A. Sorry, there were 4 people but I heard only three nationalities.

Q. Did anyone else get killed at Baing Kasey that day?

A. No.

Q. Did you ever see the Opel (which he had identified as such prior to the deposition) after the journalists were taken away?

A. I never saw the car again.

(At this point Phun was asked to identify photographs. He identified Hangen, Ishii and Sakai to be the first ones taken away. Picked pictures from many (27) without hesitation. He then picked correctly the second group of pictures stating that Waku's wife was pregnant and in Hong Kong. Hew also said that Colne had been in the French Army in Indochina in 1947 and that Colne wanted to go with Phun to PPenh by Honda if they were released. Colne spoke French and Cambodian.

Q. What do you know about Hangen? (pointing at picture)

A. Ishii (now pointing himself at correct pictures again) had military dress, fieldboots, Sakai had khaki colored shirt and trousers and a small cap. The American's dress, I do not recognize. No watches, maybe the VC took away.

Q. How long were the journalists in the Seur's house?

A. They keep them two days and one night. They slept one night in house.

Q. Did they, the VC seem very unfriendly when they started to take the journalists away?

A. They were very unfriendly, very upset, they had their rifles pointed at them when they put them in the car.

Q. How many Khmer Rouge and VC were there?

A. 4 VC and 2 Cambodians.

Q. Were the Cambodians named Noon or Kin or similar?

A. One was called Ngon and the other Hoy.

Q. Did you see the journalists put in the car?

A. Yes. Ishii, Sakai, and Hangen (pointing at pictures) first, and 4 VC and 2 Khmer Rouge.

Q. Where did they drive to?

A. They drove to Slakou village and then turned to the right at Wat Po and near the bridge they killed them.

Q. How do you know all this?

A. They discussed it after they returned to the teacher's house.

Q. Who discussed all this with you?

A. One VC major who spoke a little Khmer.

Q. How long after this was the second group taken away?

A. One hour later.

Q. What time did they taken them away?

A. About 1830 (June 1).

Q. How do you know that this group was killed also?

A. I overheard the VC Major discussing it with the Khmer Rouge.

Q. What did the VC Major say?

A. I did not understand everything. Sometimes, the Major spoke Vietnamese but he said in Khmer that they killed all of them.

Q. Why were the journalists killed?

A. I cannot tell you but maybe because some were American.

Q. Did other people mention the killings?

A. No.

Q. Did anybody mention the killings?

A. One man named Hoy (same Hoy we determined) saw them killed and talked about the killings to other people and so the VC killed him. Hoy also told me about the killings.

Q. Do you know the exact gravesite near the Wat Po bridge?

A. Yes. I cannot say exactly but if I am in the area I can point it out from the others.

Q. Were all the journalists put in the same grave?

A. One grave for one man, one for two, and one for two close together, I was told by Hoy.

Q. Were there any other Foreign prisoners in Thnal Bat before the journalists arrived?

A. I didn't see but heard that a Japanese was captured at Bain Kasey and brought to Thnal Bat one day before the journalists.

Q. Do you know anything about his fate?

A. One day before the journalists arrived, the Japanese kicked the VC and then VC kept hitting him till he died.

Q. Where do you think his grave is?

A. (he described freely one of the two graves found by NBC's San which contained a body identified by US Army mortuary, Saigon, as possible Japanese. Phun then told us that the other was a Cambodian government worker connected with agriculture.)

Q. Can you think of anything you would like to tell us?

A. Nothing.

Following is a second interview with Phun.

Q. Are you sure you saw the journalists put into the car and driven off in two groups?

A. I was with the journalists. I saw them with my own eyes. The car was in a small lane in front of the house. They were not tied up.

Q. What mood were the guards in? All of them?

A. They were in a bad mood. They were pointing rifles at them.

Q. What was your last impression of the journalists?

A. They looked scared. The VC think that they were CIA.

Q. Did Hoy the peasant (who was also Khmer Rouge) see the killings?

A. Yes, he saw all five killed.

Q. Is Hoy a trustworthy man?

A. Yes, he is only a peasant.

Q. When was he killed?

A. I only know he was killed.

Q. Did you ever talk to anyone from Wat Po?

A. Many people from Wat Po told me some Americans among five people were murdered near Wat Po.

Q. Who told the people in Wat Po?

A. Oh, from one person to another.

Q. Could you find the graves?

A. Yes

Following is a third interview with Phun. His relative Gnan has info.

Q. Phun, what did the relative tell you?

A. (at this time Phun drew a map of the Wat Po area. Map attached). The man who just came is the owner of this ricefield. (see map). He said those graves I found. Because after the VC put them in grave after three days the smell was bad so he recovered with earth. And he said many people know about these graves.

Q. How many graves and where?

A. Three graves in close to location. More than 10 meters off right side of the road in the bamboo thicket. There is a small path that leads from the road between the two bridges to the graves.

Q. What does your relative—not you—say about the journalists?

A. He heard that those people are not journalists, he heard that they are CIA.

Q. what is the man's name?

A. Gnan, a relative from Wat Po area. He said every villager from Wat Po knows exactly the place.

Q. When did Gnan see the graves the last time?

A. He said he doesn't remember the days. He covered after three days a long time ago.

Q. Where is Gnan now?

A. He is at Thnal Bat.

Q. Did Gnan see the killings or the funeral?

A. He did not see the killings, only the graves.

Q. Does Gnan go to Wat Po?

A. Yes, everyday the VC stand around Wat Po. Not too many. Most of them withdrew. Because our troops are at Slakou bridge.

Following is a fourth interview with Phun dealing with the executions.

Q. What details about the execution did Hoy or the VC Major tell you?

A. Hoy said I will get killed also sometime (meaning Phun). Before they get in the car the VC don't tie anybody. When they reach the bridge by car, the VC don't tie anybody. When they reach the bridge by car, the VC took the people out of the car and tied their hands and the VC said my bureau is not in a house only in the bamboo thicket and told those journalists to sit down and then they hit them in the back of the head with a wooden handle. The first group of journalists, among them Sakai said why do you lie and bring me to this place and not to your big box. (Phun pointed at Sakai's picture at this time.)

Q. But Sakai does not speak any Khmer or Vietnamese?

A. He said it in English, Hoy told me, and it was understood by VC. No other journalists talked to VC.

Q. Did the VC ever believe that they were journalists?

A. Because the VC saw a card, several—some had several—they believed that they were at least Generals.

Q. Were they ever interrogated?

A. I don't know because before they were ever put into the same house they questioned them.

Q. Why were you held prisoner?

A. Because I used to be a medical man on the government side. The VC look always for medical men and teachers.

Q. How did Hangen behave? Did he keep quiet? Did he talk? Did he anger them?

A. He looked sorrowful.

Q. Did he try to persuade the VC that they were journalists?

A. He never talked. Sakai (when names are mentioned Phun always points at correct picture.) was very upset. Ishii cried. Waku cried. Roger Colne also cried sometimes.

Q. Did Roger Colne ever talk to the VC?

A. He never talked to the VC or Khmer Rouge, only with me. Every 30 minutes the VC came to check and then everybody kept quiet. VC Major named Theur came and checked. He was smiling and then he would leave.

Q. Did the journalists expect to be killed or released?

A. They never think that they would get killed.

Q. What changed the mood of the VC and journalists?

A. After the first group was taken away Colne and Waku cried.

Q. When did Ishii cry?

A. When the VC took them downstairs to exercise they are happy. When he was pacing the room. But he relaxed when they took him downstairs to wash.

Q. Did the journalists never think that they were driven away to be released?

A. When the VC pushed them into the car they were not too suspicious but after more than half hour had passed they became worried.

THE ACTOR

Nop Nen, a Cambodian actor, was held at the Khmer Rouge camp for re-education at Sraka Neak in Kampot province near the Kampong Speu province border. He was released and I sent a questionnaire to him concerning the missing new men.

He answerd and his letter translates as follows:

> During captivity, I was very strong morally and I tried to find out everything about the caputured journalists and civil servants from the VC. The VC told me that the captured journalists were all send to the " higher authority". When I asked the villagers in secret what this "higher authority" means, they told me, it means being send to the sky or being killed.

The actor said, that he never saw any foreigners at the camp in the mountains.

FARMER NIN

Q. What do you remember?

A. I lived at the village during the VC occupation. I never saw the journalists with my own eyes. About 60 inhabitants saw the VC with the captured journalists. They were caught a Baing Kasey and let to my village. At Thnal Bat the VC showed journalists to the people. During the showing the inhabitants and the journalists joked together. After the display the newsmen were separated and four of them were captured at the teachers house.

Q. Which four?

A. I don't know and I dont understand the purpuse.

Q. What were you told next?

A. The inhabitants told me that the other two, an American and a Japanese, were killed. Nobody knows how they were killed, because the VC did not allow villagers near the scene.

Q. Why did you not see anything? Why did you not go out to see the journalists?

A. Because I live too far away, one kilometer. I have no bicycle and i was scared.

Q. Did the villagers tell you how they were killed?

A. The villagers heard crying and said they were beaten to death. There was no shooting.

Q. What else do you know, what happened to the others?

A. They were still in the house. They were kept only one night at the house. The next morning at six, the news men were walked to Slakou.

Q. What did you hear about Salkou?

A. Many villagers told me, even children, that the news men then were led along a path which turns off before the Slakou bridge.

Q. What did you hear then?

A. Old men from Wat Po told me in secret, because the communists were
there, that four journalists were killed East of Wat Po. I don't know how they were killed. The VC announced that foreigners must be killed, especially Westerners.

Q. What about the graves?

A. The VC kept everything secret and told the villagers that they would be shot if they tried to locate the graves of all these people.

Q. How do you explain that the bodies found in the graves were not journalists?

A. I do not understand, it is a mystery.

FORMER NBC DRIVER CHAY YOU LENG

Q. Tell us from the start what happened that day?

A. At that time I left the hotelo 8 or 9 o'clock. Only one car. The Opel. Normal car. Light green.

Q. What kind of story was the crew after?

A. I don't know. A day before there were some clashes on the road an we wanted to check on them. When we arrived on the check point, I checked two places, past Tran Khnar and I asked the military on the road and they said, they saw two cars (CBS) before us. At the last check point, I stopped the car and asked and the military said again, yes, two cars are ahead. To Hangen I spoke in French and sometimes in English.

Q. Did someone try to stop you at the last checkpoint?

A. The soldiers said, don't go.

Q. Why did you proceed?

A. Hangen said: Go, go. Because two cars went already. After the last check point, I went two klicks and saw the Mercedes on the road. I stopped the car three meters behind the Benz. I saw two Japanese sitting near the car. When I saw them I wanted to turn around and I told Mr. Hangen about my decision. Hangen said, OK, go back one kilometer and wait for me. After that, I decided to stay with Hangen. The Japanese said that they heard an explosion up the road. The Japanese thought, that the jeep had exploded.

Q. What happened next?

A. I heard the VC firing. Then the VC came to capture us, about 7 or 8. They fired at the Opel and punctured one tire. All people took cover near the car. The VC made us put up our hands. Then the VC brought us to the left off the road through rice fields without seeing the jeep and then we returned to highway 3.

Q. Were you allowed to talk?

A. No talking. We walked tow or three hours. We were captured before noon. We then walked to Thnal Bat.

Q. What happened there?

A. We saw many villagers there. They whispered. I heard them say we looked like agents. They said that we were Lon Nol people. They brought us to one house. I stayed with them in one room upstairs.

Q. What kind of house was it?

A. A regular Cambodian house. I stayed with them in one room upstairs.
There were six people.

Q. How many guards?

A. Four or five. The guards stayed downstairs with 20 or 30 villagers.

Q. Did you eat?

A. Yes, the VC gave us rice on time. We ate at about three or four in the afternoon.

Q. When you were captured, what happened to cameras and personal effects?

A. The cameras stayed in the car.

Q. When were you first searched?

A. The VC checked all people when they arrived at the house.

Q. How far is this house, the prison, off the main road?

A. About one km right off the road.

Q. Was there a little road leading from the lane to the house?

A. No

Q. And you stayed till 8 pm in this house? What happened to you next?

A. I remained at the house. The VC brought the five journalists by Citroen in direction of the road. I was upstairs sitting on the porch. I couldn't see too far because it was night time.

Q. What happened to you?

A. The VC kept me with two more drivers of regular busses. And I stayed two nights in that house.

Q. Did anybody ever tell you what happened to the journalists?

A. No.

Q. Do you remember the clothes of the journalists?

A. I don't rocognize. I don't recognize. Waku had a striped shirt. Two Japanese had khaki colored dress. One man had GI boots, CBS man. Hangen had reading glasses.

Q. Do you remember any names of the VC or Khmer Rouge?

A. No.

Q. What do you believe happened to the journalists?

A. I don't know. The VC told me to bring them to a house with journalists who were captured before. I dont know where the other house was.

Q. How many people were in the car when the journalists were taken away?

A. I don't know exactly because it was too dark. The car took them in two groups.

Q. Who was in the first group?

A. First group, two Japanese. Hangen was with second group. I don't know how many persons were in the first group.

Q. How did you get out from there?

A. After two nights fighting started coming from Baing Kasey.

Q. What Cambodian unit?

A. I don't know.

Q. Did you see the Cambodian troops coming into Thnal Bat?

A. No. I escaped at three or four o'clock. (pm)

Q. How did you get away?

A. I headed for highway 2.

Q. Did you hear firing at all times?

A. Yes, one kilometer away.

Q. You said the VC withdrew. Does that mean that all VC left Thnal Bat?

A. Some left, others stayed to fight.

THE (CATHOLIC) PRIEST

Q. What do you know about the journalists?

A. The villagers said to me: You are a very lucky man! You must have many Buddhist merits, because they did not kill you. The villagers said that all people arrested before you have been killed. I heard this story from many different people. Maybe 5o or 100. I spoke to them in Khmer, their own language.

Q. What details do you know about the journalists?

A. In Baing Kasey, I did not have much contact with the population. The villagers talked about journalists being killed in the fighting near Baing Kasey and of others who were executed near Thnal Bat. Both, American and Japanese. They also talked about one Filipino. This is what the villagers said. The Khmer Rouge have another version. They talk about a jeep being hit by a B-40 rocket. About the prisonors they   said they were led to a camp of re-education. This camp would be near the mountains in Kampong Speu province. At one time two Cambodians were freed from the camp. They spent one month in this camp. They were freed in the first week in December to be agents for propagation. I asked them: Did you see any foreigners in the camp? And their answer was: No, never.

Q. Did you talk to an eye witness?

A. Maybe the information about the killing in Baing Kasey was first hand. About the captured journalists they said they knew they were killed. The villagers presented their facts as something sure. Once near Thnal Bat, I got the word about killings a few kilometers from the place and they mentioned Americans and maybe Filipino. It was an execution and they mentioned four people.

Q. Was there a strong VC presence in the area?

A. At my time and place their were few VC. Mostly Khmer Rouge. The people did not mention who did the killing. The Khmer Rouge thought that I was a spy. They were very suspicious of me and so I could not ask questions. But there was a great feeling against foreigners, especially against Americans and especially among the VC. A Khmer Rouge leader told me: "In the beginning we made many mistakes. We killed many people and some foreigners. Now we have changed our policy."

In fact, I observed that since December 1970 till now prisonors have not been killed. At the beginning the Khmer Rouge were half bandits and killed anybody. Now they have an organization an follow the rules. I think the order comes from the top, from Hanoi. Or Peking(sic). Because we have not been killed.

SOLDIER KEO SOEUNG

Q. What do you know about the missing foreigners?

A. I heard that those journalists got captured near Baing Kasey. There are five men with the driver. the driver got released. I don't know exactly the place where they got killed. I am sure they got killed.

Q. Who told you that?

A. One boy who lived near Wat Po told me. The boy knows where the graves are. I forget because it has been a long time, but I think the graves are east of Wat Po.

Q. How did the boy find out?

A. The boy told me that the Japanese got hit in the neck and killed. Another European got shot. At this time of the killing a driver got released. The driver, I think, comes from the North of Sprang.

Q. How does the boy know all this?

A. He saw it himself. His home is near Wat Po.

Q. Did the boy say they were all brought at the same time to be killed?

A. The boy told me, first the journalists were brought by car. I don't know what kind of car. I don't know if they came together. The boy did not mention it. The boy came to see his family near here and he told them also.

Q. Can we see the family and talk to them?

A. They are very scared.

(Our escort officer said he will try to talk to the family and he left with a group of soldiers to visit the house which is in an unsecure area.)

Keo Soeung also said through the boy that he knows about a grave East of Thnal Bot with two bodies in it. (Recovered by NBC, I believe.)

Our escort officer contacted without us the sister of the young man, whose name is Phat (also Rin) in the village of Kh. Por. He found the young man's sister. She was very afraid. She was crying, he said, and reported that her brother had been led away by the VC.

A TAXI DRIVER

Q. Were you in Slakou last May during the VC occupation?

A. Yes, I was.

Q. What do you know about foreigners who were held there?

A. During this time there were only VC from Thnal Bat to Slakou. The VC
then enrolled Cambodians to help them. I was used as a helper.

Q. What was the general mood about foreigners among the VC?

A. First of all the VC made propaganda to chase foreigners, first of all Americans and then South Vietnamese. I saw a French car a 2CV drive along the highway driving from Slakou to Wat Po. I saw foreigners in the car. In the car were three to four people. I am not sure which one was American and which Japanese.

Q. How do you know that when you couldn't see it clearly?

A. I saw it from the skin when the car passed slowly my house on the way to Wat Po..

Q. When was that?

A. I forgot the date. It was around four in the afternoon sometime before the sweeping operations of the 13th Brigade.

Q. Did you see the car go more than once to Wat Po the same day?

A. I saw it the same day in the afternoon go several times with foreigners from Thnal Bot to Wat Po.

Q. What happened to the foreigners, what did the people say?

A. Eight or then days later, the Khmer Rouge Tith Phon told me that the VC asked him to kill one Japanese.

Q. How about the rest of the people?

A. The others were executed by the VC near Wat Ang Sdath.

Q. Do you know any killings near Wat Po?

A. No

Q. You say the foreigners being driven to Wat Po, now you say that they
were killed near Wat Ang Sdath?

A. Yes. Tith Phon told me that one Japanese was killed by himself near that Wat but he didn't tell me where the others were executed.

Q What happened to Thith Phon?

A. He became a government soldier, an officer in Takeo province. He was
killed by the VC.

Q. Did other villagers say anything?

A. The villigars were afraid to talk. If they know anything they will be killed by the VC.

Q. How do you know these people were journalists?

A. The VC told the people that they captured some foreigners and newsmen, but did not say antything after that.

Q. Where were these news men captured?

A. Near Bang Kasey.

TEACHER SANG SOEUR

Q. Where were you on May 31, 1970?

A. 12 kilometers from Thnal Bat village.

Q. When did you return to the village?

A. June 12, 1970.

Q. After your return, who first talked to you about any killings?

A. A man called Nin, a farmer, 48 years old, told me that two prisoners, one European and one Asian, were displayed to the people of Thnal Bot, one or two days after their capture at maybe five in the afternoon, and then let to near Mr. Nin's house which is about 500 meters from my house. My house had been used as a prison.

Q. What happened next?

A. Another man called Phan and five women heard crying noises from about hundred to three hundred meters off the highway. Nin heard
them also, but did not investigate. there were not witnesses to the killings because the VC did not permit it. After the killings Mr. Phan and some friends found 2 bodies in a shallow grave barely covered with dirt, but could not see their faces, because they were covered with dirt.

Q. How do you explain the discrepancy that the bodies found in the grave later on were not the journalists?

A. I don't know, but Mr. Nin and Mr. Phan and other villagers saw the VC returning to my house which was used as a prison without the Westerner and the Japanese. The VC returned to my house and never spoke about the killings again.

Q. What happened to the other journalists?

A. Nin and Phan sad, three other journalists were walked across rice paddies without coming to the Slakou bridge to a wooded area near Wat Po and were killed there.

Q. But why the discrepancy with the two bodies of the killings at Thnal
Bot?

A. I can't explain.

Declassified Department of Defense Intelligence Report on 3 Unidentified Missing American Journalists Reportedly Seen in Kampot Province

[0072-72.CM 03/02/96]

DECLASSIFIED PER EXECUTIVE ORDER 12356, SECTION 3.3, NND PROJECT NUMBER NN8937 597, BY RB1VSW, DATE 1/23/96

DEPARTMENT OF DEFENSE INTELLIGENCE REPORT

Note: This Document contains information affecting the national defense of the United States within the meaning of the espionage laws. Title 18, U.S.C., Sec793 and 794. The transmission or revelation of its contents in any manner to an unauthorized person is prohibited by law.

CONFIDENTIAL

This report contains unprocessed information. Plans and/or policies should not be evolved or modified solely on the basis of this report.

1. COUNTRY: CB   8. REPORT NUMBER: 6 029 0072 72

2. SUBJECT: (U) Sighting of Three   9. DATE OF REPORT: 26 Feb 72
Captured Journalists   (handwritten-W33552)

                                        10. NO. OF PAGES: 6

3. ISC NUMBER: 723.600   11. REFERENCES: DIRM: 1Q16
                                           SICR: D-7CX-49018
                                           BRIGHT LIGHT
                                           BUN BOAT ICP

4. DATE OF INFORMATION: Apr to Jun 70   12.   ORIGINATOR: US
Element, CMIC, USMACV

5. PLACE AND DATE OF ACQ: FANK G2 Hq,
    PHNOM PENH CB, 6 Feb 72

13. PREPARED BY: HARRY H. KAUPP
    CW2, USA

6. EVALUATION: SOURCE F
    INFORMATION 6

7. SOURCE: Returnee Interrogation   14. APPROVING AUTHORITY:

(SIGNED)
    DAVID L. PEMBERTON
    LTC, USA
    Dir, US Elm, CMIC

15. SUMMARY

(C) This report contains information regarding the sighting of three captured journalists in KAMPOT Province, Cambodia, in Apr and Jun 70 to include circumstances of sighting, physical description of the PW, capture data and biographical correlation. THIS IS A BRIGHT LIGHT REPORT. MACV FOR JPRC. THIS REPORT PARTIALLY SATISFIES THE REQUIREMENTS OF GUN BOAT ICP (BTAUNK).

(*Author's Note*: Bright Light was a code name for efforts to collect intelligence on missing personnel in Vietnam, Cambodia and Laos, under the jurisdiction of the Joint Personnel Recovery Center, JPRC.)

1. (C) Background Information:
a. Name: NHIM SA UM CMIC C-007 72

b. Rank: None (VC)

c. Position and Unit of Assignment: Assistant Director, Mil/Civ
    Health Committee VC/NVA region 35, Cambodia; Central Hospital,
    SRE CHENG, CHUUK District, KAMPOT Province, Cambodia.

d. DPOB: 1949; DAMNAK KANTUOT Village, TRACH District, KAMPOT
Province, Cambodia.

16. DISTRIBUTION BY ORIGINATOR:

DIA	1 cy
DIRNSA	1 cy
SAC	1 cy
INPAC	1 cy
CINPAC AF	2 cys
CINCUSARPAC	2 cys
COMUSMACTHAI	1 cy
MACJ212-2	2 cys
MACJ213-1	1 cy
MACJ23	1 cy
MACJ231	10 cys

17. DOWNGRADING DATA: GROUP 3
    DOWNGRADED AT 12 YEAR INTERVALS NOT AUTOMATICALLY
    DECLASSIFIED
    THIS DOCUMENT IS RELEASEABLE TO REPUBLIC OF VIETNAM AND
    FREE WORLD
    MILITARY ASSISTANCE FORCES AND GOC.

18: ATTACHMENT DATA: None

Page 2 of 6

e. Parents' Name as Father, MA MANN, (living);Mother, NHIM VETH, (living)

f. Circumstances of Return: Source took the opportunity to rally to FANK G2 on 1 Feb 72, while on a 5-day leave from 0a unit, during which Source was to visit his parents who resided at PHNOM DAMREY Hamlet, DAMNAK KANTUOT Village, KG TRACH District, KAMPOT Province, Cambodia. At the time of his return, Source had the following items in his possession:

(1) One leave document, valid for 5 days, signed by SAING SORY, Commander, KHMERE ROUGE Military Subdivision, KAMPOT Province, Cambodia.

(2) One Chinese instruction booklet for administering Acupuncture treatment.

(3) One set of syringes and one PINCETTE:

(4) Eleven various sized Acupuncture needles, concealed in a long hollow ball-point pen.

(5) One thermometer.

Source was dissatisfied with the oppressive policies of the KHMERE ROUGE/VC/NVA and took the earliest opportunity to return.

g. Significant Activities.

(1) DOB to Mar 70. Source attended primary school at DAMNAK KANTUOT Village. TRACH District, KAMPOT Province from 1955 to 1961. From 1961 to 1968 Source attended advanced schooling at the KIRIVON PRASAT Pagoda, DAMNAK KANTUOT Village, TRACH District, KAMPOT Province. From 1968 to Mar 7O, Source worked with VC units as a civilian sympathizer.

(2) 23 Mar 70 to DOR. On 23 Mar 7O, Source joined the VC/NVA and attended basic training SDACH KONG Mountain (vic VS49213), TUK MEAS Village, TRACH District, KAMPOT Province. Upon the completion of basic training at the end of Apr 70, Source wee assigned to the 410th NVA Infantry Bn and participated in military operations against TRACH District until US/ARVN Units appeared in the area at the end of May 70. From Jun 70 to Aug 70, Source received specialized medical training at

CENTRAL Hospital (no further designation) ORE CHENG (vic VT375097). Source attended classes taught by a Chinese doctor, TOEUV SO, with

30 other students from RVN, some Vietnamese residing in CAMBODIA, and local KHMER ROUGE. A large portion of the medical training consisted in techniques and application of acupuncture. After completing this medical training, source was assigned to the local dispensary at THNAL BATH Village, KOHTHLA District, KAMPOT Province, where he remained a member until his date of return to FANK G2 on 1 Feb 72.

Page 3 of 6

h Additional References: CMIC PW/Rallier Exploitation Guide; Photographs of Journalists Missing in CAMBODIA, published by independent News Services; Maps: INDOCHINA, Sheets No 226, East, KAMPOT, No 227, West HA TIEN, and Sheet No 217, Scale 1:100,000.

2. (C) Sighting of Three Captured Journalists. The following information is provided in accordance with SICR D-7CX-49018 (POW Intelligence):

a. Circumstances of Sighting. Source observed the first two prisoners during Apr 70, soon after their capture at THNAL BATH Village, (vic VS295882)KOHTHLA District, KAMPTO Province, CB, while they were in the process of being taken to KOMPONG TRACH for interrogation purposes. Source claims to have observed the two prisoners again, two days later, shortly before they were

supposedly executed. Source also claims the identical sighting circumstances for the 3rd prisoner, with the exception of the dates. The 3rd prisoner was captured during May or Jun 70. During these sightings Source was a member of the local dispensary at THNAL BATH Village, (vic VS295882), KOHTHLA District, KAMPOT Province, CB.

b. Description of PW:

(1) Identification of prisoner No 1:

(a) Name: Unknown

(b) Rank/Position: Journalist (hearsay)

(c) Nationality: US (hearsay)

(d) Physical Description:
   Height: 1. 80m
   Weight: 80kg
   Hair: blonde short
   Eyes: unknown
   Race: Caucasian
   Complexion: fair
   Mustache/beard: None observed
   Nose: normal
   Tatoos/birthmarks: None observed
   Build: stocky

Page 4 of 6

   Age: Approximately 35
   Glasses: None observed
Rings/Watch: None

(2) Identification of prisoner No 2:
(a) Name: Unknown
(b) Rank/Position: Journalist (hearsay)
(c) Nationality: US (hearsay)
(d) Physical Descriptions
   Height: 1.65m
   Weight: 80kg
   Hair: blonde short
   Eyes: Unknown
   Race: Caucasian
   Complexion: light
   Mustache/Beard: None observed
   Nose normal
   Tatoos/birthmarks: None observed

Build: medium
Age: Approximately 35
Glasses: None observed
Rings/Watch: None

(3) Identification of prisoner No 3:
(a) Name: Unknown
(b) Rank/Position: Journalist (hearsay)
(c) Nationality: US (hearsay)
d) Physical Description:
   Height: 1.90m
   Weight: 70kg

Page 5 of 6

Hair: Black, medium length
Eyes: Unknown
Race: Caucasian
Complexion: Dark
Mustache/Beard: None observed
Nose: Normal
Tatoos/Birthmark: none observed
Build: Slender
Age: Approximately 38
Glasses: None observed
Rings/Watches: None

(4) Clothing Worn by PW. The clothing worn by PW No 1, and PW No 2 consisted only of white undershorts. The third prisoner was wearing a light colored shirt and long trousers. (Interrogator's Note: The clothing worn by the third PW was probably a khaki uniform) (NFI).

(5) Physical Condition: Source described the physical condition of all three prisoners as good.

c. Capture Data:

(1) PW No 1 and PW No 2. In Apr 70, two US Journalists (hearsay) were captured by VC/NVA forces at the intersection of Route DAMNAK CHANG (vic VS260650). The two journalists were stripped of their personal belongings, which included radios, photographic equipment and maps (NFI). Source thought both journalists came from the town of KEP (vic VS257585), which was completely in control of VC/NVA forces. Soon after their capture, both journalists were taken to KOMPONG TRACH for interrogation. Source heard that both Journalists were executed at PHNOM BAK (vic VS425690) two days after their interrogation (NFI).

(2) PW No 3. In Jun 7O, another Caucasian, assumed to be an American, was captured in the vicinity of the same crossroads (vic VS258847), while traveling on National Highway No 3 on a red 350cc HONDA motorcycle. He was also stripped of his personal belongings, a CAPERA camera and roadmaps and was taken to POBCEUK (vic VS295882) for interrogation. Three days later the PW was also supposedly executed at the same location as the other two journalists. The motorcycle was still being kept at SRE CHENG at the time Source rallied. (Interrogator's Note: The above information has been confirmed by a previous FANK G2 Interrogation Report No. 26 dtd 23 Aug 71).

Page 6 of 6

d. Biographical Correlation and Photo Identification:

(1)Biographical Correlation. No biographical correlation was possible however as previously mentioned, the above information regarding the three Prisoners had been confirmed by a FANK G2 Interrogation Report No 26 dtd 23 Aug 71.

(2) Photo Identification: Source could not identify the three individuals from an identification booklet concerning missing Journalists in CAMBODIA, published by an independent news service.

(C) Comments: Source was cooperative during the interrogation and appeared to be of above average intelligence. Source will remain with FANK G29 PHNOM PENH until exploitation is completed.

SLAT

28